Run Strong

Kevin Beck

Editor

Human Kinetics

Library of Congress Cataloging-in-Publication Data

Run strong / edited by Kevin Beck.
    p. cm.
Includes bibliographical references and index.
ISBN 0-7360-5362-X (soft)
1 Running--Training. I. Beck, Kevin, 1969-
GV1061.5.R85 2005
796.42--dc22

2004024284

ISBN: 0-7360-5362-X

The Web addresses cited in this text were current as of November 22, 2004, unless otherwise noted.

Acquisitions Editor: Martin Barnard; **Developmental Editor:** Julie Rhoda; **Assistant Editor:** Carla Zych; **Copyeditor:** Annette Pierce; **Proofreader:** Kathy Bennett; **Indexer:** Nan N. Badgett; **Permission Manager:** Carly Breeding; **Graphic Designer:** Nancy Rasmus; **Graphic Artist:** Tara Welsch; **Photo Manager:** Dan Wendt; **Cover Designer:** Keith Blomberg; **Photographer (cover):** © Stuart Hannagan / Getty Images; **Photographer (interior):** Dan Wendt unless otherwise noted; **Art Manager:** Kareema McLendon; **Printer:** United Graphics

We thank Parkland College in Champaign, Illinois, for providing the outdoor location for the photo shoot for this book.

Human Kinetics books are available at special discounts for bulk purchase. Special editions or book excerpts can also be created to specification. For details, contact the Special Sales Manager at Human Kinetics.

Printed in the United States of America   10   9   8   7   6   5   4   3   2   1

Human Kinetics
Web site: www.HumanKinetics.com

United States: Human Kinetics
P.O. Box 5076
Champaign, IL 61825-5076
800-747-4457
e-mail: humank@hkusa.com

Canada: Human Kinetics
475 Devonshire Road Unit 100
Windsor, ON N8Y 2L5
800-465-7301 (in Canada only)
e-mail: orders@hkcanada.com

Europe: Human Kinetics
107 Bradford Road
Stanningley
Leeds LS28 6AT, United Kingdom
+44 (0) 113 255 5665
e-mail: hk@hkeurope.com

Australia: Human Kinetics
57A Price Avenue
Lower Mitcham, South Australia 5062
08 8277 1555
e-mail: liaw@hkaustralia.com

New Zealand: Human Kinetics
Division of Sports Distributors NZ Ltd.
P.O. Box 300 226 Albany
North Shore City
Auckland
0064 9 448 1207
e-mail: blairc@hknewz.com

Run Strong

Contents

Introduction

The elegance and athletic appeal of running lie in its simplicity. I've covered twice the circumference of Earth on foot in direct and indirect pursuit of various finish lines, but long before this I chased school buses, pets, and dropped report cards on windy days. Few of us have slam-dunked a basketball or sunk a hole in one, but almost all of us have run.

Some of us, wondering just how far we can push back our personal limits, never really stop. Along the way, we discover that a one-dimensional approach, no matter how dedicated we are to it, is not enough to carry us over the hump. As we grow as runners, we look outside the comfortable groove of singularity toward *everything* the best runners are doing.

We find ourselves at an unprecedented point on distance running's time line, as the worlds of coaching and exercise science become increasingly fortified with top-caliber athletes. These erstwhile competitors are introducing a variety of focused approaches and special areas of interest, creating a lively smorgasbord of advice that's high tech, yet easy to understand and build into existing training programs, all with the aim of making runners stronger and better prepared. As a result, this book contains detailed routines developed and put into practice by the very best men and women runners of our time and refined through careful study.

The aim of this book is simple: to help you develop and maximize your running performance. The basic principles governing performance in distance running have been known for a long time, and they haven't changed. Similarly, various means of strengthening the mind, body, and spirit—from ancient physical arts promoting flexibility and relaxation to cutting-edge training adjuncts such as core-muscle conditioning—are established elements in the power-building arsenal. But as athletes such as marathon world-record holder Paula Radcliffe are hammering home, successful integration of traditional training methods—from weight training to drills to time management—in an attempt to run farther and faster is an exciting, burgeoning field. This book represents the first concerted effort by experts to help strength-seeking runners use and exploit these principles.

The opening chapters provide a background in the most essential elements of running—stride, speed, and training variations. Jack Youngren's enjoyable treatise on biomechanics serves as a springboard to the rest of the book, which includes straightforward advice from top coaches and experienced competitors Greg McMillan and Joe Rubio on how to develop speed in the context of building aerobic endurance.

The middle chapters include some of the most comprehensive and specific guidelines available for strength and flexibility training for distance runners. Mark Elliott, the high-performance manager for Triathlon New Zealand whose charges claimed gold and silver medals in the men's 2004 Olympic triathlon, offers a host of pre- and postworkout routines aimed at staving off injuries and keeping the legs fresh. Michael Leveritt and Colleen Glyde Julian serve upper- and lower-body strength-training routines germane to distance runners and tailored to individual athletes' ages, overall workloads, and goals. Chris Chorak provides a compelling blend of science and spirit in her discussion of body alignment and muscle balance.

The next two chapters reinforce the "knowledge is power" credo too often ignored in a sport touched more and more by claims of the latest and greatest shortcuts to success from the less than earnest. Kyle Heffner supplies a straightforward chapter on the pros and cons of dietary supplements, while John Kellogg, leaving no stone unturned, describes precisely what's needed for long-term cardiovascular—and competitive—development.

Finally, the last three chapters explore the inextricable link between body and mind in getting and staying healthy and preparing for competition. Olympians Gwyn and Mark Coogan share strategies for preparing to race, two-time Olympian and exercise physiologist Pete Pfitzinger offers detailed tips on how to integrate cross-training into a running regimen and consistently recover quickly from workouts, and Scott Douglas, the wry former editor of *Running Times* and coauthor of several popular running books, explores ideas for staying fit—and sane—when the injury bug bites.

All of the book's contributors are impressive, not because of their advanced degrees or their world-class backgrounds, but because of their pure and indelible enthusiasm for the sport and all it encompasses. By treating running as a multifaceted and lifelong discipline, they have become not our masters but our peers. And because they can teach as well as relate, they too are part of our strength.

When I first undertook this project, I saw it as an opportunity to create a resource that, with its carefully considered orientation and holistic approach, was not available to runners. Although I feel that this goal has been met, I was unprepared for the sheer energy, personality, and outright class the contributing authors brought to the project. I am excited to be part of providing a forum for previously unpublished but enormously knowledgeable athletes and coaches such as Greg, Joe, and the Coogans to spread their wisdom, motivational powers, and strength, and I am honored to help frame the contributions of some of the sport's preeminent voices, such as Pete and Scott. Most telling of all is that I learned a tremendous amount in the course of assembling this book.

Best wishes, and run strong!

Kevin M. Beck

CHAPTER 1

Improving Stride Mechanics

JACK YOUNGREN, PHD

The chapters in this book are filled with excellent, easily understood advice from experts—practical steps that you, as an advanced runner, can take to increase your fitness, improve your running, and help reduce your risk of running-related injury. In fact, this book contains page after page of some of the most practical advice ever assembled on supplementing your basic training plans.

This chapter, however, is an obvious exception. In the following 20 or so pages, the only scrap of information you'll receive that you can apply to your own training is a basic forewarning: Get out of this body-busting sport while there's still time.

Okay, that may be overstating it, but let me elaborate. You will learn in the chapters ahead how to stretch, implement weight training, and construct a reasonable training schedule—endeavors aimed at keeping you from succumbing to the range of potential pitfalls that accompany the act of running. In this chapter, however, I save most of the practical stuff for last and begin by describing in detail the biomechanical particulars of the running motion. It will seem that in so doing I am painting a picture of an act so ridiculously complex that you will be forced to reach the same conclusion that I have: It is absolutely astounding that the haphazard Rube Goldberg devices with which we hit the roads and trails are able to keep our running careers afloat and flourishing.

I include a discussion of the safety factors involved in designing the human machine, and point out how various aspects of this contraption (e.g., two kidneys, a regenerating liver, and a rock-hard skull) are overengineered to ensure that we survive a million possible contingencies. If one of these contingencies is a controlled, daily pounding of the joints that lasts for weeks, months, and years, though, your body is going to need a little help. This chapter outlines some of the physical challenges of running and explains some of the tricks your body employs to adapt to intelligent increases in the stress that long-distance running produces. The ways in which you can in turn help your body are found in the remaining chapters.

1

Since we are discussing biomechanics, I will provide some practical steps you can take to increase the mechanical efficiency of your running stride, an issue that goes beyond injury prevention. However, if you are looking for a step-by-step guide to turn yourself into a graceful runner, this isn't it. If you're looking for ways to make the most of whatever stride your deity of choice graced you with, well, then there's hope. So let's step into the world of controlled kinetic and dynamic chaos governing the various elements of your running stride.

The term *biomechanics* itself invites us to think about the human body as a machine. So in discussing the biomechanics of running, are we suggesting that the human body is a running machine? Although watching some world-class athletes running smoothly and effortlessly at ridiculously fast speeds can make it seem so, the human body was not designed with efficient and injury-free running as the prime consideration. It's not that asking a person to run is akin to trying to get a toaster to play a DVD; it's just that for many runners, injuries and performance limitations stem chiefly from problems related to biomechanical issues. Many features have evolved in human anatomy to make bipedal walking and running much easier than it is for our nearest relatives, chimpanzees—notoriously inefficient perambulators. Still, evolutionary pressures have certainly not weeded out of the human gene pool everyone incapable of turning out regular 100-mile training weeks.

Biomechanics at its core involves a lot of mathematical equations, a keen comprehension of the principles of physics, the ability to construct and analyze force diagrams and vectors, and the capacity to drop into conversation terms such as *net angular impulse* and *peak extensor torque*. Thus, experts in biomechanics make excruciatingly tedious dinner companions. I once sat in an undergraduate physics lecture that was interrupted by a student who stood up in the middle of the auditorium and announced, "I'm dropping this class. You're too (expletive deleted) boring." Inspired by this example, I've elected to omit equations and as much jargon as possible from this chapter. What I do cover is the components of the running stride and the biomechanical issues related to running efficiency and stresses applied to the structural components of the lower body. I provide just enough scientific jargon that you'll be able to impress your future physical therapist when you discuss how you ended up with Achilles tendinitis.

One term I frequently use throughout these pages is *running economy*, which is simply the metabolic energy required to run at a certain speed. Usually, we measure energy consumption in terms of the rate of oxygen consumed because this is the easiest way to estimate the metabolic cost of performing an activity that is primarily aerobic. A highly economical runner, therefore, is one who requires relatively small amounts of oxygen and energy to run at a given speed. A runner's biomechanics are a chief determinant of his or her running economy; it follows that stride mechanics are closely tied not only to injury prevention but also to improving competitive performance. Later in this chapter I cover whether runners can increase their running efficiency and therefore run faster at a given energy expenditure.

Structural Considerations

There are two main objectives in exploring how to improve stride mechanics in order to strengthen your running. The first is to increase the efficiency of your running motion. In theory, if we can use knowledge about proper running form to our advantage, we can improve performance. The second is to keep things from breaking. It is with respect to our breakability that it is most helpful to think of our bodies as machines.

The fact that the seemingly simple act of running involves a lot of moving parts means that there are many potential trouble spots, or "weak links," in the structural components of running; these spots differ among individuals as a result of biomechanical quirks. Such quirks may be modifiable (as with relative muscle strength imbalances) or not (as with basic skeletal architecture), but in any case they create a different injury-risk profile for each runner. Still, the design of the structures makes them robust enough that with proper training, they should be able to withstand the normal wear and tear of running, provided that the loads applied are not too great. The extent to which a mechanical structure is designed to withstand greater-than-normal loads is termed that structure's "safety factor." For example, a passenger elevator is constructed to withstand 10 times the expected maximal load. This is a tremendous amount of overconstruction, but the public safety issues surrounding passenger elevators demand that extra resources be allocated to these structures, given the horrible consequences of a structural failure.

The esteemed physiologist and evolutionary biologist Jared Diamond has written eloquently about the safety factors that are built into all physiological systems. These factors vary widely depending on the potential consequence of failure and the cost to the organism of "overconstruction." An understanding of these issues helps explain why we have two kidneys when only one is needed and a liver and pancreas that have a capacity far beyond that required for normal function, but only one brain, whose function is absolutely critical for most tasks apart from distance running.

Very few anatomical structures in the human body have the sort of backup seen in passenger elevators because of the energy cost to the individual of overconstructing these tissues. For instance, a human backbone has a safety factor of about 1.35; this means it can withstand about 35 percent more than the maximal expected load. Some tendons have safety factors much higher than this, but others that need to withstand very large strain forces—such as the Achilles tendon—may not withstand forces much greater than 30 percent of their expected peak load. The stress that a tendon will allow itself to be subjected to without failure is a function of both its size in relation to the size (and therefore force-generating capacity) of the muscle it connects to and the speed of loading it experiences.

As with other components of the musculoskeletal system, the properties of tendons are greatly affected by fatigue. Repeated loading of either tendon or

3

bone over time dramatically reduces the amount of stress the tissue can withstand before it fails, resulting in injury. In this way, our biological structures are much like general building materials. For instance, a building made of wood must be constructed to a higher safety factor than one made of steel because of the capacity of wood to fatigue—or lose its ability to withstand stress—over time. The reduced capacity of bone and connective tissue to withstand stress because of fatigue is a function of the applied load, the number of repetitions, and the frequency of loading. For endurance athletes fatigue is largely a function of the number of repetitions and the frequency of loading; high levels of repetition and frequency are more likely to produce tissue injury than the application of a single traumatic load. Tales of ultramarathoners suffering sudden bone fractures after 40 miles of running are as instructive as they are nauseating.

One difference between the human body and inorganic machines is that our bodies can rebuild themselves at any time if load requirements are altered. The metabolic adaptations to an exercise program represent one way in which muscles "retool" themselves to meet increased loads. The addition of mitochondria, glycogen stores, and capillaries—elements of muscles' hallmark response to repeated exercise—is an adaptation necessary to avoid metabolic failure during prolonged physical activity. Luckily, the body can also beef up the structural

© Human Kinetics

Given the chance, the human body can use its unique properties to shore up its structures and adapt to increased demands.

safety factors in response to the repeated application of physical strain on the connective tissues. Structural failure is what shelves an athlete's training ambitions in a hurry. To prevent this sort of failure in response to repeated mechanical loading, connective tissues such as bones and tendons bulk up—strengthen their core structural elements—and enjoy an increased capacity to withstand stress. This adaptive response takes time, but it allows an increased capacity for the body to withstand the high repetitive training loads required for success in endurance sports. This is also why we observe many running injuries in novice runners despite training volumes that are relatively low compared to those of more experienced athletes—the more experienced runners' bodies have adapted to the training loads.

Excess bone is normally deposited in response to compressive forces, e.g., the impact of weight-bearing exercises such as running. Excess bone is also deposited at the sites of tendon attachments when increased tensile forces applied through muscle produce an increase in the diameter of not only the muscle, but of the tendon that connects it to the bone in order to shore up this potential weak link in the muscle–tendon–bone chain. This is normally a beneficial adaptation that helps reduce the risk of failure-associated injury; however, in cases where excessive stress is applied chronically, this remodeling of connective tissues to withstand increased loads has a downside. Injuries such as heel spurs, which are common in runners, and Osgood-Schlatter syndrome, which is not, involve the deposition of bony formations at the site of tendon attachments; this often painful condition is the result of excessive stress applied to the muscle–tendon–bone structure, usually caused by excessive motion.

Another way in which the human body differs from a typical machine is in the materials the body employs. Biological tissues have mechanical properties that are more complex than simple construction materials. The unique performance properties of anatomical structures have made attempts to replace them with synthetic replacement parts, such as artificial knee ligaments, mostly unsuccessful. Many of these hard-to-replicate properties arise from the water-holding properties of the molecular components of the connective tissues. The ability of the body's connective tissues to use fluid dynamics allows, for example, the meniscus in your knee to absorb impact forces repeatedly and not break down as quickly as the midsoles of your last pair of training shoes. In addition, the various types of connective tissue are composed of various ratios of elastic and collagenous fibers that make these structures either very rigid or highly deformable. Tendons, as we shall see, have a highly elastic component that allows them to stretch and store energy before snapping back to generate propulsive force. Ligaments, on the other hand, consistent with their role in stabilizing joints, can absorb large amounts of force without stretching or deforming at all.

The elastic properties of muscle and connective tissue are critical in powering running. Energy stored in the stretch of these tissues is used to propel the body forward when the muscles shorten. To describe this in mechanical terms, our legs function similarly to simple springs. In fact, it has been suggested that at faster running speeds, the muscles of the calf provide minimal work and the majority of the propulsive force imparted by the foot comes from energy stored and released by the Achilles tendon. As we discuss the basics of the running motion next, you will notice that all of the stages of the running gait ultimately depend on both the storage of energy as muscles and tendons stretch upon impact with the ground and the subsequent utilization of this energy to propel the body forward and upward.

Stride Basics

Everyone knows what running looks like, and even if you can't precisely describe what good running form is supposed to look like, you surely recognize it when you see it. The body leans slightly forward from the pelvis with the back kept straight. The shoulders are relaxed and the arms are carried loosely between the waistline and chest. The arms balance the motions of the lower body; as one leg pushes off against the ground, the opposite arm drives downward. The knee drives up as the hips rotate to pull the swing leg forward, and the upper body balances this movement with a rotation in the opposite direction.

The gait cycle is the period from initial contact of one foot with the ground to the next contact of the same foot with the ground, so the cycle consists of

a   b

Figure 1.1 Each stride of the gait cycle includes the stance phase—footstrike *(a)*, midstance *(b)*, and toe-off *(c)*—as well as the swing phase *(d)*.

6

one stride with each leg. We typically break down each stride of the gait cycle into two phases: a stance phase (figures 1.1a-c), during which the foot remains in contact with the ground, and a swing phase (figure 1.1d), during which the leg swings through the air in preparation for the next footstrike. The progression from walking to running is associated with reducing time spent in the stance phase and increasing the time spent aloft in the swing phase. While walking, the ratio of time spent in the stance phase to that spent in the swing phase is about 60 percent to 40 percent. The difference between running and walking is that, even at slower running speeds, more time is spent in the swing phase than in the stance phase, and running includes two double-float phases when both feet are off the ground simultaneously.

The following paragraphs detail the general components of the gait cycle; in outlining the different phases of this cycle, I offer practical tips on how you can optimize these components and thus strengthen your own running.

Stance Phase

To discuss the intricacies of the running gait, I break the stance phase into three separate aspects: the events surrounding footstrike (figure 1.1a), an intermediate or midstance phase that occurs as the body's center of mass moves over the

c   d

Figure 1.1 *(continued)*

7

foot (figure 1.1*b*), and a later stance phase leading to toe-off (figure 1.1*c*). We'll ignore the opposite leg, although the movement of the whole body is obviously determined by the movements and positions of both lower limbs and, to a lesser extent, the arms.

Footstrike

Our discussion of the gait cycle begins with the moment the rubber meets the road—the footstrike. For about 80 percent of runners, this means a heel strike, in which the heel or rear foot makes initial contact with the ground (see figure 1.1*a*). The other 20 percent of runners, the midfoot strikers, land on the outer portion of the middle section of the foot. While it's clear that there are definitely two distinct footstrike camps—the rear-footers and the midfooters—it's not clear that runners should spend much energy deciding where to pitch their tent. Much of this decision may have been made for you based on your particular architecture. So, if you are landing on your midfoot, for example, it is likely due to your skeletal structure and other innate factors. However, running speed can also influence a runner's footstrike, with increasing speeds and longer strides pushing the site of contact farther toward the forefoot and sprinting speeds usually moving the contact to the toes or the balls of the feet. Also, despite the consequences of each "style" that a biomechanics expert could list (for example, heel-strikers spend more time in the stance phase), it's not clear that there are significant functional differences between landing fore versus landing aft.

At the time of footstrike, the muscles in the front and the rear of the lower leg are active, stabilizing the foot in preparation for impact. The foot draws back beneath the runner, coming closer to his or her center of gravity, but is still moving forward relative to the ground. On impact, the muscles of the leg must absorb the braking forces as the foot contacts the ground (see figure 1.2). These forces, and

Figure 1.2 Even with an efficient stride, considerable force is produced when the foot strikes the ground.

8

the excess work necessary to overcome them, can be exaggerated by overstriding, as I discuss later in this chapter. An efficient stride therefore involves the foot striking closer to the center of the mass, thereby minimizing the braking forces applied by the ground.

Of course, you can't talk about footstrike without discussing impact. The main impact force encountered on landing is the vertical ground reaction force. This is the bone-jarring component of the force of impact that is transmitted straight up the limb. In sprinting, vertical ground reaction forces can reportedly exceed six times the body weight with each stride. At paces encountered in distance running, the body absorbs ground reaction forces on the order of two and a half to three times its weight with each footstrike. These forces are twice those encountered while walking, and they are generated in half the time. Because strain is a measure of force applied per unit of time, this means that compared to walking, running produces four times the strain imposed on the connective tissues exposed to this force.

Peak forces do not seem to be significantly different between heel- and forefoot-strikers, but forefoot-strikers should realize that virtually all the forces requiring absorption are concentrated under the front of the foot, whereas heel-strikers absorb the impact over the full length of the foot as they go through the stance phase. Thus, the forefoot-striker needs to select footwear that features substantial cushioning under the front portion of the shoe because some shoes all but ignore this area in favor of nice cushy heels.

Another potential source of consternation for runners is the issue of just where to put the foot when it comes down. Both the angle at which the foot contacts the ground and the distance from the midline of the body can greatly influence the forces that are transmitted to several muscles and connective tissues. Severe inversion or eversion (landing "pigeon-toed" or "duck-footed," respectively) causes significant torque on the joints and tissues because the rotational forces through the knees and hips are increased as the body passes over the foot later in the stance phase. Ideal foot placement leaves the ankle and knee joints aligned in the same vertical plane, minimizing lateral twisting of these joints as the body moves over the support leg.

A related factor is the distance that the feet land from the midline of the center of mass. In most runners, both feet fall on the same line underneath the center of mass; if asked to run using a normal stride along the lane line of a local track, most people would see both of their feet land pretty much on the line. This differs from walking, during which the feet land on separate, parallel lines. If this "two-line" pattern occurs during running and the feet are not aligned under the center of mass during the stance phase, this places too great a load on the muscles stabilizing the hip. Conversely, many runners run with more of a crossover pattern, in which the feet cross the midline and fall under the opposite side of the body; this running pattern increases stresses on the outer portions of the knees and leads to an even greater amount of rotational movement during the stance phase.

9

Midstance

The midstance stride phase includes everything between the initial footstrike and the point at which the body's center of gravity passes over the foot (see figure 1.1*b* on page 6). The transition from footstrike to midstance is all about absorbing energy. Some of this absorption serves to reduce the force of impact on the body, but much of it serves to store energy for powering the propulsive stages of the gait cycle. A major means by which the body absorbs the forces of impact is pronation. Pronation is the eversion, or turning outward, of the bottom of the foot as pressure moves from the outer rear part of the foot to its inner front aspect (see figure 1.3). Owing to the odd angles involved in the foot joints, rolling the top of the foot inward—and the sole of the foot outward—causes the lower leg and knee to rotate inward. Therefore, while some pronation is beneficial for absorbing the shock of impact, excessive pronation—which may be caused not only by running but by standing or walking for long periods in high-heeled shoes or other footwear lacking adequate arch support—can introduce rotational forces that can add stress to the knee and hip joints.

Pronation from an inverted to an everted position occurs within 30 milliseconds of heel strike, five times faster than during walking. How fast is that? Well, it has taken you approximately nine minutes, or 540 seconds, to read this chapter to this point, meaning that 30 milliseconds is about 1/100th of the

a   b

Figure 1.3 Normal pronation helps absorb the shock of impact, transferring pressure from the outer heel *(a)* to the inner toe section of the foot *(b)*.

10

time it took for you to lose all interest in whatever calculations were about to be thrown at you. In other words, it's pretty fast. What that means to physicists is that the stresses applied to the structures of the foot and lower leg as a result of this motion are great indeed. What it means to runners is that it's not surprising that so many injuries are associated with overpronation, and what it means to shoe manufacturers is that there's a gold mine out there in designing and marketing "motion control" and "stability" running shoes. Bear in mind that pronation is a normal phenomenon; the chief signs of overpronation are sore arches, marked compression of running shoes on the inner part of the sole compared to the outer one, collapse of the shoe's heel counter, and pain on the inner lower shin, often accompanied by a noticeable turning outward of the foot at the ankle.

Foot structure plays an enormous role in determining the ground reaction forces absorbed during midstance. The simple model is that feet with high insteps or arches, termed "cavus feet," tend to be quite rigid and inflexible and do not pronate well. This foot type absorbs ground reaction forces very poorly. Force is transmitted up the lower leg in these runners, a pattern that is associated with an increased risk for stress fractures. The heads of the metatarsals in the foot bear the brunt of impact forces in this foot type. A well-cushioned shoe with an emphasis on the forefoot is therefore recommended for runners with high-arched, rigid feet. Correction with appropriately designed custom orthotics can help provide necessary support for the high-arched foot as well as promote adequate pronation for shock absorption and efficient motion. To do so, the orthotics must be designed around the normal motion of the foot during the stance phase and not just fitted to the shape of the foot. This requires that the podiatrist analyze the patient's gait in addition to making a mold of the bottom of the foot.

Conversely, excessive pronation is, on the surface, more likely to occur in runners with low arches. Generic advice therefore steers runners with this foot type into motion-control shoes. However, a podiatrist or experienced shoe expert should analyze the pronation and confirm the runner's actual shoe needs. Working anatomically from the bottom up, excessive pronation is linked to plantar fasciitis, Achilles tendinitis, shin splints, tibial compartment syndrome, stress fractures, and chondromalacia (damage to the articular cartilage of the knee). There is some evidence that increasing the strength of the muscles that stabilize the ankle can reduce the amount of pronation (regardless of arch height); however, this has not yet been proven using standard physical therapy treatments for ankle strength, such as a balance boards or toe raises.

During midstance, the full weight of the body is (obviously) supported by the support leg. Maintaining a relatively level pelvis at this point requires the concerted actions of the medial gluteal muscles, the muscles of the low back, and the abdominal muscles; weakness in these muscles can lead to excessive pelvic motion and strain in the joints of the hip. For details on strengthening these muscles, refer to chapter 6.

Toe-Off

The second half of the stance phase generates propulsive force, primarily by using the energy stored in the elastic component of the muscles and tendons during stretch (see figure 1.1c on page 7). As the body's center of mass passes over and in front of the weight-bearing foot, the corresponding knee and hip begin to extend (the leg straightens out). This is partly due to the active contraction of the thigh and gluteal muscles and partly due to the elastic recoil from the stretch loading. The foot, having been in an everted position after pronating, supinates (rolls toward its outside edge) because of the rotation of the lower leg that follows the rotation of the hips as the opposite leg swings forward. This supination, aided by contraction of the calf muscles, locks the foot in a rigid position and helps generate force at toe-off. An often overlooked fact is that some runners who underpronate—and whose body weight, therefore, does not roll toward the inner aspect of the foot—experience a loss of propulsive force because they underutilize the big toe if toe-off occurs under the middle or outside of the foot. This can be a problem for runners with alterations in the normal pronation and supination motion of the foot, but can be corrected by custom orthotics designed specifically to evert the foot and move the center of propulsive force inward toward the big toe.

In theory, toe-off is where increased rigidity and stiffness in the muscle and tendon structures help runners; muscles and tendons cannot be too flexible and compliant or they will not store enough energy during the loading phase to provide adequate propulsion. However, if this stiffness includes reduced mobility of the ankle joint, problems ensue. This is because as the lower leg pushes forward over the foot (dorsiflexion at the ankle joint) late in the stance phase, a greater degree of ankle flexion produces a greater amount of prestretch on the calf, which will produce a greater amount of force for the same energy cost, caused by the simple snapping back of the elastic components of the tissues. (Think of this system as a bow and arrow; if the bow is too rigid to be bent, no tension can be generated in the string and the arrow cannot be fired.) With diminished joint mobility, then, the loss of stretch and recoil means that more force for toe-off must come from a greater active contraction of the calf muscles, which costs energy. It is no surprise, then, that increased ankle flexion at this stage of the running cycle is associated with more economical running. You can find exercises to increase the range of motion of your ankle in chapter 4.

Swing Phase

Following toe-off, the hamstring muscles contract to bring the lower leg up toward the gluteal muscles and to hold the knee in this flexed position as the leg swings out ahead of the center of mass (figure 1.1d on page 7). This is an important action because more energy is required to swing a limb with its weight distributed toward the end than is needed to swing a limb with its weight concentrated near the joint. This is why a figure skater pulls her arms against her body to spin faster, and why some baseball sluggers cheat by corking their bats. A more economical running form is associated with a more flexed knee during the swing phase. This doesn't mean that you should try to literally kick your own butt with every stride; this would lead to a highly peculiar and inefficient running style. Instead, runners should ensure that the hamstrings do not have to work against too much resistance to keep the knee flexed during the swing phase.

Knee flexion during the swing phase depends to a great extent on quadriceps flexibility. Try this exercise: Stand with your weight on one leg. Keeping the thigh of the other leg perpendicular to the floor, slowly contract your hamstring muscle and bend your knee to bring your foot up against your glutes. Can't do it? Well, it's not because the muscle is not inherently strong enough to lift the leg; it's just not strong enough to overcome the resistance to stretch that the quadriceps impose. Therefore, minimizing energy expenditure during leg swing depends on balancing the efficiency gained by reducing the weight moved during the leg swing against the energy cost of contracting the hamstrings against the resistance of the quads. As a matter of fact, much of the knee flexion that occurs during the swing phase is accomplished passively, so under ideal conditions, energy expenditure by the hamstrings would be minimal. Obviously, increasing quadriceps flexibility could potentially pay off in the form of improved running economy, as the same energy output could produce more knee flexion. You'll find exercises designed to increase quadriceps flexibility and therefore improve running economy in chapter 4.

During the stance phase, the body stores energy in the abdominal muscles and hip flexors when these muscles stretch as a result of the pelvis rotating and the hip of the support leg extending backward just before toe-off. Now, as this leg swings forward with the knee flexed, the body takes advantage of this stored energy, and the contraction of these muscles powers the swing of the leg forward through the air. Ideally, energy is transferred through the body segments with the efficiency of a skilled golf swing. To swing a club with maximal power, golfers first stretch their muscles during the backswing. Then, to bring the club forward with as much power as possible, they begin their swing with the legs and hips, leaving the arms and club back. The hips rotate, which causes a stretch of (and therefore a transfer of energy to) the muscles of the trunk, which then begin to contract before movement of the shoulders is initiated, stretching and transferring energy to the shoulder and arm muscles and so on until finally, all the energy is transferred into the club head and, finally, the ball (or, in my case, the divot).

For runners, the efficient transfer of power through the trunk to the lower leg requires some degree of abdominal muscle strength, low back and pelvis rotation, and flexibility of the hip flexors to allow optimal stretch loading. In runners who lose rotational capacity in the low back because of age or general inflexibility, the driving force for the forward leg swing loses virtually all input from the abdominal muscles and must therefore come entirely from the hip flexor muscles. The net effect of this is a loss of power and increased stress on the hip flexors, which can lead to strain injuries of this muscle group, especially with speed or hill training. Strength of the abdominal muscles (the body's core) should be a focus for all runners. Chapters 6 and 7 provide more information on improving core strength and flexibility.

It is predominantly during the swing phase (see figure 1.1*d*) that tight hamstring muscles team up with weak abdominal muscles to cripple the efforts of many an unfortunate runner. Running, when serving as an individual's only regular form of exercise, tends to work the muscles of the low back at the expense of the abdominals, and the repetitive sweeps of the hamstrings through a relatively limited range of motion further promote their inflexibility. As the leg swings forward—especially as the knee begins to extend in the latter half of the swing phase—stretch applied to tight and unyielding hamstrings results in a forward tilt of the lower pelvis. The runner is then pulled into a slouching posture, especially if abdominal strength is insufficient to resist the forces acting through the leg. This anterior tilt position is not only inefficient (it limits the hips' range of motion), but contributes to several common chronic problems that runners face, such as piriformis and hip-flexor injuries. You can find exercises designed specifically to target tight hamstrings in chapter 4.

Extrinsic Factors Affecting Biomechanics

So far we've considered factors that relate to the body itself—the levers, joints, and pulleys that drive runners through the gait cycle. The following sections, on the other hand, describe what happens when outside variables—the work rate (or speed), angles (that is, uphills and downhills), or even shoe types—change. These external factors produce very different stresses. These modifiable factors can increase the risk of injury in susceptible runners, or even aggravate existing injuries that could otherwise be trained through.

Running Shoes

There are those who argue that running in modern cushioned shoes reduces the work that your feet need to do to absorb and generate force. In other words, big, cushiony shoes make you soft. Wrong. Driving your SUV two and a half blocks to get a half-decaf, vanilla hazelnut, nonfat, low-foam cappuccino makes you soft. Properly fitting, cushioned training shoes are a godsend.

Face it—we like getting new running shoes because they are nice and cushiony. They absorb a lot of the shock that would otherwise be transmitted to the bony structures of the body. Ideally, they return most of that energy for use in forward propulsion just like the elastic components of our connective tissues do; otherwise we might as well be running in sand. Compared to running in shoes, which most of us do, barefoot running usually results in increased pronation. This exaggeration of the normal rolling of the foot from an everted to an inverted position is a necessary compensation for the loss of shock absorption resulting from running without shoes; this underscores the important role that normal pronation plays in dissipating the impact of running. Some studies have shown that running economy increases in well-cushioned shoes compared to stiffer models. This effect is attributed to the increased muscular work necessary to absorb impact forces that are passed on by less-forgiving footwear.

It has been shown that modifying the midsoles of shoes to prevent overpronation significantly reduces the inward torque transmitted to the foot and lower leg in susceptible runners. So, shoes can do good things. The type of shoe you should choose, however, depends heavily on your foot type (i.e., flat versus high-arched) and running style. You can employ corrective orthotics to correct biomechanical issues beyond the bailiwick of a motion-control shoe.

Of course, shoes add weight to the feet, and as discussed earlier, weight applied to the end of the limb is the most costly in terms of energy. It has been calculated that adding 50 grams (1.8 ounces) of weight to each ankle increases the energy cost of running by 1 percent. Given that a typical pair of training shoes weighs about 300 grams (10.6 ounces), there is a definite metabolic cost for wearing shoes. This is why racing flats sacrifice a significant amount of support and cushion to cut the weight to about half that of training shoes.

Heel height can also significantly affect stresses applied to the Achilles tendon. Most training shoes incorporate more heel lift than do racing flats, which have a flatter profile. The difference between training and racing flats can be accentuated if orthotics are worn in the rear of a training shoe. Switching to racing flats—or in a more extreme case, track spikes—means that increased stretch is applied to the posterior calf muscles–Achilles tendon complex (because of these shoes' lower heel) at the same time that the greater than normal propulsive forces of racing are applied to them.

In addition, susceptible individuals may experience increased lateral torque to the Achilles as a result of the reduced support and stability of racing flats. Therefore, take care to allow your body to adapt to racing flats gradually; for example, wear them for a few reps during a track workout first, then on the roads for a three-mile stretch, then over a few hills, and finally in a race.

Running Speed

Increasing running speed has very predictable effects on the gait cycle. Faster speeds are accomplished mostly by increasing the length of each stride, with smaller increases in stride frequency. These changes obviously require greater propulsive forces to increase the distance covered during the "flight" phase, when both feet are off the ground, and greater limb velocities to cover an increased range of motion in a slightly shorter time. Impact forces are greater at faster speeds and are absorbed through a smaller area of the foot because a forefoot strike becomes more prevalent. Stresses on the Achilles tendon are much greater during running at faster speeds because the calf muscles generate increased force to power the increased flight, and the resulting increased range of motion produces an increased stretch of the tendon before toe-off. Additionally, landing on the forefoot at higher speeds in conjunction with increased ground impact forces transmits tremendous stretching forces to the calf muscle–Achilles tendon complex. Because running fast often means wearing lower-profile racing shoes or track spikes with low heels that produce even greater stretch, acute strains of the Achilles can occur from racing or speed work. Taking all of this into account, it's often advisable to avoid faster speeds when recovering from Achilles injuries.

Running Surface

The descriptions of running form presented so far all presume an ideal (i.e., smooth and flat) running surface. In fact, for practical purposes, most scientific investigations of running biomechanics are done using treadmills, upon which runners likely use a somewhat different gait than they use to run across a nonmoving surface. Runners are forced to train on treadmills because of weather and other considerations, and expect that the training loads applied on the treadmill will translate into performance on the track.

There are, however, a few noteworthy differences between treadmill running and running on land. For one thing, treadmill running probably results in a slight increase in the range of leg motion and can therefore produce more stretch of hip flexors and other muscles than running on a nonmoving surface does. More important, treadmills provide a much more cushioned running surface than most outdoor terrains (even newer track surfaces) do. The amount of cushion inherent in the treadmill can affect the energy cost of running by as much as 10 percent. Therefore, it is difficult to accurately extrapolate performance on the treadmill to performance on the roads. Empirically, many runners have difficulty shifting from treadmill-only running to running on the roads, mainly as a result of increased pounding on harder road surfaces. Much of the muscular work performed by many muscle groups during running involves shock absorption and eccentric, or lengthening, contractions, so it is to be expected that treadmill running may not adequately train certain muscles for the work necessary for running on asphalt.

In addition to being harder and less forgiving than a treadmill belt, the real world also has a tendency to deviate from the horizontal. As most of us know from experience, running uphill or downhill induces alterations in running biomechanics. Uphill running increases both the forward lean of the trunk and the hip flexion during the swing phase that lifts the leg high enough to match the rise in the ground. This reduction in the angle between the leg and the trunk requires a greater degree of stretch in the hamstring and more abdominal strength to hold the low back and pelvis in line. Runners who experience a forward pelvic tilt and forward slouch of the spine under normal conditions will experience an even greater breakdown in form on uphills, resulting in a loss of power and an increased strain on muscle groups acting at the hip. At the end of this chapter as well as in chapters 6 and 7, there are exercises to help forestall such conditions.

Downhill running creates a few more functional consequences. Predictably, the general changes in running form and gait are opposite those seen in running uphill. The trunk leans farther back, and the knees are somewhat more extended at footstrike and quickly flex to a much greater degree as the quadriceps absorb much of the increased landing force. This "negative work" performed by the quadriceps is the main reason that downhill running is associated with increased postexercise soreness, particularly in the quads. The soreness that results from excessive eccentric contractions is due to actual structural damage within skeletal muscle fibers. Following exercise that induces soreness, enzymes normally found only in muscle cells are found in the blood and urine, indicating significant damage to the muscles. This ultrastructural damage is observable when muscle biopsies taken after exercise are examined under a microscope.

Although you may not feel the pain from a hard downhill run until the next day, and the discomfort may not peak for 48 hours after the run, the trauma to the muscles nonetheless has immediate consequences. Comparing steady 40-minute runs on the level and downhill, it has been found that downhill running results in a steady increase in both oxygen consumption and muscle activation while the level run does not. Evidently, damaged muscle fibers drop out of the fight and new muscle fibers are recruited during the run to keep the pace constant. The cost? A decrease in running economy.

Of course, downhill running is more efficient initially than is running on the flat. Using the force of gravity to drive the forward running motion means that you can run at the same speed while expending less energy. (Side note: When seeking your next point-to-point personal-record course, be aware that the most efficient slope to run down is a 5 percent grade, a drop of 50 meters per kilometer or about 250 feet per mile. Any steeper than that and you'll begin to expend too much energy in braking.)

In much the same way that overpronating and underpronating runners should choose different shoe types to help them achieve normal pronation, different running surfaces can have opposite effects on the two types of runners. Because most underpronating runners constantly battle the repetitive pounding effects of running, they eventually learn that the more mileage they can cover off the pavement, the better off they are from a health perspective. Grass and dirt trails absorb much more of the impact than concrete or asphalt, and all runners can benefit from the reduced pounding they get off-road. However, these surfaces also offer less friction and increase the amount of motion that can occur while the foot is in the stance phase. This can be an issue for overpronating runners because the act of pronation produces a rotational force on the foot that is normally resisted by the frictional component between the outsole of the shoe and surfaces such as asphalt and concrete. A surface such as dirt offers little resistance to these forces, and the result is that the heel of the foot tends to rotate inward as the body weight pivots over the forefoot. These rotational movements are transmitted up the leg and produce strain on the knee and hip. So, individuals who are susceptible to injuries related to pronation may find that they can aggravate their condition by running on dirt and other low-friction surfaces.

Achieving an Efficient Running Gait

To this point, I have mainly discussed how the various aspects of stride biomechanics—structural and external factors—are related to injuries. Now I focus on how these factors collectively contribute to running economy.

Probably no one has contributed more to the understanding of the biomechanics of human running—especially the determinants of running economy—than Dr. Peter Cavanagh of Penn State University. Dr. Cavanagh has studied and compared novice runners, experienced runners, collegiate runners, and elite distance athletes, and has come up with a model of what constitutes a highly efficient running gait. Among other factors, he has listed

- average to below-average height,
- a leg structure that distributes mass closer to the hip (in other words, no beefy calves; larger upper legs than lower legs),
- a narrow pelvis,
- smaller-than-average feet (again, better to have less weight at the end of the limb),
- an optimal stride length,
- a low vertical oscillation of the center of mass (in other words, minimal bouncing up and down, with the center of mass staying lower because of increased knee and hip flexion during stance and less of an upward trajectory in flight),
- a more acute knee angle during swing (still beating that weighted-pendulum theory into the ground),
- decreased ankle extension at toe-off,
- some degree of stiffness in the muscle–tendon structures (which increases energy storage during stretch), and
- a nonflamboyant arm action.

In reading that list, many of you will notice that, unfortunately, many of these routes to improving economy are closed to you. Sure, it would be nice to surgically narrow your pelvis, and binding your feet may have worked during development, but it's hardly an option now. Still, one factor might jump out at you as something you *can* control: an optimal stride length. Alterations in this realm are eminently possible. So what makes a stride length optimal, and how does one go about choosing wisely?

Choosing Optimal Stride Length

Every runner has a single maximally economical stride length for each speed. As mentioned earlier, running at faster speeds is accompanied by increasing stride length out of proportion to increasing frequency; therefore, a runner's optimal stride length is different at each speed. At a given speed, however, if you run with a stride longer or shorter than optimal and adopt a slower or faster turnover, you will use more energy. If you study a group of experienced (but not elite) runners, you'll find that many of them select stride lengths longer or shorter than their personal ideal, suggesting that many runners have some room to improve their running economy—and therefore their performance—by tinkering with their running stride. However, most experienced runners select a stride length that does not differ dramatically from the ideal, implying that overall running experience has something to do with the capacity to self-select an optimal stride length. When collegiate runners were studied across their college careers, researchers found that running stride lengths tended to decrease from their first year to their final year. This is in line with the findings that elite runners tend to have shorter strides than experienced, but less accomplished, runners.

This is all fine and good, but does it help an individual runner to optimize his or her stride? After all, some runners self-select stride lengths that are shorter than optimal. So what makes an optimal stride length? Well, it would be great to answer that question, but in fact, no one knows. As a general rule, taller runners with longer legs have longer optimal stride lengths (on average their optimal strides were 1.4 times their leg length while running seven-minute miles). On an individual basis, though, height and leg length are poor determinants of optimal stride length. In a study of 10 experienced runners, the subject with the shortest leg length had the longest self-selected and the longest optimal stride length. The runners, on average, chose stride lengths just four centimeters from optimal.

The problem is that without true predictors of what an optimal stride length is for an individual (and even a trained coach would probably have a hard time determining whether a runner was overstriding or understriding), there's not much a runner can do except let his or her body adjust to an optimal stride through experience. It is also possible that the biomechanics researchers have been looking at this problem backward. Because stride length has to balance with stride frequency, or stride rate, to produce a given speed, and because each runner's stride length varies widely across speeds while stride rate stays relatively constant (increasing slightly with increasing speeds), it is possible that runners choose a stride rate that is most efficient, regardless of the speed, and adjust stride length to obtain the desired speed.

Noted exercise physiologist and coach Jack Daniels places an emphasis on nudging new runners toward a faster stride rate. Daniels, who has helped more runners than his namesake has destroyed livers, selects 180 steps per minute as a target to reduce pounding forces associated with longer strides. Although beginning runners have a tendency to overstride somewhat, it is by no means certain that any runner can increase his or her running economy by arbitrarily choosing a different stride frequency; the same can be said for attempts to make oneself a forefoot-striker or a heel-striker. Both lead to fighting one's most natural tendencies. One classic study of elite distance runners showed self-selected stride rates of 190 steps per minute at 5:24 mile pace. However, among less accomplished runners, efficiency was highest at frequencies slightly below 180 strides per minute, albeit at a much slower treadmill speed. Therefore, many runners can probably benefit from adopting a somewhat shorter stride length and faster turnover. There are, however, no magic numbers that can be applied to all runners looking to optimize their running form.

Training to Improve Stride Mechanics

With radical pelvic and foot surgeries out of the question, it still may be possible to train the body you're stuck with to improve biomechanical efficiency. Because running economy seems to be a matter of maximizing the energy storage and return that occurs through the stretch–shorten cycle, adaptations that improve the efficiency of this system should decrease the energy cost of running at a given speed. Exercises aimed at achieving this generally fall under the heading of plyometrics.

Plyometrics are a form of dynamic exercises that have been hypothesized to improve energy return through the stretch–shorten cycle. Plyometric training exaggerates the stretch–shorten cycle of muscle groups used in running, using propulsive movements that follow excessive stretch preloading. Plyometric training—involving exercises such as drop-jumping, hopping, and bounding—can increase jumping ability and performance in other activities requiring high power outputs. There are reports that plyometric training can improve distance-running performance, although this has not been demonstrated conclusively. Still, these exercises are a staple of sprint training programs and may enhance running economy for distance runners who have less need of the all-out ballistic power that sprinters seek. Many coaches advocate the judicious application of plyometric exercises to supplement distance-training programs.

The unproven theory is that plyometric training enhances the function of the muscle spindle reflex in muscle. As mentioned previously, prestretching a muscle–tendon unit enhances the subsequent contraction through a simple recoil effect of the elastic components of the tissue. In addition, the stretch activates sensory nerves in the muscle called spindles. Neural activity of the spindles then initiates a reflex loop leading to an increased muscle contraction response in the muscle. Unlike the elastic recoil of muscle, however, this is not a purely passive process in that it stimulates the active contraction of muscle. Although it carries an energy cost, this contraction may still serve to increase muscle stiffness and increase elastic recoil. Therefore, although the spindle reflex helps in movements that require maximal force production by generating a more forceful contraction, it may or may not improve the energy cost of running at submaximal speeds.

Plyometric training will likely increase all-out sprinting speed and muscle endurance at high power outputs—both of which are components of running performance—and will strengthen the connective tissues involved in running. However, these exercises carry a high risk of injury for the same reasons. Plyometric exercises are designed to load muscle and connective tissues with forces sufficient to amplify the stretch reflex. After a point, these loads begin to cut into the "safety factors" of the structures involved. Therefore, you should undertake the following plyometric exercises with caution. Incorporate them into your training program gradually, starting with one set of a couple of exercises, then adding other exercises after the body has adapted to the dynamic loads. Do plyometric workouts a maximum of twice per week; one session a week is usually adequate for distance runners. Reserve these workouts for the early season, when the amount of high-intensity running training is low.

Do the following exercises on a smooth, grassy surface to reduce the risk of injury. Allow complete recovery between sets to minimize the negative effects of fatigue on connective-tissue integrity and to give the muscles the chance to recover so that they can effectively stabilize the joints and thus absorb the large forces that are applied. Also, avoid hard training the day after a plyometric session to allow adequate recovery.

In-place jumps. These serve primarily as a warm-up. Simply bend your knees slightly and jump straight up (as shown in the photos below). Concentrate on pushing off with a "snapping" movement of the ankles.

Depth jumps. This serves as the cornerstone of the plyometric exercises. Start this exercise using boxes 12 inches (30 centimeters) or shorter and build up height in 6-inch (15 centimeters) increments. Athletes typically use drop heights of one to three feet, although physiologists suggest that maximal power development occurs at heights as great as 44 inches (122 centimeters). It is unlikely that the potential benefits to distance runners offset the risks of absorbing such great forces. If you are susceptible to injury, keep the box height no more than 12 inches even as you progress. Standing on top of a box, jump (or drop) off the box and land on the balls of the feet. Allow your knees to flex to absorb the impact of landing, flexing past 90 degrees before springing up rapidly, jumping as high as you can with both arms raised (see photo below). Do no more than 10 of these exercises per session.

Box jumps. This exercise is similar to a depth jump. Set two boxes of equal height a couple of feet apart, one in front of the other. After jumping off one box to the ground, jump directly onto the other box. This actually requires a modicum of coordination. Use box heights similar to those used for depth jumps. Stick to 5 to 10 repetitions of this exercise.

Box bounds. For this exercise, arrange four or five boxes in a row about two feet apart. Keeping both feet together, hop over each box in rapid-fire succession. Try to land softly between the boxes, absorbing energy by flexing the knees, and quickly rebound up and over the next box. Do no do more than four or five of these sets.

Squat jumps. These are not true plyometrics because they lack the dynamic preload. They do however, increase the dynamic strength of your quadriceps and can help your body handle the strains of running and doing plyometrics. Standing with your legs apart, slowly lower yourself until your thighs are nearly parallel to the ground, as if you were doing a barbell squat. Pause in this position and then explode upward as quickly as you can (see photos below). The brief pause prevents the stretch reflex from aiding in the force of contraction and reduces the elastic recoil resulting from the prestretch.

Bleachers. These exercises are basically box jumps, except that jumping is done "uphill" as a result of landing on successive stadium bleachers. Make sure your coordination is tested via box jumps before trying these exercises, also known as "widowmakers."

Power bounds. To bound, adopt an exaggerated running style in which you toe off with maximal force to achieve as long a stride as possible (see photos below). Use your arms to help with your "super takeoff." Land lightly, with your knees bending to absorb shock on impact, and bounce back into the next big stride as quickly as possible. Get a high knee lift and as much spread between your front and back legs as possible while you float through the air. Start with four to six repetitions of whatever distance you can manage without losing form, building up to 40 to 50 meters of continuous bounding.

CHAPTER 2

Creating Leg Turnover and Raw Speed

GREG MCMILLAN, MS

All distance runners want to be faster—faster over the entire distance of their chosen event and especially in their finishing kick. Runners love the feeling of blowing away the competition in the finishing straight with a sizzling kick. But training to improve your finishing kick has other benefits that make leg-speed training important during every phase of your training cycle, not just when entering a sharpening racing phase.

Training to increase leg speed, or "turnover," as it's often called, can yield several benefits. First, and most obviously, leg-speed training does indeed help your finishing kick. Although each runner has a genetically determined ratio of fast-twitch muscle fibers to slow-twitch muscle fibers (see sidebar on page 28) and therefore a specific amount of innate leg speed, all runners can improve their ability to sprint at the end of a race. Sometimes, this is just a matter of practicing sprinting every so often, so that when you *do* kick for the finish, your body has some idea of what you're trying to get it to do!

Second, by including leg-speed training, you may lower your risk of injury. Most surveys suggest that two-thirds of all runners incur an injury serious enough to cause them to miss a week or more of training each year. Since I began incorporating leg-speed training into my training programs, very few of my runners have gotten hurt despite often training more—and harder—than ever before.

Many health professionals who treat running injuries—physical therapists, chiropractors, podiatrists, massage therapist, kinesiologists, and so on—suggest that leg-speed training works the smaller "accessory" muscles of running that are not recruited to an appreciable extent at normal training speeds. Leg-speed training also strengthens the major running muscles and tendons, improving their resistance to injury. When doing this type of training, you also move your legs through a greater range of motion, which helps improve flexibility and thus better prepares your body for hard training and racing.

Finally, and perhaps most important, leg-speed training adds another type of workout to your program, and overall variety in training seems to be one of the keys to staying healthy and continuing to improve. The body responds well to the training stresses it receives provided that the intensity and the volume of these stresses are varied. Very fast, short runs seem to add zip to your legs *and* your mind. By incorporating leg-speed training, you escape the distance runner's "shuffle" that can develop as a result of doing only slower, aerobic running. And don't think that marathoners—notorious for shuffling—are the only ones who do it; it's common in 5K and 10K runners too.

What Is Leg-Speed Training?

Leg-speed training improves your ability to sprint for short distances. Don't let the word "sprint" cause your FT fibers to curl up in your hamstrings—not all sprinting is of the Michael Johnson variety. For distance runners, leg-speed training is defined as *any workout in which maximum or near-maximum speeds are maintained for durations of less than 90 seconds*. With this sort of training, you move your legs and arms at near-maximum speed and push off of the ground with maximum force to generate the highest velocity possible across the ground. However, you must perform this without straining or tightening up, which compromises running form.

Because technique is critical for leg-speed training, I actually find these workouts to be the perfect opportunity to fine-tune and improve running form. With each repeat, you can try moving your legs or arms in a slightly different way or try holding your body in a subtly different position. When you do this, monitor the outcome. Do you get more speed with less effort? Do you get less speed with more effort? Over time, you will learn the body position, leg action, and arm swing that generate the greatest speed in the most efficient manner for you.

When I do leg-speed workouts, I try bringing my rear leg closer to my gluteal muscles. Then I try pushing harder against the ground, or bringing my knees higher. Then I can fine-tune how to best move my legs for the greatest speed. I do the same with body position—more forward lean, less forward lean. Then I do the same with my arms—pumping higher, holding them lower. Once you find the best technique, additional leg-speed training consolidates this technique in your neural patterns as your fastest running form. Then, when it comes time to sprint for the tape in a race, you'll be ready.

Although there are many subtleties in arm and leg action, the most important technique to work on is your push against the ground. You initiate this motion when the leg is in front of you, before ground contact. Once the leg has swung fully forward, forcefully pull it down and back as the foot makes contact with the ground. Continue this backward pull then push of the leg as you move toward push-off. When I concentrate on pulling my leg down and back and empha-

© M. Sandkuhler / Jumphoto

Experiment to find your personal fastest running form, then train so that it is fully engrained by race day.

sizing my push backward, I increase my stride length and speed. Simply put, I cover more ground. Please note that it's important to accentuate the backward push against the ground and not just a forceful push downward—otherwise you'll bounce up and down rather than propel your body horizontally across the ground. A biomechanist friend of mine suggests that this forceful contact with the ground is the key to running faster.

Once you improve your "paw-back" and push-off motion, you can work on forcefully swinging your leg through as it moves from behind you to in front of you. This improved swing phase (see chapter 1) also helps optimize your stride length.

I want to emphasize this: Don't consciously focus on increasing your stride length. Let your stride length increase as a result improving the paw-back motion and push-off. When you focus on the right technique, your stride length, as discussed in the previous chapter, will optimize on its own. Athletes who focus on increasing their stride length instead of concentrating on technique often overstride.

Muscle Fiber Types

Whole muscles are comprised of bundles of individual muscle fibers, or myocytes. These individual fibers can have different traits and have been categorized into two general types: slow twitch (ST) and fast twitch (FT). Because different scientists have used different terminology to identify fiber types, you also see the ST fibers called Type I, red, or slow oxidative fibers. Likewise, you may see the FT fibers called Type II, white, or fast oxidative fibers. Type II fibers can be further broken down in to Type IIa (fast oxidative-glcolytic) or Type IIb (fast oxidative).

A key difference between the fiber types relates to their respective speeds of contraction. As you might guess, ST fibers take longer to contract (~75 milliseconds) than do FT fibers (~35 milliseconds). Another important difference relates to the fibers' metabolic tendencies and capacities. Slow-twitch fibers are resistant to fatigue; they contain more mitochondria (cellular "energy factories") and more enzymes that produce aerobic energy than do FT fibers, and therefore, are very important for distance running. Fast-twitch fibers, on the other hand, tend to fatigue more quickly but contain better capabilities for quick energy production using carbohydrate, and are essential for fast running.

Some FT fibers, though, are like chameleons: They maintain some of the key benefits of FT fibers, such as fast contraction, but can become more resistant to fatigue by acting more like ST fibers, exhibiting an increased ability to produce energy aerobically. These are frequently called fast oxidative-glycolytic, or Type IIa, fibers to denote their hybrid nature. It now appears that with endurance training, more and more of your FT fibers may morph into this fast oxidative-glycolytic type.

Nearly all of the muscles used in running contain both ST and FT fibers, but the overall contribution from each can vary greatly depending on the type of muscle under scrutiny and individual genetics. For example, the soleus, or deep calf muscle, is predominantly composed of ST fibers, whereas the gastrocnemius, or superficial calf muscle, typically has a more even distribution of ST and FT fibers.

The bottom line is that you want to maximize the endurance capabilities of both the ST and FT fibers while maintaining your ability to sprint (recruiting the FT glycolytic fibers) when necessary; hence the requirement for a varied, well-designed training program.

How Can I Increase Leg Speed?

Within this general definition of leg-speed training for distance runners, we can distinguish two subtypes of training: neuromuscular and lactic-acid tolerance. As with most types of running training, there are as many workouts for each of these subtypes as there are coaches and athletes. Following are descriptions of the subtypes and examples of workouts for each that I've had success with as a coach.

Neuromuscular Training

Neuromuscular training (NMT) is a popular buzzword in leg-speed training theory these days, and refers to training the neurological system (the brain and nerves) to best activate, or fire, the muscles involved in running. Training the neurological system to call upon more muscle fibers in a coordinated fashion is what ultimately improves speed.

In this type of leg-speed training, little if any lactic acid builds up in the muscles, either with each repetition or throughout the entire workout. This is because in exercise bouts lasting less than 30 seconds, the primary energy source is stored ATP and creatine phosphate. The system that produces lactic acid is activated only briefly; thus little lactic acid is produced, and the amount that is produced is quickly removed. Contrast this with repeats lasting more than 30 seconds, wherein a large amount of lactic acid accumulates, not only after each repeat but also throughout the course of the workout. In practice, this alactic training results in recruiting individual muscles more effectively and more coordinated firing of several different muscle groups. Put together, this means that you can generate more speed.

It's sometimes easier to understand NMT by thinking of a baby learning to walk. Before walking, and even crawling, a baby learns how to fire the individual muscles for movement. We see this in the kicking of the legs and arms and all the squirming around. The urge to squirm, kick, and move is the impetus for developing neural patterns that reinforce these and more complex movements. As maturing infants develop more and more neural patterns, not only for each individual fiber but also within muscles and between muscle groups, the body and mind can progress to more and more complex movements—first standing, then walking, then running, and so forth. When it comes to standing and then walking, however, the baby must coordinate the individual muscles and muscle groups with other muscles so that balance, posture, and coordinated movements that use the entire body can occur. Over time, these movements become more coordinated and produce faster and more defined movements.

NMT involves the same principles in producing faster running—learning how to better activate individual muscles and how to best coordinate these individual muscles with other muscles to achieve the overall effect: faster leg speed. When considering the advantage of improved speed, many runners think only of a better finishing kick. However, possessing greater speed allows you to maintain a faster pace throughout the range of your training and racing, and also to better handle midrace surges. As your body gradually finds its best position for fast running, it becomes more efficient while in this position; this ultimately translates into faster paces for all training at the same effort level.

You don't need an exercise scientist to tell you that a buildup of lactic acid interferes with the neuromuscular recruitment in the muscles, resulting in poor technique. Just watch the last 100 meters of a 400-meter race: most competitors have greatly reduced knee lift, turnover, and overall stride coordination. As mentioned earlier, during neuromuscular training (NMT) you want to practice proper technique as well as cover ground quickly. Therefore, you must take a full recovery between repeats to avoid lactic acid buildup during the course of the entire workout; this will allow you to maintain efficient form. When done correctly, you should find that you can run your last few repeats much faster than your first few. Take full recoveries.

Some examples of NMT workouts include the following:

Straights and curves. This is one of my favorite NMT workouts on a track. After a thorough warm-up of 20 to 30 minutes, jog the curves but sprint the straightaways. Always start with the jogging portion, then sprint the straights for a number of laps appropriate for your fitness level and training phase. I start runners with four to six laps at the beginning of the base phase, and progress to a maximum of 10 laps (20 total sprints). It sounds like an easy workout, but trust me, it's not. Regardless of your fitness level, this kind of training demands considerable focus if you do it properly.

I suggest that runners maintain a medium-intensity level for the first few straights and then gradually get faster, so that the last two to four straights are completed at near-maximum speed. As I mentioned earlier, this is an excellent opportunity to work on your technique. After all, you want to promote and practice the most effective running form. Play around with your leg action, your body position, and your arm action; find what works best for you. You should never quite reach 100 percent effort. When athletes try to run at 100 percent effort, their form invariably deteriorates.

Make sure that you're jogging the curves very slowly—the idea is to maintain a large difference in speed and effort between the straights and the curves. To prevent lactic acid buildup, a slow recovery jog or walk is necessary. And don't skimp on the postworkout jog: After taking your muscles through a large range of motion and exerting a lot of force, you need to cool down adequately. Jogging slowly for 10 to 30 minutes (depending on your training level) is a great way to cool down after an NMT workout. Also be sure to allow adequate recovery before your next key workout.

Stride workouts. Stride workouts are a great way to introduce leg-speed training into your program. In fact, I call the fast portions of leg-speed training "strides" instead of sprints, as the word "sprint" conjures bad memories for many runners or makes them think that they must run at an all-out speed, which can lead to straining and poor form.

In a stride workout, warm-up by jogging slowly for 10 to 30 minutes, then begin to alternate 15- to 30-second strides with 45- to 60-second jogs.

A great advantage of this workout is that it does not require a track and can be done on trails, grass, or roads. I start runners with 10 or 15 strides and gradually increase the number to 15 to 25. Remember to jog slowly between each stride to allow full recovery. Stride workouts are especially great for people without access to a track or who are so time-obsessed that they'll start racing themselves if they only do straights and curves.

You can also do stride workouts at the end of an easy run; it's your choice. My suggestion is to do them in the middle of your runs, so that your body and mind are not tired and you can maintain good form. Sometimes runners get sloppy with strides at the end of a run.

Lactic-Acid Tolerance Training

Lactic-acid tolerance (LAT) training consists of workouts that train the muscles to better tolerate a large buildup of lactic acid. Lactic acid is the end result of the conversion of carbohydrate (glucose and glycogen) to energy through the glycolytic metabolic pathway. Once produced, the lactic acid quickly breaks apart into a lactate molecule and a hydrogen ion. The lactate molecule quickly diffuses out of the muscle cell, where it can be shuttled to other muscle fibers and the heart for energy, or to the liver. The hydrogen ion, meanwhile, is buffered by the sodium-bicarbonate system, thereby neutralizing its acidic effect.

Lactic acid is quickly overcoming its reputation as the "bad boy" of metabolism. Physiologists are learning that lactic acid is not the enemy but a substance whose measurement may—like heart rate, $\dot{V}O_2$, and perceived exertion—serve as a useful parameter for monitoring and prescribing training.

A key to incorporating knowledge of lactic acid into your training and racing is understanding that even when your body is at rest, it produces lactic acid. As you run faster and faster, more and more lactic acid is produced; this production is balanced by the body's ability to remove the lactate and hydrogen ions using the lactate-shuttle and sodium-bicarbonate systems. Both of these systems, however, have a maximum capacity. As the capacities are reached, more and more lactate and hydrogen ions accumulate in the blood and in the cells of working muscles.

The point at which the production of lactate begins to outpace its removal is often identified as the lactate, or anaerobic, threshold. As the hydrogen ions accumulate, the environment inside the muscle cell becomes more and more acidic; eventually, this acidity interferes with the production of energy and the contraction of the muscle cells—as anyone who has run all out for 400 or 800 meters knows too well.

Using this information, you can see that training at intensities resulting in varying levels of blood lactate (which is a direct indication of the amount of lactic acid produced) can induce adaptations in the efficiency, capacity, and removal systems related to carbohydrate metabolism. For even more information on lactic acid, see Tim Noakes' *Lore of Running*, Fourth Edition.

Thus, unlike neuromuscular training, with LAT training you work to build up lactic acid in your muscles. The goal is to teach the muscles to continue to operate despite the flood of hydrogen ions in the muscle cells and a large drop in muscle-cell pH. You also want to enhance your body's ability to remove lactic acid quickly. Over time, LAT creates muscles that are better able to function despite a large buildup in lactic acid—a benefit of particular importance in the last half-mile or so of most races. The result is an increased ability to sustain leg speed.

Because the two types of speed training relate to lactic acid in opposite ways—NMT with no buildup of lactic acid and LAT with a large buildup—it's important to know which type of speed training you're doing; otherwise, the results won't be as predictable. "You have to understand the difference between the workouts," says World Indoor and Outdoor 800-meter bronze medalist Rich Kenah. "You can't properly perform both types of training in the same workout."

The study of physiology tells us that lactic acid begins to build up in the muscles after 20 to 30 seconds of fast (mile race pace or quicker) running. Therefore, the neuromuscular workouts consist of repeats lasting approximately 30 seconds or less and include long recoveries (45 to 90 seconds) between reps so that no lactic acid builds up. This is a very important point. If you are trying to do an NMT workout, such as the strides workout noted on page 30, make sure you don't build up lactic acid. You want to perform each repeat perfectly. You want to maintain good running technique and be able to move your arms and legs as quickly as possible for NMT training to affect the body as it should. A buildup of lactic acid compromises the internal mechanisms that NMT training focuses on. This manifests itself as deteriorating form (the head tilts back, the arms start to flail, and so on) and the inability to move the arms and legs as fast as possible. Keeping the repeats in the NMT workouts to less than 30 seconds and taking 45- to 90-second recoveries allows your body to remove any lactic acid that might have built up before it interferes with the muscles' ability to work.

In LAT workouts you *do* want a large buildup of lactic acid to help teach the body to manage it more effectively and at higher speeds. Therefore, the repeats should last longer than 30 seconds and up to 90 seconds to effect maximum lactic acid buildup. However, don't perform repeats lasting longer than 90 seconds. Remember, not only are you trying to improve your tolerance of lactic acid buildup, but you are also trying to build leg-speed and practice good technique. Running for longer than 90 seconds necessitates a slower pace, and you may not be able to hold your form this long. Therefore, keep your repeats in LAT workouts within the 30- to 90-second range.

Recovery between each repeat should be sufficient (usually two to three times the duration of the repeat) so that the body has time to remove most of the lactic acid before the next rep begins. The recovery between each rep should also be long enough that you can maintain or increase your speed with each successive repeat. Over time, the muscles learn to operate despite large amounts of lactic

Outlasting the Competition: Rich Kenah

Rich Kenah had the rare ability to maintain his leg speed during the last 100 meters of his 800-meter races to a greater extent than his fellow competitors. While all 800-meter runners slow in the last 100 meters of the race, Kenah had the ability to close the last 100 meters better than most, resulting in bronze medals at both the 1997 World Indoor and 1997 World Outdoor Track and Field championships. His personal best of 1:43.38 still ranks the Olympian in the 2000 Games fourth on the all-time U.S. list.

How did he do it? Kenah believes that his closing speed was due to the specialized training he used. Like Peter Snell (see sidebar on page 38), Kenah attributes his ability to outlast his opponents to his aerobic endurance and to the development of the specialized traits necessary for middle-distance success: aerobic endurance, stamina, "speed-endurance," and leg speed. But unlike Snell's, Kenah's training week was composed of workouts geared toward improving each of these traits throughout an entire training cycle, building the speed of each workout as the cycle progressed. By gradually increasing the intensity of each type of workout across a training cycle, Kenah saw his body adjust to faster and faster training, and with so much quality running in each week, his body developed the ability to race well through multiple rounds of races in major competitions. This was also what produced his ability to maintain his speed over the last 100 meters of his races. Kenah states, "I emphasized the total package, not just one aspect."

For improving leg speed, Kenah used very short but fast repeats with long recoveries—classic LAT training. In these workouts, he limited his repeats to distances no greater than 300 meters and focused on running them fast. Long recoveries were taken so that each repeat could be done at near-maximum speed. Because this type of training is strenuous, the total volume of leg-speed training was limited to no more than 1,000 meters of total work. He cautions that attempting to work on both leg speed and speed-endurance (repeats longer than 300 meters) simultaneously is a mistake. "You can't work on both in the same workout," he says. "They are different types of work, and you must understand this if you want to fully develop each one."

Kenah supplemented his track work with hill workouts early in his training cycle as well as explosive workouts in the weight room. As he says, "To be a better middle-distance runner, you need to lift like a sprinter in the weight room and train like a distance man when running."

Developing leg speed and racing ability like Kenah's does not occur overnight. Kenah believes that with a comprehensive plan to fully develop each trait that contributes to successful distance running and with a focus on the long term, you can improve your leg speed and therefore your racing performance.

acid, and the blood buffers improve their ability to remove lactic acid during the recovery between repetitions.

To perform an LAT training session, simply run for 30 to 90 seconds at near top speed. There are a multitude of combinations you can use for an LAT workout. You can go to a track or marked course, and—depending on the time it takes you to complete each repeat—you can perform 200- to 600-meter repeats. Alternatively, you can do a workout where you simply vary the pace of your run, mimicking the fast running followed by recovery running that you would do on the track. This type of varied running, called a "fartlek" run, doesn't require a marked course, so it is great for the roads, on trails, or when traveling. In a fartlek workout, simply surge for 30 and 90 seconds. The key variables to manipulate are the intensity and duration of the repeats and the recovery between each. For any LAT workout, the intensity must remain high enough to ensure a considerable accumulation of lactic acid; for most competitive runners, 800-meter to 3,000-meter race pace achieves the required intensity.

© M. Sandkuhler / Jumphoto

LAT workouts can be performed anywhere; the key is to alternate bursts of enough high speed running to build up lactic acid with recovery times sufficient to permit its removal.

As mentioned earlier, the recovery between each repeat must be long enough to allow the muscles to practice removing the lactic acid. The goal is a cycle of producing a lot of lactic acid, removing it, and then producing it again. Generally, if athletes take recoveries lasting two times the duration of the repeat for 30- to 45-second repeats and three times for 45- to 90-second repeats, they will be ready for the next repeat and will be able to complete the entire workout. For example, if you do repeats of 200 meters in 45 seconds, then a recovery of 90 to 135 seconds is a good rule of thumb. I recommend that you also mix up the distances and durations of your repeats within single workouts, a pattern that creates a ladder workout. In a ladder, you may do a workout such as 400, 300, 200, 300, and 400 meters. A ladder workout not only teaches your body to tolerate lactic acid, but it also challenges your ability to judge pace and dole out your effort appropriately over a variety of durations, to change pace, which is invariably needed in a race, and to maintain focus, which usually results in faster racing.

Be creative when designing your LAT workouts. As long as you follow the basic guidelines, you'll get the adaptations you want regardless of the specific permutations you choose. Once you find a workout you like, use this as a marker throughout your training cycle and throughout your running career so that you can track improvements in your fitness. I discuss more about how to use marker workouts later in this chapter.

Combination NMT and LAT Workouts

A few workouts can achieve the goals of both neuromuscular and lactic-acid tolerance training:

Ins and outs. This is a combination neuromuscular and lactic-acid tolerance workout and provides a great transition into the type of traditional speed training (400-meter to one-mile repeats) that runners typically incorporate into their programs. Ins and outs are similar to straights and curves, but the relevant distances are twice as long. With this workout, you jog for half a lap of the track and stride for half a lap. The exertion guidelines for straights and curves still apply. It's best to start with 8 laps and progress to a maximum of 20 laps, although 12 laps seems to work best for most competitive runners of all distances.

Because you are now running very fast for 200 meters rather than 100 meters, it's likely that it will take you longer than 30 seconds to complete each repetition. You therefore will accumulate more lactic acid than in the NMT workouts, but will also have a longer recovery (200 meters versus 100 meters). Ins and outs provide a good combination workout.

Hills. Like ins and outs, hill workouts can provide a great combination workout, but can also be strictly NMT or LAT with proper structuring. The difference is in the direction you run the hill. There are two main types of hill repeats—uphill and downhill—and each yields different results.

To perform an *uphill* workout, find a hill of moderate slope (a 6 to 10 percent grade) that will take you approximately one minute to ascend at a steady, but not exhausting, pace. (A grade that causes you to noticeably change your form is probably greater than 10 percent; most steeper grades on secondary highways are in the 6 to 10 percent range.) Try to find a hill with a soft surface like grass or dirt. Run up the hill at about 5K race effort, focusing on the forceful push against the ground that springs you up the hill. Again, it's vital to note that the goal is not to simply run up the hill as fast as possible. As three-time Olympic gold medalist and exercise physiologist Peter Snell says, "The goal is to focus on a forceful push-off, or thrust, up the hill, so that you almost 'bound' uphill. With uphill repeats, you are trying to develop leg power, an important component of leg speed." As you thrust your body forcefully up the hill, keep in mind that you must move forward as well as upward or you may find yourself bouncing virtually in place. Because uphill repeats are stressful on the body, it's best to start with 4 to 6 repeats and increase by two repeats each week until reaching 10 to 12.

To perform a *downhill* workout, find a hill with a very gradual slope (a 1 to 3 percent grade) that will take you 15 to 20 seconds to descend. Because there will be additional pounding while running downhill, it is imperative to find a grass or dirt area for downhill repeats. Unlike uphill repeats, where the goal is to focus on a powerful push-off, the aim of downhill repeats is to improve leg turnover. As Snell suggests, "Focus on a very high cadence with the legs on the downhills." Downhill repeats afford an opportunity for you to turn your legs over at a rate that is not possible in flat running. However, they are stressful on the body, so begin these more gradually than uphill repeats. Start with 3 to 5 repetitions and build up to 8 or 10. In order to avoid unnecessary braking and its damaging effects on your legs and your pace, try leaning forward slightly and staying on or toward your toes, letting gravity pull you down the hill. You may feel somewhat out of control initially, but with practice you will adjust to the sensation.

How Do You Implement Leg–Speed Training?

The longer I coach, the more I believe that leg-speed training should be included in the training program year-round. Knowing which types to include and when is the trick to developing and completing a successful training program.

A key aspect of a successful year-round training program is dividing your program into several periods, or cycles. As with other aspects of training, the type of leg-speed training performed will change as you move through the cycles.

During base training, the only type of speed training I recommend is the NMT type. NMT workouts help you maintain your fast running form, keep you injury free, and spice up your training because most training during your base phase is steady aerobic running. You'll also find that when you begin doing more fast training in later phases, your body will be better prepared and your race sharpness will return more quickly.

New Zealand coach and training pioneer Arthur Lydiard used to say, "Don't pull the pH down during your base-building phase." The pH is a measure of acidity: The lower the pH, the more acidic the environment. Accordingly, when lactic acid builds up in the muscles, the pH of the muscle drops. When the muscles become acidic, the enzymes involved in generating energy are inhibited. Additionally, the muscle cells themselves are compromised and the

enzymes can "leak out." If you are trying to increase your aerobic endurar
you don't want to harm the enzymes associated with this energy system. This
is why I advocate neuromuscular training, not lactic-acid tolerance training,
during your base period. It allows you to maintain your leg speed but does not
interfere with the development of your aerobic endurance. Lydiard said this 30
years ago, and it holds true today.

If you are new to leg-speed training, the following eight-week program is a
great way to start building your turnover and leg speed. Remember to always
include a thorough warm-up and cool-down.

Week 1—Straights and curves: 4 to 6 laps

Week 2—Straights and curves: 6 to 8 laps

Week 3—Straights and curves: 8 to 10 laps

Week 4—Stride workout: 10 to 12 × (30 seconds with a 60-second recovery
jog)

Week 5—Stride workout: 12 to 15 × (30 seconds with a 60-second recovery
jog)

Week 6—Ins and outs: 8 to 10 laps

Week 7—Ins and outs: 10 to 12 laps

Week 8—Straights and curves: 8 to 10 laps

I also use this program with beginning runners. Prescribing this type of
training once a week brings about faster fitness improvement. However, beginners usually walk rather than jog the curves or half-lap recovery segments.
After you've completed this program, you can include other types of leg speed
workouts once a week to add zip to your legs.

As you enter your transitional phase and build strength and stamina through
hill workouts and so forth, you can begin to incorporate an LAT workout once
every two to three weeks in addition to the weekly NMT workout. It's important
not to do too much LAT training too early in your training program; doing so
can bring you to peak fitness too early in your season.

Distance runners focusing on the 10K or shorter events can do LAT workouts
once every one or two weeks during the competitive phase, whereas longer-
distance runners (half-marathon to marathon) will benefit from performing these
workouts every two to four weeks or incorporating them as the final portion
of a workout made up of 800- to 5,000-meter repeats. Again, a weekly NMT
workout keeps your legs fresh.

Of course, an important consideration is how much running to do in an NMT
or LAT workout. Opinions vary, but I find that between 800 and 3,000 meters
of NMT or LAT is sufficient for one workout, depending on the time of the
year, experience, and goals of the athlete. Kenah kept his NMT training to no
more than 1,000 meters per session, and for LAT training, he ran no more than
2,400 meters per session. Most coaches and athletes keep the volume of NMT

The Proof Is in the Pudding: Peter Snell

Peter Snell, 1960s middle-distance legend, was not merely the best of his day. His times, 1:44.3 for 800 meters and 3:54.1 for the mile, would be respectable in many contemporary competitions. In fact, he still holds the New Zealand national record for 800 meters—and remember, he ran on grass and dirt tracks!

Snell was characterized by his incredible strength and power. He seemed to be able to run forever, and when racing, to always maintain his top speed, particularly in the last 100 meters.

These qualities can be attributed to his training as well as his talent. An athlete of legendary New Zealand coach Arthur Lydiard, Snell regularly included the long-distance running that was contrary to popular middle-distance training of his day. In fact, his training was even more voluminous than that of many of today's competitive marathoners. He regularly ran 80 to 100 miles per week with long runs lasting two to three hours. The philosophy was that athletes needed a large base of aerobic endurance that could only be gained by weeks and weeks of steady aerobic training. Then, as the major competitions of the season drew near, athletes shifted into race-specific training. This, combined with a peaking program designed to produce maximum performance, allowed Snell and his teammates to dominate their events in the mid-1960s.

Today, Snell is an exercise physiologist at the University of Texas Southwestern Medical Center in Dallas. I asked him about his training and how he developed his legendary strength and speed. Snell's training to fully develop leg speed consisted of three steps, which he recommends for runners today. First, he says, athletes must fully develop their aerobic systems. This is accomplished through the base phase of steady aerobic running. But the trick is that the training must also activate, or recruit, as many muscle fibers as possible. There are two ways to recruit a lot of fibers: run very fast for short periods or run a moderate pace for a very long time. Snell says that research has shown that during exhaustive exercise, not only do the slow-twitch (ST) fibers become depleted of glycogen, as expected, but in runs of sufficient duration, the fast-twitch (FT) fibers become depleted as well; this indicates that FT fibers are activated even when the pace is slow. So, over time, the body's ability to consume and utilize oxygen increases, and both the ST *and* the FT fibers are trained.

The benefit of long-duration, steady aerobic running, says Snell, is that in contrast with running very fast for short periods of time, there is no buildup of lactic acid even though the FT fibers are activated. A buildup of lactic acid lowers the pH in the muscles and can destabilize the cell membranes, resulting in the loss of important enzymes used to produce energy. The lowered pH also interferes directly with the functioning of these enzymes as well as with the contractile mechanisms of the muscles themselves. As a result, Snell contends that athletes should train the FT fibers during their base-building phase with long-duration running.

How fast should these runs be? Fast enough to tap into glycogen stores in all available muscle fibers, but not fast enough to produce lactic acid. How far? Far enough to deplete the ST fibers, which leads to the recruitment of FT fibers. If you run long enough frequently enough, all the fibers are trained, which conditions the FT fibers to adapt more quickly to, and therefore benefit to a greater degree from, the race-specific speed training that comes as the primary competition nears.

After completing the aerobic-base phase, the second step in gaining speed for performance is to develop leg power, leg turnover, and efficiency at race pace. To gain leg power and leg turnover, Snell used hill training—both uphill and downhill (see pages 35 to 36 for more on hill running).

The final component Snell used to produce his world-record performances was race-specific track workouts. He capped his preparation with workouts such as 400-meter runs at race pace with enough recovery to repeat them six times. Snell also added 150-meter accelerations, building up to top speed in the first 100 meters, then holding the last 50 meters at maximum speed to further fine-tune leg speed.

The end result was that Snell won three gold medals, set four world records, and dominated his events. Although the track world is different today, with a greater number of competitions spread throughout the year, he believes these concepts can help runners achieve faster performances. And, as they say, the proof is in the pudding!

One note: A frequent criticism of the training Snell used as espoused by Lydiard is that the athlete loses basic speed during the base-building phase. Snell says not to worry. That speed will be regained in the race-specific phase. He goes on to say, though, that there is no problem with an athlete incorporating a leg-speed workout once a week throughout the year as long as he or she understands the goals of each training phase and adheres to them.

and LAT training within a tight range regardless of overall training volume; the amounts of other types of training are typically calculated as a percentage of overall volume, but NMT and LAT are exceptions.

Mark Wetmore, the successful coach of the University of Colorado cross country and track teams, varies the amount of speed training based on athletes' primary events. For middle-distance specialists (800- to 1,500-meter runners), 200 percent of the race distance is deemed adequate for one workout, whereas for long-distance types (3,000- to 10,000-meter runners), 100 percent of the race distance is used. "I don't think our leg-speed training is that much different than other programs," he says. "The difference is that we sit at 5,500 feet above sea level." At this elevation, the air is thinner and running is more difficult. As a result, Wetmore has to adjust workouts to achieve the proper adaptations. Says Wetmore, "We have to be careful with anaerobic work at altitude. We find that the repeats have to be shorter. We're not able to run 400-meter repeats like our sea-level counterparts. We use 300-meter repeats. We also have to take a longer recovery time between repeats."

For NMT training, Wetmore's athletes perform strides after runs each week. During the winter and spring, the Buffaloes hit the weight room to work on ballistic power and explosiveness as well as on flexibility (see chapters 4, 5, and 6 for details about developing strength and flexibility). Hill workouts per se aren't used, but the terrain itself ensures that the athletes get in some hill training. Part of Wetmore's success is his ability to alter the guidelines for training based on individual athletes' proclivities and the environmental conditions.

Because each athlete is unique, experiment with different amounts of NMT and LAT training to see what seems to give you the best results. In fact, once you find the NMT and LAT workouts that seem to work best for you, you can perform them once every four to eight weeks as a way to track your improvement in leg speed. Over time—not only across your training plan but also from year to year—you'll be able to use your marker NMT and LAT workouts as a way to predict when you are most ready for a stellar race performance. Combined with the information you gain from other marker workouts in different types of workouts, you—like Kenah, Snell, and Wetmore's athletes—will be able to reach your peak performance in your key races.

Turnover and leg-speed training are vital aspects of becoming the strongest runner you can. The workouts are fun, provide you with added injury protection, and allow variety. When these workouts are implemented correctly across your training cycle, you will find that not just your finishing kick, but *all* areas of your fitness, are improved. And, boy, then they'll eat your dust when you go flying by!

CHAPTER 3

Devising an Efficient Training Plan

JOE RUBIO

If you consider yourself a competitive distance runner, chances are that much of the enjoyment you derive from running depends on racing your best. Depending on your ability level, "racing your best" may mean qualifying for the Boston Marathon, making the Olympic Trials, setting a new personal best, or beating your training partner at the local 5K. Whatever the stakes, competition and racing well on the big day are important to you. If this describes your running purpose, then you have probably played around with your training schedule in an attempt to improve your race performances, and maybe you've had mixed results.

In a never-ending search for improved race times, competitive runners are constantly on the prowl for a better weekly plan, improved workout routine, or new addition to their training diet that will help them race faster. There is a seemingly endless supply of articles on the Internet or in the magazines on your grocer's shelf each month that fuel this desire. These articles tout a new "flavor of the month" workout that promises to deliver outstanding race results in five easy steps, yet each "new" workout looks suspiciously similar to the secret workout from last month. Unfortunately for many runners, attempts at varying their own training menu rarely produce significantly better race results. Thus, the question arises after several seasons of trial and error: Is there a consistent training program that I can use to achieve success, or is this really as fast as I can run?

If you are in this boat, you have probably tried most of the suggestions in various magazines with zeal. Still, even after incorporating these suggestions as prescribed, you continue to wait patiently for the promised results. You have tried a little of everything, such as upping the mileage, doing occasional long

41

runs, and incorporating an interval scheme; you have tried the tempo runs and strides and hill repetitions; you have even considered performing plyometrics, lifting weights, and doing Pilates.

Still, with all these additions here and there to your training routine, your race times are not going anywhere, at least not as fast as you would like. What *specific* elements must you include in your training routine *consistently* to enjoy success as a competitive distance runner?

Learning From Experience

When I look back on my competitive marathon days and read over the training I did to run my personal bests, I'm struck by the simplicity of it. It was really due to dumb luck that I happened on a successful training plan, particularly because I did not have a coach to set it up for me. In addition, I thought I knew everything there was to know about training at the time. I did not even consider looking at other runners' training diaries to see what I could learn from them; I just went about running workouts based largely on trial and error. To determine my schedule, I looked over my old training logs, picked out a few workouts I liked, and then proceeded do these workouts over and over until the big day. Sometimes this process worked well, while at other times it was a disaster.

Before my fastest marathon, I happened to throw together a program that involved a few consistent workouts. Tuesday of each week, I performed 800- to 2,400-meter intervals on the track at 5K to 10K pace. Later the same week I ran a second, faster workout that amounted to a hard 15-miler. This 15-miler was not timed; instead, I ran by effort, with the goal of completing each successive five-mile section at an ever-increasing pace. The first five miles served as a warm-up, the middle five miles were run at a marathon race-pace effort, and the final five miles I ran about as hard as I could manage. On weeks that I couldn't face the 15-miler, I performed 400-meter repeats at faster than 5K pace to aid my leg turnover. I added to these workouts a standard weekly long run of 90 to 120 minutes, double days several times a week, runs of 45 to 90 minutes the other days of the week, and a scheduled recovery day of 30 to 40 minutes easy every Friday. Using these workouts over the course of four months, I ran 2:18:08 at the 1990 California International Marathon, which not only resulted in my best-ever time and a five-minute personal record, but also resulted in my first U.S. Olympic Marathon Trials qualifying mark.

For some reason, after a personal-best performance, certain nutty runners think they can continue to improve on their training. I was one such nut, and I immediately devised ways to improve upon what I had done the previous December at Cal International. In my bid to make the Olympic team in the 1992 Trials, I decided that I needed more speed work. Why? I don't really know, but speed became the name of the game in my mind. I decided to throw out the progressive 15-mile run completely, and instead I replaced it with an additional track workout each week, such as mile repetitions, 800s, and 400s at fairly brisk paces. I attempted to overcompensate for the lack of a midweek 15-mile progressive tempo run by adding a few miles here and there to my daily routine; I also ran even more miles on Sunday by adding a second easy run of 40 minutes on top of the 105- to 120-minute run in the morning. The rest of the training week included the same training elements as the program that had led to my 2:18:08.

This new plan seemed to be working; I ran my fastest workout times before heading into the big day—surely a sign of good things to come. However, what I ended up running on the big day was a nearly last-place finish at the Trials, with a 2:37 finish time. I started out fine through 10K, but fell apart by halfway and struggled home. I spent the days following this performance drinking my sorrows away. During this time, I was struck by the revelation that the training for my 2:18 race, which had included the progressive 15-miler that allowed me to maintain my race pace the last half of the race distance, was far superior to the preparation for my humbling 2:37 effort, which lacked this single element. As best as I could tell—then and looking back now—the reason I wound up 19 minutes slower was simple: I'd omitted a single type of workout. This was a tough lesson to learn, but learn it I did. I decided to give the marathon another go.

In 1994, I made an assault on the next Trials' qualifying mark after being largely uncompetitive the previous two years. I went back to using the training program that included the consistent 15-miler at progressive efforts along with 800- to 2,400-meter intervals at 5K to 10K pace, consistent 400s at better than 5K pace, a weekly long run, the standard 45- to 90-minute runs, double days, and a recovery day each week. This schedule came through again: I ran a 2:19:40 Olympic Trials qualifier in December after being only a 31:30 10K runner the previous August. For the 1996 Trials, I used these same training elements once again to obtain a 26th place finish in 2:20:30, a personally satisfying performance given the difficulty of the course, the 26 degrees Fahrenheit weather, and, of course, the level of competition.

Based on this series of fortunes and misfortunes, it became apparent that to race my best marathon, I had to include six elements into my training schedule *consistently* to achieve success. These six elements follow:

1. A weekly long run of 90 to 120 minutes or longer
2. General training runs of 45 to 90 minutes and consistent double days
3. Progressive tempo runs
4. Intervals of 800- to 2,400-meter intervals at 5K to 10K race pace
5. 200-, 300-, or 400-meters at faster than 5K race pace
6. A recovery day each week

In coaching other runners, I have found that if they consistently incorporate these same six variables into their training, they realize the same solid performances I did. This holds true for 1,500-meter specialists, marathoners, and everyone in between.

I recently used these same six variables to design training programs for 10 athletes. Of these 10, six set significant personal records. One ran a three-second personal record (PR) in the 1,500 meters, earning an Olympic Trials qualifying standard; another ran PRs in the 800 and 1,500 meters, mile, and 5K. My wife, after recently giving birth to our daughter, earned her first PRs (mile, 5K, and 12K) in eight years after competing as a collegian for Cal Poly at San Luis Obispo. A local runner improved his 5K PR by 10 seconds to 14:12, while his 10K improved by 30 seconds to 29:33. Two of our female marathoners who competed in the 2004 U.S. Olympic Trials in St. Louis ran their best performances ever; one had the second-largest improvement of anyone in the field, running a PR by nearly eight minutes while earning 13th place overall, while another ran close to a four-minute PR to finish 22nd. Training for all these athletes was based on—you guessed it—the six variables. You can incorporate these same six elements into your program to train more efficiently and become a stronger runner.

Including the Six Training Elements

Every top distance runner's training arsenal includes many different workouts. However, on close examination, it's easy to see that all of these workouts fall into one of six types. These variables form the cornerstone of the successful competitive runner's training and serve as the backbone of a successful athlete's training diet; as you'll see from the examples that follow, this holds true whether his or her event is the 1,500 meters, the marathon, or any distance in between. Use these elements consistently in your program, tweaking them a bit here and there to account for individual variability, and you'll enjoy success.

The six training elements that I stumbled on fall into four essential training zones as classified by David Martin, PhD, and Peter Coe in *Better Training for Distance Runners* (1997). This book is regarded as one of the best available works on the science and theory of distance-running training. Each of Martin and Coe's four basic training zones has clearly defined characteristics and potential benefits.

Aerobic conditioning. Training in this zone is achieved primarily through moderately paced sustained runs of 30 to 120 minutes at 55 to 75 percent of $\dot{V}O_2$max. What does this mean in terms of "real-world" paces? These runs range from a warm-up jog to everyday conversational-pace running. Most general training runs during the week fall into this category. This pace also encompasses recovery runs performed at less than 65 to 70 percent of $\dot{V}O_2$max. This particular training zone is responsible for the following:

- Improved oxidative capacity in cardiac muscle and the muscles used in running
- Improved joint and tendon strength
- Increased capacity to store fuels such as carbohydrate and fatty acids

- Increased number and size of mitochondria (the powerhouses of the cell)
- Improved O_2 delivery and CO_2 removal through increased blood volume and capillary density

Anaerobic conditioning. Training in this zone involves runs primarily of 15- to 25-minute efforts completed at 75 to 90 percent $\dot{V}O_2$max. These runs are generally defined as tempo or steady-state runs and range from slightly slower than marathon race pace to as fast as 10K race pace. The main goal of training in this zone is to complete a comfortably hard effort for a sustained amount of time. This training zone is responsible for the following:

- Increased ability of Type IIa fast-twitch muscle fibers to use glycolytic and oxidative enzymes
- Increased stroke volume (the amount of blood pumped in a single contraction or beat of the heart)
- Increased capillary density and blood volume

Aerobic capacity. This type of training is performed primarily through two- to eight-minute repetitions at 90 to 100 percent of $\dot{V}O_2$max, where $\dot{V}O_2$max pace is the pace that well-trained distance runners can hold for roughly 10 to 11 minutes when running all out. These are classically defined as interval workouts or fartlek runs, whereby the athlete runs at a particular pace and then takes a recovery jog between hard efforts. In this case, the harder efforts are performed at primarily 5K to 10K race pace. This is the fastest of the aerobic paces. This particular training zone is responsible for the following:

- Increased ability of working muscles to use glycolytic and oxidative enzymes
- Increased blood-buffering capacity
- Continued activation of fast-twitch muscle fibers

Anaerobic capacity. This type of training is performed primarily through 30- to 120-second repetitions at faster than 100 percent of $\dot{V}O_2$max. This effort is anaerobic and is considered speedwork to most. (See chapter 2 for detailed instruction on implementing this type of training.) Intervals are generally performed at roughly one- to two-mile race pace for most distance runners, although middle-distance runners are known to regularly run repetitions at 800-meter race pace and faster. This particular training zone is responsible for the following:

- Improved functional leg strength and overall speed
- Increased ability to tolerate high levels of lactic acid through increased buffering capability
- Increased plasma volume and improved neuromuscular recruitment

Most runners know the purpose of the various workouts that they do; they're just not quite sure *which* workouts they should do consistently as part of their training program or if they are doing the *right mix* of workouts to gain the greatest possible increases in event-specific fitness. Runners generally end up focusing on one, or maybe two, of the four available training zones and bypassing the others. Not on purpose, perhaps, it just tends to work out that way. Many athletes, left to their own devices, will do the workouts at the general pace they are proficient at while avoiding workouts they have trouble with. Some runners may occasionally incorporate the training zones that are not part of their normal training routine, but not with conviction and rarely for long enough to affect their fitness significantly—that is, they are not consistent. This leads to a one-dimensional athlete whose progress is delayed because he or she does not train in all of the training zones; these athletes are missing a key piece or two of the fitness puzzle.

© Empics

For maximum improvement, runners must train beyond their preferred workouts at paces outside their comfort zone.

When improvement is the name of the game—and this is a point that most people miss—increased racing fitness is best achieved by following a well-rounded program based on consistently training within each of the four training-pace zones. Now, given these four training zones, let's look at how each zone fits into the six training elements.

The first and second elements, the weekly long run and the general training runs of 45 to 90 minutes and consistent double days, specifically address aerobic conditioning. By training consistently with easier to moderately paced runs of 55 to 75 percent of $\dot{V}O_2$max for roughly 30 to 120 minutes at a time, the body builds the fitness elements required for a competitive distance runner. Increases in joint and tendon strength, in size and number of mitochondria (the powerhouses of the cell), and in stored fuels such as carbohydrate and fatty acid as well as enhanced O_2 delivery and CO_2 removal form the foundation of future training success.

The third element, progressive tempo runs, addresses anaerobic conditioning. By training consistently at paces ranging from slightly slower than marathon race pace up to 10K race pace for sustained periods, athletes increase their plasma volume, capillary density, and stroke volume, all necessary ingredients for faster performances. An additional benefit is an adaptation by Type IIa fast-twitch (FT) muscle fibers that results in an increased density of glycolytic and oxidative enzymes, which is a fancy way of saying that a greater percentage of FT fibers take on aerobic characteristics, allowing them to assist in distance races (see also sidebar on page 28). This is particularly important because it allows athletes to use a larger percentage of their available $\dot{V}O_2$max for a longer period of time (i.e., an increased fractional use of $\dot{V}O_2$max), resulting in faster overall race times.

The fourth element, interval work using distances of 800 to 2,400 meters at 5K to 10K pace trains aerobic capacity. By training consistently at 5K to 10K race pace, the athlete trains at roughly 90 to 100 percent of $\dot{V}O_2$max pace, the exact pace necessary to develop maximum oxygen uptake by the muscles, a key component in distance-running performance.

The fifth element, 200s, 300s, and 400s at faster than 5K race pace, develops anaerobic capacity. By training consistently at paces faster than 5K pace, the athlete effectively incorporates consistent speedwork and anaerobic adaptation into the training mix. Primary benefits include increased tolerance to lactic acid (see chapter 2) and lower-leg strength. Additional benefits include improved efficiency, or running economy, developed through increased neuromuscular recruitment. The body becomes more efficient at the actual act of running, which is a key component in distance-running performance, because improved efficiency at racing speeds results in faster race times, all other factors of fitness being equal.

The sixth element, a recovery day each week, is not specifically addressed in the training zone list but is addressed in nearly every manual on competitive distance training because it is essential to the training process. Unfortunately, overly competitive athletes often do not take an easy day unless they are forced to. Most athletes view a recovery day as wasted: "Why run easy when I can get in extra training?" By scheduling a recovery day each week, you can be fairly certain that you get at least some, if not all, of the rest your body needs to adapt and improve. This is probably the one ingredient that keeps many athletes from improving. Basic physiology and the noted physician Hans Selye—who described in great detail how stress of any sort can positively or negatively influence humans—tell us that improvement relies on adequate recovery that allows adaptation and overcompensation to occur.

Recovery—a subject covered more fully in chapter 11—need not entail a complete rest day; a recovery run can be defined as 20 to 40 minutes at a very comfortable aerobic-conditioning pace. Recovery can also be defined as the absence of a hard training day once or twice during the week. This could include easier aerobic-conditioning runs in place of harder workouts such as anaerobic-conditioning, aerobic-capacity, or anaerobic-capacity runs.

I achieved my best athletic performances when I based my training on these elements, and largely because of this, I still use them today with the runners I coach.

Applying the Six Elements to Different Runners

After speaking to many runners over the years, I have the distinct impression that in spite of a wealth of available information, most are utterly confused about what elements the training schedules of successful runners include. By using specific athletes with different running goals as examples, I can show that there really is an established path to success—one that milers through marathoners can follow to fruition using the same six training elements.

The following three athletes adhered to training programs based largely on the same principles I used to set my personal bests. Two are marathoners; the other is a miler. Two of these athletes ran personal bests off the training I suggested, while the other ran her fastest marathon in nearly five years at the age of 42. All three ran some of the top performances by American athletes in 2003 at their goal distances.

The Miler

In the fall of 2002 and spring of 2003, I had the pleasure of working with a female middle-distance athlete named Aeron Genet. Aeron ran for Cal Poly at San Luis Obispo in the late 1980s, focusing on the 400 and 800 meters. She was a solid runner, garnering NCAA Division II All-American honors in the 4×400-meter relay, 800 meters, and 1,500 meters in her senior year. When she finished her eligibility, she did what most college athletes do: She stopped competing. Eleven years later, she watched the 2000 U.S. Olympic Track and Field Trials in Sacramento and decided that she wanted to qualify for the 2004 edition. This was an athlete who had become quite a surfer in the decade-plus since college but had not run much during this time. She decided that she wanted to become a miler. She ran cross country events in the fall of 2000 and followed that up with a full track season in the spring of 2001. That year, she recorded a best of 4:27 for 1,500 meters (approximately a 4:47 mile). Not a bad start.

In the fall of 2001, she decided that racing and training for cross country was not much fun; coaching high school kids and watching them hurt instead seemed like a better option than toiling in the mud and slop herself. She did little serious training from June of 2001 through February of 2002. She was running a bit to stay in some sort of shape, but there was very little intense training—anything in the anaerobic-conditioning, aerobic-capacity, or anaerobic-capacity zones—to speak of in her fall or winter program.

In February, with track season looming a month away, she started working out on the track with zeal. She performed workouts consisting mostly of fast 200s, 300s, and 400s. She did very few 800s, 1,000s, or mile intervals at 5K to 10K race pace. Her long runs amounted to roughly 70 to 80 minutes; double days and tempo runs were not a part of her program. Focusing primarily on the single training element of 200s, 300s, and 400s at faster than 5K pace, she ran 4:34 for her best 1,500m of the 2002 season (approximately a 4:54 mile), seven seconds slower than the year before.

Aeron and I sat down during the summer of 2002 and came up with a routine of workouts for September 2002 through March of 2003. Mainly, we addressed the components that were missing from her previous season. First, we scheduled consistent workouts of mile intervals, 1,000s, or 800s at 5K to 10K race pace. A sprinter at heart, Aeron didn't like these workouts at all, but she ran them. Next, I asked her to add a second workout, an easy run, several days a week. She didn't like this idea either, but again, she followed through. The duration of these easy morning runs started at 20 minutes so that Aeron could comfortably establish them in her training routine, and eventually she worked up to 30 to 40 minutes consistently. Additionally, we scheduled a tempo run every week or two. These she absolutely hated, but again, she did them anyway. Added to these new elements were the familiar workouts she loved, such as 200s, 300s, and 400s at faster than 5K race pace. Given that Aeron was shooting for a fast mile, her 200s, 300s, and 400s were run at 1,500-meter race pace, and she occasionally added 200s at 800-meter race pace. In addition to the 800s, 1,000s, or 1,600s at 5K to 10K race pace, the double days, the tempo run, and the middle distance–specific pace work at faster than 5K race pace, she included a standard Sunday long run of 90 to 105 minutes. We scheduled runs of 45 to 90 minutes the other days of the week and scheduled a recovery day every Thursday or Friday, which amounted to one or possibly two easy runs of 20 to 40 minutes followed by light strides. In some cases it was a complete day off.

After following this revised training schedule for seven months, Aeron ran her first 1,500-meter race of the year in 4:22. Although there were slight modifications in the scheduled workouts to account for increases in fitness level, the six training elements remained the cornerstone of her training program. This personal-best performance—a good 14 seconds faster than her time from nine months earlier—was enough to win her heat of the prestigious Stanford Invitational. This was also her first victory ever at 1,500 meters, which enhanced her confidence greatly and showed that her training was on the right path. She would continue to improve to 4:18.10 by July, falling short of the 2004 U.S. Olympic Trials B qualifying standard by just 0.60 seconds. She continued training in this fashion, and in 2004 she made the Olympic Trials B standard with a 4:15 performance at the 2004 Stanford Invitational, an improvement of seven seconds from the previous season as well as another three-second PR.

The lesson? The elements I had used to run my personal marathon best were the same elements that Aeron used to run her personal best at 1,500 meters. Even though there was a difference of more than 25 miles (40 kilometers) in our respective race distances, our personal-best performances were the result of the same six training elements.

The Marathoners

During the same time that I worked with Acron, I was also fortunate to work with two athletes pointing toward the 2003 World Track and Field Championships in Paris. Jill Gaitenby (now Jill Boaz) and Linda Somers Smith were both scheduled to represent the United States in the marathon. In setting up their training schedules, I took the schedule that had brought me marathon success and incorporated much of what Jill had learned from her time in the Fila Discovery Program. The training used in the Fila program was a carbon copy of the training that many of Kenya's top marathoners used to achieve their success. In the Fila program, a few basic workouts form the backbone of the training. One of the primary harder workouts was "minutes"—60-second repetitions at faster than 5K race pace followed by a 60-second recovery, which addressed anaerobic capacity. They also performed 1K, 2K, 3K, or 5K intervals at roughly 5K to 10K race pace, thereby addressing aerobic capacity. "Progression runs" in which athletes ran each 5K segment of a 14- to 22-miler (23- to 35-kilometer run) at an ever-increasing pace, covering the last 5K at a fast clip, increased anaerobic conditioning. Double days were scheduled most days of the week.

I modified Jill's program slightly so that it fit the parameters of my training scheme. I included her previous training elements of 1K and 2K intervals at 5K to 10K pace. Some days, Linda and Jill ran these repetitions on the track, while on other days they ran them on a 900-meter dirt field known as "the cornfield." At other times, Jill ran this workout as a fartlek, or variable-pace run, on dirt trails or roads. To accommodate the "minutes," some weeks Jill and Linda ran 400s at faster than 5K race pace on the track, while in other weeks Jill ran her minutes on a road or on the trails in a local state park. Linda and Jill also ran 14- to 16-mile (23- to 26-kilometer), and sometimes even 20-mile (32-kilometer), progressive tempo runs. On most weekends that didn't include a progressive long run, they ran a standard Sunday long run of 18 to 22 miles (29 to 35 kilometers). The remaining workouts of the week were usually 45- to 90-minute runs, plus a second run most days of the week. Finally, I included a recovery day in Jill's training—one that had not been scheduled during her time in the Fila program.

To review, Linda and Jill's training schedule included the following training elements:

1. A weekly long run of 90 to 120 minutes
2. General training runs of 45 to 90 minutes and consistent double days
3. Progressive tempo runs
4. Intervals of 1K to 2K at 5K to 10K pace

5. "Minutes" or 400s at faster than 5K pace

6. A recovery day each week

Jill used this schedule—which was based on the same elements that Aeron used to run her 1,500-meter personal best and that I used to run my marathon best—for about two months, following this with a three-week taper. She finished as the top American in the World Championship field in 2:34:54, a new personal record by 90 seconds. Linda had a very strong performance as well, finishing as the second American with a 2:37:14, her fastest time in nearly five years at the age of 42 and following several years of injury. Here are Linda's thoughts on the effectiveness of the training program:

More important, after five years of on-and-off injury, the program allowed me to train injury free for almost two years, which is a good point to make—getting to the starting line healthy is the primary goal for any runner, regardless of any other goal.

These real-life examples illustrate pretty clearly that, even though there is a significant difference between a mile and a marathon, the training programs for each contain the same training elements. And in the case of these three national-class athletes, combining these elements resulted in solid race performances.

Many distance runners try to make training infinitely more complex than it needs to be. However, successful training is surprisingly similar across the spectrum of distances from 1,500 meters to 3,000 meters to 5K to 10K to the half-marathon to the marathon. The six elements form the cornerstone of all successful competitive distance runners' training. If you get these right, rest assured that you are training as a majority of Olympians do. Miss one of them and you are, in effect, missing at least half the puzzle. In my case, I slowed by 19 minutes—about 45 seconds a mile—in the marathon by leaving out the progressive tempo run. In Aeron's case, she ran 18 seconds slower for 1,500 meters by focusing her training almost exclusively on the single element of 200-, 300-, and 400-meter repetitions at faster than 5K pace. If you start with these six elements and then branch out from there with solid ancillary training such as plyometrics (chapter 1), weight training (chapters 5 and 6), range-of-motion exercises (chapter 4), and so on, you can expect to race very well.

Designing Your Own Training Week

Based on my experience as an athlete and a coach, I believe that the most valuable tool for any self-coached runner is an outline to guide decisions regarding which workouts are appropriate. The various types of training, such as long runs, interval work, tempo runs, and so on, are all important and necessary for helping you improve as a runner. The key is classifying the various workouts and then scheduling them into your training consistently. Following a map—one that successful runners have used time and again—can ease the uncertainty and doubts that creep into every athlete's mind. Following an outline that has led to success allows runners to train with greater focus and purpose, knowing their work will achieve long-term results. A workable training schedule brings workouts together to form a routine that addresses every relevant energy system necessary for top racing performance and continued improvement over time.

I cannot name one individual heroic workout that will take someone to the next level, but there are a few workouts that, when done consistently and repetitively as part of a training schedule, can lead to substantial progress for the majority of runners. The surprising thing for many runners is realizing that the training principles are the same for any distance you want to race. It doesn't matter if the event is the mile, 5K, 10K, marathon, steeplechase, or cross country; the same training elements and concepts apply. As a coach, if I base an athlete's training on the key elements, the athlete invariably maintains his or her health throughout the season, improves his or her race performances throughout the year, and competes well at specific goal races. It's basic, it's fairly brainless to follow, and most important, it works.

The following suggestions will help you fit each of the six elements into your training consistently within your standard training cycles. Some advanced athletes who recover quickly can address all six within a single week. Athletes who require more time between hard efforts to recover fully should consider fitting these within a two- or three-week cycle. You can also try a 10-day cycle if one week doesn't work for you, but given that most people have schedules that revolve around a standard 7-day week, we tend to stick with 7, 14, or 21 days as the standard options.

For my athletes, I generally schedule two harder workouts every week, cycling through anaerobic-conditioning, aerobic-capacity, and anaerobic-capacity training. Once we've addressed each of these individually, we start the sequence of workouts over again; this allows us to elevate the athlete's fitness level by concurrently working all of the energy systems necessary for distance running success. For athletes who recover especially quickly, I schedule a separate anaerobic-conditioning, aerobic-capacity, or anaerobic-capacity session each week, thereby allowing the athlete to address all energy systems within a single training week. For those who require additional recovery, a single session each week of one of these types of training is sufficient, allowing the athlete to address all relevant energy systems within a three-week period. Here's the most effective route to incorporating the six elements in your program:

Step 1. Designate Your Recovery Day

Because most of the athletes I work with have families and careers, a recovery day is usually one on which they'd like to complete additional chores around the house, spend time with their families, or socialize. It may be a day to do little or nothing except read a book and relax. Others travel frequently for business and have a floating schedule; these runners need a day on which they can miss a run without feeling guilty. View the recovery day as a day to let your body and mind unwind and allow modern life to take priority over training. As an added benefit, it'll keep you healthy, allow you to improve, and help keep you motivated.

Step 2. Determine Your Long-Run Day

This is pretty simple because most athletes do their weekly long run on either Saturday or Sunday. Whatever works for you is fine, as long as you do it consistently. I don't have a hard and fast rule regarding spacing recovery days around the long run. In most cases, my athletes run a harder effort on Saturday, run long on Sunday, and run an easier day on Monday. This allows Saturday to be fairly hard and Sunday moderate while providing a recovery day following these back-to-back harder run days.

Step 3. Determine Your Primary Workout Days

On primary workout days you run scheduled harder workouts. My athletes schedule primary workouts every Tuesday and Friday in the fall. In the spring, the longer-distance athletes maintain this schedule, while the middle-distance runners adopt a Monday, Wednesday, and Saturday schedule. Depending on the length of your workout cycle, combinations of hard days vary. A 7-day cycle might include primary workouts on Tuesday, Thursday, and Saturday. Runners on a 14-day cycle might designate Monday and Thursday as primary hard-workout days. On the other hand, some runners can only tolerate a single hard workout each week and are therefore on a 21-day cycle. Based on your particular goal event, rotate workouts in this order:

1. 200s, 300s, or 400s at faster than 5K race pace (anaerobic capacity)
2. 800- to 2,400-meter intervals at 5K to 10K race pace (aerobic capacity)
3. Tempo run of approximately 30 minutes at threshold pace (anaerobic conditioning)

On the fourth hard-effort day, start over again with the 200s, 300s, or 400s at faster than 5K pace and work your way through the lineup again. In this manner, you address all the relevant energy systems needed for top-level performance. The 800- to 2,400-meter intervals at 5K to 10K pace handle aerobic capacity, the tempo runs address anaerobic conditioning, and the 200s, 300s, or 400s at faster than 5K race pace develop anaerobic capacity (economy).

Most runners use a 14-day schedule of two primary, harder workouts each week during the two-week period. The question arises: There are four harder workout days and three primary workouts to do, so should I adjust the schedule? Rather than starting again with workout one on the fourth workout day, would there be a benefit to focusing on one area of fitness more than the other? I allow for the following slight variations based on the fact that most athletes see the greatest improvement in race times by giving increased focus to aerobic-capacity development.

Week 1: Aerobic-capacity workout, anaerobic-conditioning workout

Week 2: Aerobic-capacity workout, anaerobic-capacity workout

During the final four to eight weeks of the training year before the championship racing season, I make the following adjustments based on event focus:

1,500 meters. Each week perform an aerobic-capacity workout on one day and an anaerobic-capacity workout on another.

5K to 10K. During week one, perform an aerobic-capacity workout one day and an anaerobic conditioning workout the second harder day of that week. During week two perform an aerobic-capacity workout one day and an anaerobic-capacity workout the second harder day.

Marathon. Each week perform an aerobic-capacity workout on one day and an anaerobic-conditioning workout on another.

Step 4. Schedule Your Double Days

I generally schedule double days on the primary harder workout days of the week because I want the athlete's hard days to be hard. Without exception, my top athletes do a minimum of two double days per week on Tuesdays and Fridays, the same days we schedule either the 200s, 300s, and 400s, the 800- to 2,400-meter intervals, or the tempo run. The more experienced athletes add double days on an additional two to four days per week as they see fit.

Step 5. Fill In Rest With Aerobic-Conditioning Runs

The remaining days should consist of runs varying in distance from 45 to 90 minutes. Whether you choose to do two-a-days and whether you keep to the shorter end of the 45- to 90-minute range or the longer end is as much a matter of preference and "recoverability" (see chapter 11) as it is a function of your chosen race distance.

To help illustrate the previous concepts in detail, tables 3.1 through 3.3 provide some sample training weeks using this program. These are not set in stone, but rather are intended to illustrate how to apply the training principles to the everyday training of fast competitive athletes who also happen to have careers and family obligations.

So that's it. Designing a training plan is important yet simple. I've described the elements it should include and provided examples of runners across the race-distance spectrum who have used these elements to form training plans that have taken them to the top of their game. Now, it's your turn. Reread this chapter along with the other information in this book, set clear goals, grab a pen and paper (or a mouse and computer), and go to it.

Table 3.1 Jill Gaitenby's Marathon-Specific Training—July 13 through 26

Day	Workout	Elements used
Sun	22 miles—5 miles easy, 5 miles at MP (marathon pace), 5 miles easy, 5 miles at MP—2-mile cool-down	1, 3
Mon	AM: 9 miles moderate PM: 8 miles easy	2 2
Tues	AM: 5 × (double cornfield [approx 1,800m] starting at 10K effort and working down to 5K effort with 3-min recovery) PM: 8 miles easy	4 2
Wed	AM: 13 miles in hills at progressive effort PM: 8 miles easy	3 2
Thurs	AM: 9-mile progression PM: 8 miles easy	3 2
Fri	8 miles very easy	6
Sat	3 miles easy, 3 miles at MP followed by a workout within a local 10K race on the beach—10 min at MP/tempo, 60-sec surge, 8 min at MP/tempo, 60-sec surge, 6 min at MP/tempo, 60-sec surge, 4 min at MP/tempo, 60-sec surge, 2 min at MP/tempo, hard to finish	3, 5
Sun	22 miles	1
Mon	AM: 9 miles moderate PM: 8 miles easy	2 2
Tues	AM: 22 × (60 sec on at better than 5K effort, 60 sec off) PM: 8 miles easy	4 2
Wed	AM: 13 miles in hills at progressive effort PM: 8 miles easy	3 2
Thurs	AM: 9 miles easy PM: 8 miles easy	2 2
Fri	AM: 12 × (single cornfield [approx 900m], starting at 10K effort and working down to 5K effort with 2-min recovery) PM: 6 miles easy	4 2
Sat	AM: 10 miles very easy PM: 4 miles very easy	6 6

Jill's goal was the World Track and Field Championships in Paris, August 31, 2003. Her finish time off this training was 2:34:54 (PR). Note that marathoners only incorporate number 5 every other week.

1 mile = 1.609 kilometers

55

Table 3.2 Aeron Genet's 1,500 Meter-Specific Training—February 10 through 23

Day	Workout	Elements used
Mon	AM: 4 miles easy	2
	PM: 4 sets of 2 × (200 at 800m pace with 100m jog), 400m jog between sets	5
Tues	5.5 miles easy	2
Wed	AM: 4 mile easy	2
	PM: 8 × (400 at 3K pace with 200m jog)	5
Thurs	11 miles in hills at progressive effort	3
Fri	4 miles very easy	6
Sat	AM: 4 × (1,600m ins/outs [MP/5K/MP/5K = an average at tempo pace] 400m jog)	3, 4
	PM: 4 miles easy	2
Sun	1:40 easy to moderate	1
Mon	2 × (200m at 800m pace with 100m jog); 4 × (150m accelerations with 250m jog), start at 800m race pace and finish at best top-end relaxed speed	5
Tues	9.5 miles easy	2
Wed	AM: 4 miles easy	2
	PM: 2 sets of 3 × (400m at 1,500m pace with 200m jog), 400m jog between sets	5
Thurs	11 miles in hills at progressive effort	3
Fri	AM: 4 miles very easy	6
	PM: 6 miles very easy w/ light strides, drills	6
Sat	6 × (800m at 5K pace with 400m jog)	4
Sun	1:40 easy to moderate	1

Aeron's goal for this training was the CanAm High Performance Distance Circuit in July of that year. Her performances there for 1,500 meters were 4:18.15 and 4:18.10, both PRs.

1 mile = 1.609 kilometers

Table 3.3 Joe Rubio's Marathon-Specific Training— January 14 through 27

Day	Workout	Elements used
Sun	2:10 easy to moderate	1
Mon	AM: 65 min easy PM: 35 min easy	2 2
Tues	AM: 40 min moderate PM: 10 × (800m at 10K pace with 2-min recovery)	2 4
Wed	85 min moderate	2
Thurs	AM: 40 min very easy PM: 35 min very easy	6 6
Fri	AM: 40 min moderate PM: 16 miles—middle 4 miles at marathon pace (MP), last 4 miles at tempo	2 3
Sat	70 min easy	2
Sun	2:10 easy to moderate	1
Mon	AM: 55 min easy PM: 35 min easy	2 2
Tues	AM: 40 min moderate PM: 1,600m, 2,400m, 1,600m, 2,400m, 1,600m at 10K pace with 3- to 4-min recovery	2 4
Wed	80 min moderate	2
Thurs	AM: 35 min very easy PM: 35 min very easy	6 6
Fri	AM: 35 min moderate PM: ins/outs: 8 × 400m at 5K + 400m at MP	2 5
Sat	50 min easy	2

My goal for this training was the 1996 U.S. Olympic Trials in Charlotte. I ran 2:20:30 off this training. Note that marathoners only incorporate number 5 every other week.

1 mile = 1.609 kilometers

[handwritten: why considered a 5 + not a 4?]

57

CHAPTER 4

Stretching Your Range of Motion

MARK ELLIOTT

The title of this chapter alone may lead many runners to place this topic in the "too-hard" basket. Speedwork and strength training often seem much more appealing than flexibility training when it comes to making an investment in improving performance. For the majority of distance runners, achieving optimal range of motion does not come naturally. Many runners feel that the effort and time spent improving their range of motion could be better spent doing something that would more directly affect their running training; these runners feel that adding stretching, yoga, Pilates, flexibility, core conditioning, or a strength and weights class into an already hectic personal and professional schedule just won't work. Specificity of running is, with good reason, the focus for the majority of distance runners.

However, limited research links performance gains in running to increases in flexibility or range of motion. Numerous studies over the last 10 years have been unable to link increased range of motion through static stretching to increased performance (Pope 1999). However, it is intuitively clear that possessing a body that is stronger and has a greater range of motion will lead to greater efficiency in any athletic discipline, including running.

The latest research indicates that *static* stretching before training or competition actually *reduces* performance strength or power output (as you'll see later, the situation is different following a workout). Static stretching before intensive exercise is thought to inhibit components of the neurological system in a manner that limits the efficiency of muscle contractions. Thus this chapter is not aimed at converting you to endless hours of stretching and flexibility work, but rather at providing you with simple, practical, time-saving tools for maximizing your running-specific (i.e., functional) range of motion, thereby allowing you to maximize your performance and to become an injury-free athlete.

Range of motion for a runner is a matter of striking a balance—an equilibrium—between two physiological components of body symmetry: *strength* and

59

functional movement. Symmetry in the body arises from possessing comparable levels of strength and functional movement in key muscle groups; the combination of these two factors enables a greater efficiency of athletic movement patterns. When an athlete runs, it is the combination of the actions of vascular tissues, muscles, nerves, tendons, and ligaments that creates the "performance package." In many runners, certain muscles become tight, while other muscles become stronger or weaker. Excessive flexibility in the absence of satisfactory muscle control may be detrimental to a runner's performance and may predispose him or her to injury. A restricted range of motion resulting from tight muscle groups can be placed in the same category.

The movement patterns we use in daily life often create specific strengths, weaknesses, and increases or decreases in our mobility. For example, spending hours sitting at the computer can lead to tight hip flexors, weak gluteal muscles, tight hamstrings, weak quadriceps, tight calf muscles, and poor upper-body posture. Driving a car for extended periods with one leg always placed on the accelerator and the other leg tucked up, rotated off to the side, or intermittently using the clutch can cause an imbalance between the left and right sides of the body. All these daily activities of modern life influence body symmetry.

When athletes lose functional mobility or strength, it is most often because they have chosen not to use the muscle through its complete range of motion. The neurological pathways that allow the body to move will initiate certain movement patterns only if the body consistently uses that functional pattern. In simple terms, if you don't use high knee lift when running up a hill, you will not achieve high knee lift merely through stretching your quadriceps. Hip flexibility, hamstring flexibility, hip-flexor strength, upper-body posture, arm drive, and head position all influence the body's ability to gain the full range of running-specific motion and balance during a knee lift.

Decreases in functional movement are often the result of certain muscles being too tight; this causes the opposite muscles to become weakened or lengthened. The equilibrium between opposing muscles thus gives way to an imbalance, which accordingly compromises strength and functional movement for a specific muscle group.

Because a great deal of available research literature deals with the physiological or technical aspects of flexibility, I do not cover those topics in detail here. The heart of this chapter instead covers two practical areas that will help you achieve "balance" as a runner:

1. Making the most of your existing range of motion
2. Determining the best situations in which to use the simple strategies currently recognized as best practices for increasing range of motion

Using both static and dynamic methods, you can employ a number of simple, practical tools that fit the busy lifestyle of the modern runner.

I apply range-of-motion principles to establish balance in two distinctive areas of sport performance: pretraining and precompetition, and posttraining and postcompetition. In this chapter I explain the goals of each in depth and describe specific exercises to achieve balance in these areas.

The biomechanical process of running involves the mutual relationships of hundreds of muscles, nerves, joints, tendons, and ligaments that work together to create movement. The speed and efficiency of this movement creates runners' performances. The dynamic and static stretches I provide later in this chapter target the primary muscles and nerves active during the running cycle (see also figure 6.1 on page 108 for some key muscles of the lower extremity). These include the calf muscles, hamstrings, quadriceps, hip flexors, iliotibial band, piriformis, gluteal muscles, abdominal and lower back muscles, and the latissimus dorsi as well as the sciatic nerve and the upper limb nerve complex.

© Human Kinetics

The right type of stretching at the right time will enhance your range of motion.

Range-of-Motion Options

The latest research indicates advantages to using one specific set of flexibility techniques for pretraining and precompetition and another for posttraining and postcompetition. A good general warm-up such as 10 to 15 minutes of jogging followed by dynamic warm-up exercises has been shown to consistently produce an increased range of motion compared to a program of static stretching alone (McNair and Stanley 1996). Consistent static stretching for specific periods of time has been shown to maintain range of motion in athletes (Bandy and Irion 1994). However, this type of stretching must be done at specific times, such as after working out or competing and not before, to benefit performance because research has shown that static stretching actually *inhibits* muscular performance during the period immediately following the stretching by decreasing peak force production and rate of force generation (Rosenbaum and Hennig 1995). The body is less able to absorb force, and electromyography (EMG) wave amplitudes are decreased for up to an hour after static stretching (Fowles, Sale, and MacDougall 2000).

Several current authors have proposed that limitations on flexibility—in particular dynamic flexibility—are neurological rather than purely musculoskeletal (Rosenbaum and Hennig 1995). Although this chapter focuses on the musculoskeletal aspects of flexibility, I describe one more "neural-based" stretch, the straight-leg hamstring–sciatic nerve stretch. It is important for runners to address the sciatic nerve because of its major influence on the lower body. To address other specific nerves of the body, athletes should consult a qualified sports physiotherapist or physical therapist.

Most runners tend to develop set patterns, or rituals, before training or racing—some without conscious thought. These may include specific ways of tying their shoelaces, wearing specific racing flats, a set warm-up time or distance before racing, or settling into a good rhythm or stride.

One of the most important rituals you should follow before any range-of-motion work is to ensure that your body is suitably warmed up and mobile. Because of the structural physiology of tendons, joint capsules, muscles, and ligaments, your body is more pliable if it has been lightly active before you initiate flexibility or strength work. The physiological basis for a warm-up jog before stretching includes the following:

- Increased core body temperature
- Increased elasticity of connective tissue
- Increased heart rate and a subsequent increase in the blood flow throughout the body, which increases the amount of blood directly supplied to the main working muscles
- Improved efficiency of oxygen uptake and carbon dioxide removal, and assistance in the removal and breakdown of anaerobic by-products such as lactic acid, because of the increased blood flow
- Increased coordination and rhythm due to activation of the central nervous system through the pattern of movement

A standard warm-up jog of 10 to 15 minutes is sufficient for most athletes to initiate these factors. Start any training or competition session with a 10-minute jog and walk. Similarly, you can enhance postrace recovery or intensive training by performing light exercise after completing the event; this allows your body to more effectively remove lactic acid and allows the body to slowly decrease its metabolism postactivity. Some athletes may prefer a nonweight-bearing cooldown, such as swimming or cycling, following an intensive training session or competition.

Pretraining and Precompetition Flexibility

Partaking in a full range-of-motion program before a long, slow, distance training run or a 45-minute jog around the park is not necessary, but if you plan to push yourself into a steady to moderately hard training zone, ensuring that your body is fully mobile and able to achieve its functional range of motion is vital.

A warm-up for training or competition must be based on one fundamental principle—dynamic movement. Dynamic movement involves patterns that systematically increase the functional range of movement of the body. Dynamic flexibility takes the body's muscles and tissues through an initial functional range of motion using small, slow, controlled movements. This then increases functional range of motion by building the intensity using controlled ballistic movement patterns. The concepts outlined are aimed at achieving a balance in your warm-up in both flexibility and strength, and will optimally prepare your body for immediate training or competition. One key advantage of using a dynamic range-of-movement pattern in your pretraining or precompetition warm-up is that the consistent movement patterns keep your core temperature elevated from the general warm-up jog. A 5- to 15-minute static stretching regimen, on the other hand, causes the warm-up body temperature to drop. Combined with the neurological factors described earlier, this negates the effect of the initial warm-up.

Dynamic flexibility increases a joint's range of motion throughout different planes of movement, for example, increasing the range of forward-and-backward and side-to-side limb flexion and extension at the hip or shoulder joint. As athletes warm up and perform these exercises, they become functionally stronger through the increased activation of muscle groups under specific loads.

An ideal dynamic flexibility program before training or a competition takes only 10 to 15 minutes to complete. It should be done after a 10-minute walk or jog to ensure complete readiness for a quality training session or for "loosening up" on the starting line for competition. In hotter, more humid conditions, you can halve the time of this warm-up, while in colder conditions you may need to lengthen the warm-up by repeating many of the movement patterns three or four times to ensure maximum system activation.

You'll notice that the key muscles you activate in this warm-up parallel the muscles you predominately use in the running cycle. The exercises described are recommendations to maximize your system activation. The order in which you perform these exercises is not important; the initial warm-up and gradual increase in intensity is. A gradual increase in the grade and level of movement patterns is fundamental to maximizing range-of-motion benefits.

Once you have completed your gentle warm-up walk or jog, find a sheltered, flat area to carry out the following movement patterns. To ensure that you maintain your elevated body temperature, follow each dynamic movement pattern with an easy 50-meter jog.

Hot Steps

This activity is aimed at activating the cadence and firing of your calf muscles. Start slowly and build in intensity over three or four repetitions.

1. Stand in the position you would use to run.

2. Starting off with slow movements, run "on the spot," staying on your fore-feet—do not let your heels touch the ground. Drive the speed of your feet with the cadence of your arm swing. The tendency is for athletes to "sit in a bucket" with this exercise. The movement pattern is not one of running low to the ground; athletes should make a conscious effort to "run tall" with the hips up and forward and the upper chest and head high. Remember to drive your arms to set the cadence of the feet.

3. Carry out this pattern for a burst of 10 to 15 seconds, jog for 50 meters, and repeat this movement pattern twice.

Ankle Lifts

Attaining a high knee lift as described here provides a low-intensity means of preparing the muscles for the running motion.

1. Start in a standard running position. Try to bring your heels directly up under your buttocks without looking down or flexing forward from the hips.

2. Start the pattern with step one—drive one leg up, concentrating on leg and arm drive on the opposite side.

3. Progress to step two, involving both legs but with one leg always on the ground, and finally to step three, driving with both legs in a running-on-the-spot motion. Note that this exercise is not simply running on the spot. The focus is purely on ankle lift under your buttock in a manner that activates your quadriceps and calf muscles.

4. Perform steps one and two 10 times each with leg. Once you reach step three, repeat only 8 to 10 times with each leg—the final phase of this exercise is very explosive and should be limited for most athletes.

Hip Holds With Ankle Rotation

The aim of this movement pattern is threefold: activating ankle mobility, opening up the hips, and activating the opposing gluteus maximus muscles.

1. Standing upright, bring your right knee to your chest and hold it there with your hands.

2. Contract your left buttock muscle and straighten your left leg for support and activation of this muscle group. Do not allow your body to sway backward. It is important to keep your center of gravity over the left midfoot.

3. Once you are stable with your right knee held to your chest, rotate your right ankle around in big clockwise and counterclockwise circles.

4. Do three rotations in each direction, and then repeat the same movement with the left leg and ankle.

Stepping Over the Fence

The focus is on increasing hip and adductor range of motion and activating the opposing gluteal muscle group.

1. Standing with your hands on your hips, lift your right leg up and out to the side.

2. Rotate your leg forward, rising up onto your toes. The movement is similar to that of stepping over a low fence.

3. Carry out a smooth pattern of stepping forward and "over the fence" using your left and right legs. Keep your hips as stable as possible; imagine having two headlights on the front of your hips and pointing the beams of light forward. Athletes with tight hips tend to rotate their hips backward during this exercise if they have limited range of motion.

4. After stepping over the fence four to six times with each leg, jog for 15 to 30 seconds, and repeat the movement pattern.

Leg Swings

Strained hamstrings can be a long-term curse for any runner. From my experience as a sports physiotherapist, injury to the hamstrings tends to occur in more explosive-type athletes such as sprinters and hurdlers, athletes who have large quadriceps muscles, or athletes with sedentary jobs that involve lots of sitting or driving. Dynamic flexibility of the hamstrings starts with small, controlled movement patterns and builds up to intensive, far-ranging movements.

1. Hold onto the side of a fence or bench. Position your hips perpendicular to the object you are holding onto. Gently swing your right leg back and then forward, with your toes pointing forward and your hips remaining stable. The key to activating your hamstrings is ensuring that your pelvis remains stable.

2. As you progress through a greater range of motion and velocity of movement, be sure that your low back does not flex excessively as your leg moves backward. The swinging leg and toes should remain pointing forward and should not rotate out to the side; an outward rotation of the leg dynamically stretches the adductors rather than the hamstrings.

3. Repeat these movement patterns 12 to 18 times each with leg, then repeat using the opposite leg.

Walking Lunges

The lunge is one of the most important exercise patterns for any runner or endurance athlete. With slight adaptations, you can use the lunge to stretch and strengthen the majority of major muscle groups in the lower and midbody. The lunge can be either a dynamic or a static movement, depending on your goal. A simple walking lunge systematically stretches and activates the legs using a smooth, controlled pattern of movement. (I describe static lunges later in the posttraining and postcompetition section of this chapter.) Explosive rotational and jump lunges are more strength based, but are also an excellent form of conditioning for serious runners.

The basic exercise pattern described here focuses purely on stretching the hip flexors and quadriceps (rectus femoris portion) and on strengthening the hamstrings and gluteal muscles. To ensure that you obtain maximal benefits from the lunge, correct technique is essential.

1. Hold your hands on your hips.

2. Maintain a stable pelvis position by drawing your belly button in and posteriorly tilting your pelvis. If you have your hands on your hips, you can easily feel your pelvis maintaining this stable position. An anteriorly tilted pelvis does not allow you to place pressure on your hip flexors, which renders the stretch ineffective.

3. Step forward enough to feel a light stretch on the top of your back leg.

4. Do not rock your weight onto your forward knee, instead lower your body to the ground by dropping your weight through the knee of your back leg. The reasons for dropping the weight in this manner are fourfold:
   - It activates your hamstrings and gluteal muscles to control the deceleration of your body.
   - It prevents you from overloading the patella (kneecap) of your front leg and evenly distributes the weight between both legs.
   - It ensures that you stretch the rectus femoris and hip flexors.
   - It keeps your upper body perpendicular to the ground.
5. Once you establish this position, simply step from the right to the left leg, concentrating on a slow, controlled rhythm, systematically opening up your left and right hip flexors, and activating key running muscles.
6. Perform six to eight steps per leg, followed by a 50-meter jog, then repeat the movement pattern using a wider lunge, bringing the back knee closer to the ground on the second set.

Walking Lunges With Extension Stretch

The focus of this exercise is not the hip flexors, although these are activated and stretched, but rather opening up the chest and latissimus dorsi muscles. Runners have a tendency to omit flexibility work for the upper body. Most runners have the simple but misguided idea that running is about using the lower limbs, not the upper body. This exercise features a great, yoga-based movement pattern that will ensure that you have an open chest and ribs for breathing.

1. Use the principles outlined in the walking lunge exercise, but clasp your hands together above your head.
2. As you step forward with each lunge movement, reach up high with your hands and gently exhale. You should be able to feel the insides of your arms brush your ears if you are reaching up with your arms.
3. As you drop through your back knee, you will feel a strong stretch from your hip flexors up into your abdominals and sides. Do not "go deep" during the first few weeks you do this stretch.

Walking Lunges With Rotation

The basic lunge position is described previously. By rotating the upper body during the movement pattern, a dynamic force is transferred to the lateral aspect of the thigh. This places a dynamic stretch on the iliotibial band (ITB) and tensor fasciae latae (TFL) muscle.

1. As you step forward, maintain an upright position.
2. When you begin to drop the weight down through your back knee, rotate your upper trunk and arms to the same side as the knee in front. As with the basic walking lunge, the emphasis is on a stable pelvis position. The pattern with this dynamic movement is always slow and controlled.
3. Carry out a maximum of six lunges per leg, jog for 50 meters, and repeat.

Sideways Running With Rotation

This exercise focuses on increased trunk range of movement and activation for the adductor and lateral gluteal muscle groups. The pelvis should always remain as stable as possible, and the head should face the direction you are traveling.

1. Running sideways from left to right, alternate by crossing the left leg in front of the right and then crossing the left leg behind the right.
2. To increase the activation of the exercise and the amount of trunk rotation, simply swing the arms—held at shoulder height—in a more forceful pattern.
3. Once you have repeated the full crossover sequence 8 to 10 times, stop and run in the opposite direction, this time crossing the right leg in front of, then behind, the left leg.

Posttraining and Postcompetition Flexibility

The principles behind a more passive form of flexibility after training and racing center on controlled, static stretching. Dynamic flexibility is also important following training or competition; however, the focus should be more on relaxing your muscle groups. Research has shown that the benefits of postexercise static stretching—with individual stretches held for periods of up to 30 to 60 seconds—are sufficient to maintain range of motion (Shrier and Gossal 2000). Stretching immediately after exercising maintains and increases range of motion by decreasing the resistance of muscle structures and increasing your "stretch tolerance." After several weeks of stretching, your muscle resistance does not drastically change; instead, increases in range of motion occur because you can apply more force to the muscle before you feel discomfort. Table 4.1 shows the muscle groups and the specific exercises recommended for each.

An easy cool-down jog and cross-training activity should precede range-of-motion work done after training or racing. The objectives of a cool-down are to gradually lower body temperature from that attained during strenuous exercise and to ensure a lower blood lactic-acid level.

Static stretching can be a time-consuming activity, which is one of the fundamental reasons runners avoid it. To make maximal use of your time while stretching, the best options are the following:

- Stretch in front of your favorite TV program—that always keeps you focused longer.
- Stretch two muscle groups together using a similar pattern or body position. A number of the static stretches outline muscle groups that can be combined.

Table 4.1 Flexibility Exercises for Muscles Used in Running

Muscle group	Recommended exercises	
	Pretraining and precompetition	Posttraining and postcompetition
Gastrocnemius and soleus	**Hip holds with ankle rotation** **Hot steps** **Ankle lifts**	*Soleus stretch* *Gastrocnemius stretch* <u>Sciatic-nerve stretch</u>
Hamstrings	**Leg swings** **Lunges**	*Bent-knee hamstring stretch* *Stork-position hamstring stretch* <u>Sciatic-nerve stretch</u>
Quadriceps Rectus femoris	**Ankle lifts**	**Combination quadriceps, hip flexor, iliotibial band, latissimus dorsi stretch**
Hip flexors and iliotibial band (ITB) Tensor fasciae latae (TFL)	**Walking lunges** **Walking lunges with rotation** **Hip holds with ankle rotation**	**Combination quadriceps, hip flexor, iliotibial band, latissimus dorsi stretch**
Adductors	**Sideways running with rotation** **Stepping over the fence**	*Adductor stretch*
Gluteal muscle group	**Hip holds with ankle rotation**	*Piriformis stretch*
Lateral obliques and abdominal muscles	**Sideways running with rotation**	**Sideways running with rotation** (if desired)
Quadratus lumborum Trunk and spinal muscles	**Sideways running with rotation**	**Quadratus lumborum stretch**

Bold = dynamic, *Italic = static,* <u>Underline = neural</u>

72

Soleus Stretch

Stretching immediately after running may delay the onset of muscular fatigue as well as prevent or mitigate muscle soreness caused by a bout of exercise. You may want to wear a stable pair of shoes during this stretch; flat-footed athletes may struggle to isolate the soleus (deep calf muscle) if they excessively pronate in bare feet. You can also adapt this stretch by placing a three-quarter-inch wedge under the toes of the leg to be stretched.

1. Stand approximately three feet (one meter) from a wall or a high fence and lean forward with your palms against the wall or fence to initiate a standard calf stretch.

2. Place the back leg about a foot behind the front leg, with the back heel planted firmly on the ground. Keep the rear heel perpendicular to the wall in front of you; this ensures that your rear foot does not pronate, or collapse medially, when you "load up" the stretch.

3. Lean the upper body forward only slightly. Drive the weight down through the rear heel and drop the back knee forward.

4. As you feel the load come onto the lower Achilles region, keep the knee cap directly over the middle toe.

5. Hold this stretch for approximately 15 seconds, then try to load the calf for another 15 seconds with additional pressure.

Gastrocnemius Stretch

Again, stretching postworkout may help stave off rebound tightness, soreness, and fatigue. As with the soleus stretch, wear a stable pair of shoes if you don't feel the stretch in bare feet or place a three-quarter-inch wedge under the toes of the leg being stretched. You might also try the stretch with your toes a few inches up on the wall and your body closer to the wall. You need to wear shoes in this case.

1. Start just as you did for the soleus stretch.
2. Contract the quadriceps of the rear leg to ensure that the leg remains straight.
3. Maintain a downward force on the rear heel and slowly lean the upper body forward, bringing the pressure onto the back leg. The tension of the stretch should start in the middle of the calf and expand either toward the knee or down to the Achilles tendon. Ensure that the weight of the rear foot is driven primarily toward the heel.
4. Hold this stretch for approximately 15 seconds, then try to load the calf for another 15 seconds with additional pressure.

Bent-Knee Hamstring Stretch

Keeping the hamstrings loose and strong is the key to preventing muscle imbalances between the front and back of the thighs and may even help forestall low back pain. Because of its increased range of motion, faster running in particular relies on limber hamstrings.

1. Kneeling on the ground with the right foot forward, support the back leg and knee on a soft surface. Ideally, only the heel of the front foot should touch the ground, with the toes pointed skyward.

2. Lean forward and place the right hand on the right knee. Then place the left fist on top of the right hand.

3. Lean forward from the upper body to place the chin onto the left fist.

4. Shift some of your weight to the back leg by slightly straightening the right knee; sink backward from the front knee. You should, from this position, feel a slight stretch in the hamstrings. If not, try removing one or both fists to lower your chin position. If you still don't feel a stretch, place your chin on your knee. Keep the pelvis perpendicular to the left leg.

5. Hold the position for 20 to 30 seconds, and repeat on both sides two or three times.

Stork-Position Hamstring Stretch

The benefits of this stretch mirror those of other hamstring stretches. Athletes with limited flexibility will struggle to maintain a stable position from the pelvis during this stretch. It is critical to push this exercise only to the point that your pelvis and lower trunk are aligned with the ground. If you twist your lower spine and pelvis, you will not place the load directly on your hamstrings.

1. Standing near a chest-high table or wall, place all of your weight on the left leg.
2. Lean forward from the hips, extending the right leg directly backward. Also extend the arms out to maintain your balance.
3. Keep the left leg straight by activating the quadriceps.
4. Lean forward until the upper body and right leg are almost parallel to the ground. To assist with stability, lightly place your fingers on the wall or table for balance.
5. Hold the position for 20 to 30 seconds and repeat on each side two or three times.

Adductor Stretch

Also known as a groin stretch, this exercise can help alleviate tightness in the adductors. The adductors tend to work constantly in a short range of motion to stabilize the leg in the stance phase.

1. Place the feet about twice hip-width apart.
2. Turn the feet outward and sink into a partial squat position, keeping the back straight. To keep the back straight, distribute your weight on the heels rather than the forefeet.
3. Depending on your flexibility level, place either the forearms or the elbows on the insides of the knees. If you have trouble keeping the back straight, hold the insides of the knees with the palms.
4. Push the knees apart until you feel the adductors tighten. Make sure that your knees are not inside the line of your toes.
5. As the adductors tighten, sink into the squat another inch (2 to 3 centimeters) or so.
6. Hold this form and pressure for 20 seconds.
7. Stand and walk around briefly, then repeat the movement.

Combination Quadriceps, Hip–Flexor, Iliotibial Band, Latissimus Dorsi Stretch

Maintaining flexibility around the hip joint—which depends on stretching the muscles of the lateral (iliotibial band) and anterior (quadriceps) thigh and the muscles of the lower trunk—is critical to maintaining proper posture while running and while at rest. Many runners suffer low back and hip-flexor pain as a result of tightness in the pelvis after years of activity unaccompanied by exercises aimed at achieving balance.

The basis of this stretch is the quadriceps and hip-flexor stretch. The quadriceps is a unique muscle group because it crosses two major joints (hip and knee) and works in conjunction with key hip-flexor muscles. The best way to statically stretch the quads is through a combined quad–hip stretch.

1. Kneel on the ground with the right knee approximately 8 inches (20 centimeters) from a couch or low chair and the right ankle resting on the edge of the couch or chair. Keep the pelvis parallel to the couch.

2. Place the knees on a pillow or other soft surface to protect the patella. Ensure that the hips have a slight posterior tilt. Achieve this tilt by holding the sides of the hip bones and imagining that you are trying to tuck an imaginary tail between your legs. The hips should also be parallel to the couch and not twisted.

3. Take a deep breath, and as you push forward from the hips, gently let your breath out.

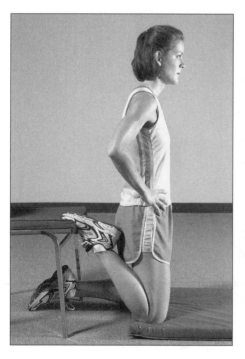
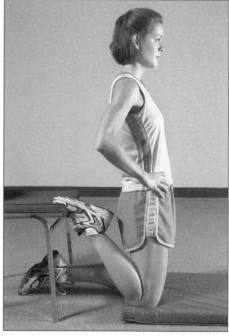

4. Adjust the tension on the quads by changing the distance between the left patella and the couch; the closer you place the knee to the couch, the greater the quad stretch, all else being equal. Squeeze the buttocks to assist in the activation of the quads.

5. To isolate the hip flexor, place the right foot on the ground and push forward from the hips until you feel pressure just below the left hip bone. It is essential for the trunk to remain upright with the pelvis posteriorly rotated to maximize the stretch on the hip flexors.

6. To increase the quad stretch, push forward from the center of your abdominals without tilting your pelvis forward.

7. Hold this position for 15 seconds, relax, and push the stretch slightly more forward from the hips for another 15 seconds. Repeat on the left side.

Once you've mastered the quadriceps hip-flexor stretch, you can further the stretch by also targeting the iliotibial band (ITB). Because of the structural nature of the ITB, you will feel this stretch in the abdominals, hip flexors, and quads—everywhere but the ITB itself. The ITB is a band of fascia with limited stretch receptors. Because of the structural attachments of the ITB to the hip and knee, this extended-hip position is ideal for placing pressure on the ITB.

1. As you stretch the left hip flexor, rotate the upper trunk to the right. This places tension on the front and lateral aspects of the left hip.

2. As you rotate the upper body to the right, push the left hip directly sideways. It will only move about half an inch to an inch (one to three centimeters) because of the pressure of the hip-flexor stretch.

3. Hold this position for 20 to 30 seconds.

4. Try to rotate the upper body more to the right and slightly push the left hip farther forward.

5. Hold for another 15 seconds. Repeat on the right side.

Now you can further the stetch by adding the lats (latissimus dorsi). The lats are the large muscles running from beside the armpits toward the center of the back that form the V shape of the trunk in heavily muscled specimens. Invoking the lats in range-of-motion exercises is especially useful for runners who develop tight shoulders and rounded upper backs.

1. Return to the standard hip-flexor stretch position, with the back leg fully supported on the ground.

2. As you push the left hip forward, reach the left arm high above the head and reach over slightly toward the right.

3. Take a deep breath in; as you exhale, tilt the upper body slightly to the right and reach as high as you can, keeping the knee on the ground.

4. Hold for 20 seconds, and repeat with the right leg, reaching your right arm toward the left.

Sciatic-Nerve Stretch

The sciatic nerve is the major nerve originating in the low back, and it serves both the anterior and posterior leg compartments. Keeping the surrounding hip muscles from tightening around the nerve is critical for avoiding downtime due to sciatica, piriformis syndrome, or other insults to the nerve at the point where it passes through the pelvis.

1. While lying on your back, extend the left leg until the left quad is perpendicular to the trunk.
2. Place the hands flat on the floor.
3. Keep the right leg straight and not rotated outward. Maintain the head in a neutral, relaxed position.
4. Keeping the left quad stable, extend the left knee until you feel tension in the area behind the knee and calves. Adjust the tension by flexing the ankle back toward the head. Focus on keeping the thigh perpendicular to the ground and keeping the knee stable.
5. When you feel you cannot pull the toes back any farther, gently oscillate the knee around one-half inch (one to two centimeters) forward and backward from this position. This movement should be very slow and controlled; only carry out this movement in a pain-free range. The movement should cause only mild discomfort from behind the buttock, knee, or calf.
6. Oscillate the movement backward and forward 10 to 15 times per leg. Repeat each side twice.

Quadratus Lumborum Stretch

Many runners do not see spinal rotation as beneficial to their performance. As I have described, however, maximizing performance is all about balance. There are endless means of achieving trunk and spinal balance. The trunk is a multidirectional complex of joints. Focusing on simple rotational movement is a strong starting point for any endurance athlete. Try combining this stretch with the sciatic-nerve and piriformis stretches in a group of three movements, and then repeat them on the opposite side.

1. Extend the left arm to the left with the palm facing down.
2. Bring the left leg over to the right with the knee crossing the chest at a 90-degree angle to the spine.
3. Hold the left knee with the right hand to maintain balance. Firmly drive the left arm and shoulder blade into the ground to maintains stability.
4. Try to rotate the spine by pulling the left leg with the right hand.
5. Hold this position for 20 seconds, and repeat twice on each side.

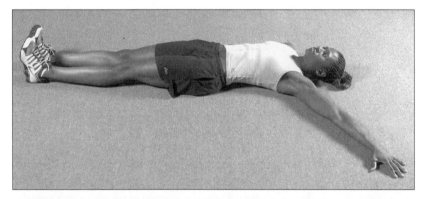

Piriformis Stretch

The piriformis muscle is deep within the hip region and is extremely active during the running cycle to control medial rotation of the thigh during the stance gait phase. It is also responsible for stabilizing the hip joint.

1. To isolate the piriformis and some of its fellow hip-joint rotators, lie on your back and bring the left knee up toward the chest.
2. Hold the left knee with the left hand while holding onto the left ankle (just above the joint) with the right hand. Keep the left knee in the midline of the chest and bent at a 90-degree angle. The left knee should be right in front of the face.
3. To bring extra pressure onto the left piriformis, keep the left hip firmly on the ground.
4. Hold the left knee in the midline and bring the left shin and ankle toward the head.
5. Hold the pressure in this position for 20 seconds, relax slightly, and reintroduce the tension by pulling the ankle into a dorsiflexed position.

Many distance runners are loath to stretch for a variety of reasons: discomfort, time considerations, and the lack of a perceived benefit. However, many runners—especially those who have been competing for many years—are prone to developing imbalances in opposing muscles groups, for instance the hamstrings and quadriceps, and tightness in particular muscles or muscle groups. It is clear that the optimal treatment for, and prevention of, such states is dynamic range-of-motion exercises performed when muscles are warm. Without these exercises, many runners will find themselves consigned to the sidelines, victims of preventable injuries. The exercises in this chapter address the most common injury sites among runners and, if performed diligently, may play a large role in both forestalling injury and advancing performance through stabilization and improved dynamic range of motion.

CHAPTER 5

Gaining Ground Through Upper-Body Strength

MICHAEL LEVERITT, PHD, CSCS

Strength training for the upper body is an important training component often overlooked by many runners. A stronger upper body can lead to increased respiratory efficiency, improved core stability, and enhanced running economy. Although upper-body strength training might not affect running performance as much as other forms of training, such as aerobic conditioning, it can benefit serious runners seeking an extra couple of percentage points in improved performance. This chapter not only discusses how upper-body strength training can improve your running performance, it also shows you how to incorporate upper-body strength training into an overall running training program.

Understanding the physiological responses to resistance training enables runners to more effectively design an upper-body resistance-training program based on their individual needs. Let's briefly review the neuromuscular adaptations to resistance training. For a more detailed review, refer to Fleck and Kraemer (1997) and National Strength and Conditioning Association (NSCA 2000).

The major benefit of resistance training is an increase in muscular strength, which can improve performance and help prevent injury. Resistance training can increase strength by increasing the size of the muscle or by increasing the nervous system's ability to coordinate the contraction of muscle fibers to create greater force. Increasing the size of the muscle fibers, or hypertrophy, rather than increasing the number of muscle fibers results in larger muscles; the cross-sectional area of a muscle correlates to the amount of force the muscle can produce. Thus, an increase in muscle-fiber size can increase muscle strength. As with any gains in training, the amount of muscle hypertrophy achieved from resistance training depends on the duration, volume, and intensity of training.

When an individual begins a resistance-training program, muscle strength increases almost immediately. However, little muscle hypertrophy is evident in the first six to eight weeks of training. This suggests that other factors—likely adaptations of the nervous system—are responsible for the initial gains in muscle strength. Once an athlete continues resistance training beyond six to eight weeks and up to several years, increases in muscle size are responsible for improvements in strength.

However, very little is known about which factors cause long-term increases in strength after several years of training; most research studies do not continue for long periods because of the burden they place on subjects and the high costs. However, some suggest that hypertrophy may reach a ceiling in response to long-term resistance training. For example, research has shown that very experienced strength-trained athletes can still increase strength without further increases in muscle hypertrophy. Therefore, neural factors may play a part in the initial and long-term strength gains that result from resistance training.

In response to training, the nervous system can synchronize the contraction of muscle fibers so that more fibers contract at the same time, thus producing more force. It is also possible that training causes an increase in the number of muscle fibers contracted during a particular task. Furthermore, inhibitory mechanisms in the neuromuscular system that protect against injury may decrease after a period of training, allowing the muscle to produce greater strength. A reduction in the co-activation of antagonistic muscles during a particular activity may also contribute to strength gains. Because it is difficult to measure anatomical and physiological changes in the nervous system in humans, scientists continue to debate the exact nature of the neural mechanisms underpinning gains in strength.

The fact that we can increase strength without muscle hypertrophy has particular significance for runners wanting to perform upper-body resistance training. Ideally, an upper-body strength-training program for runners would increase strength without increasing muscle size. Otherwise the runner would have to carry extra weight while running, and whether it's muscle or fat, extra weight is likely to hinder running performance. Therefore, it is important that upper-body strength-training programs manipulate training variables in a manner that minimizes hypertrophy while ensuring adequate strength development. Such programs benefit performance by yielding more force to propel the body forward without the extra weight. As I discuss later in this chapter, this is possible by judiciously choosing training exercises.

Principles of Resistance Training

As with any other component of training, the key principles of resistance training are specificity, progressive overload, reversibility, and individuality.

Specificity refers to the capacity of the body to adapt specifically to the demand imposed on it. This means that the specific type of training activity dictates the nature of the body's adaptation. For example, training the body with fast, explosive movements is best for athletic events such as serving in tennis and throwing in baseball. Training the body with slow, controlled movements might be best for occupational tasks that involve lifting and manual handling. Upper-body exercises that are unilateral, such as a dumbbell one-arm lateral row, are more specific to running than bilateral exercises, such as a barbell bent-over row, because running does not involve both limbs moving in the same direction simultaneously.

Progressive overload refers to the progressive application of a stimulus with increasing levels of intensity. To produce optimal adaptation, the resistance-training stimulus must impose a demand that is greater than what the body is accustomed to. The body then adapts to this stimulus and becomes stronger. It is important to keep increasing the overload in a progressive manner to ensure continued improvements in performance. For example, you may need to increase the weight lifted in some dumbbell exercises by one to two kilograms (two to four pounds) every couple of weeks to ensure that your muscles are overloaded in a progressive manner.

Reversibility refers to the tendency to lose the gains achieved during training when training ceases. This means that it is not possible to maintain strength gains if you stop training. As a general rule, strength gains can be maintained by performing resistance training once per week. However, if resistance training stops, strength tends to decrease at roughly the same rate at which it was gained. For example, if you had a 20 percent improvement in strength after training for six weeks, it would take approximately another six weeks without training to lose this gain. However, this is only a general rule; there can be significant individual variation in the reversibility response.

The principle of individuality recognizes that each person responds slightly differently to a particular training stimulus. This is important to remember when devising a program based on results of research studies or anecdotal reports of training regimens undertaken by certain athletes. Research studies can indicate what the average response to training will be in a specific group of people, while anecdotal reports give an example of how a specific athlete responds to a particular training regimen. It is best to use these as guidelines when formulating your own training program, remembering to monitor your own progress, because it is likely that your response to training will be slightly different than those of other athletes. Monitoring and evaluating your individual response to training will let you fine-tune your training program to ensure optimal performance.

Adhere to the principles of specificity, progressive overload, reversibility, and individuality when designing your own upper-body strength-training program.

Benefits of Upper–Body Strength Training

To understand how upper-body strength training can help running performance, let's briefly review the physiological factors that determine running performance. It is generally agreed that $\dot{V}O_2$max, lactate threshold, and running economy determine running performance. $\dot{V}O_2$max, or aerobic power, is the maximal rate at which the body consumes and uses oxygen. Although it is important to have a high $\dot{V}O_2$max, the ability to work at a high percentage of your $\dot{V}O_2$max is also a key predictor of success in endurance running. A high lactate threshold enables a runner to work at a high percentage of $\dot{V}O_2$max over a long period of time. Running economy refers to the ability to use energy specifically to propel the body forward and is determined by measuring the oxygen required at a given running velocity. The more oxygen required to sustain the given velocity, the poorer the economy; the increased oxygen demand means that extra energy is being used by muscles that do not contribute to the forward propulsion of the body (for example, muscles that shake the head and clench the jaw require oxygen).

Several research studies have investigated the effects of resistance training on $\dot{V}O_2$max and lactate threshold, and most have found that resistance training does not improve either of these factors. The studies that do show an increase in $\dot{V}O_2$max or lactate threshold have usually used untrained or sedentary subjects whose fitness levels were so low that any form of training would have provided sufficient stimulus to improve their aerobic fitness.

On the other hand, there is evidence that you can improve running economy through resistance training. Because most studies have used a whole-body resistance-training program, the contribution of the upper and lower body to the improvements in running economy is unclear. However, it is fair to assume that both upper-body and lower-body strength training can improve running economy. The improvement in running economy with resistance training is generally about 4 to 8 percent, and the impact on actual performance is probably even smaller. The improvement in running economy that occurs with resistance training is probably due to improved mechanical efficiency, enhanced muscle coordination, and superior motor recruitment patterns—all of which improve neuromuscular efficiency and reduce nonessential upper-body muscle contraction, resulting in a decrease in oxygen consumption at a given running velocity.

As mentioned earlier, one of the keys to improving running economy is to reduce the amount of nonessential upper-body muscle contraction; this can be achieved by improving balance and core stability. During running, every time the foot strikes the ground, a cascade of muscle contractions occurs to stabilize and prevent the runner from falling over. Although it may seem that this would require little effort, these muscles all require oxygen, which means that less oxygen is available for the muscles doing the main job at hand—propelling the body forward. By strengthening the core muscles, however, you reduce the effort required to stabilize the body during each footstrike. Core stability training comes in many shapes and forms, and it is important to choose appropriate exercises to improve running economy and performance. Core stability exercises are discussed in detail in chapters 4 and 7.

Recent studies by Dr. Alison McConnell in the United Kingdom show that resistance training targeting the respiratory muscles can improve endurance performance. Most of the studies have been performed on rowers and cyclists, but it is likely that inspiratory muscle training would also enhance running performance. Although most exercise physiologists agree that lung capacity does not limit endurance performance (the amount of oxygen entering the lungs far exceeds the amount that enters the blood during exercise), it does appear that training the respiratory muscles may actually contribute to small but significant improvements in performance. For example, the air that is taken into the lungs in each breath contains about 21 percent oxygen. The air expelled in each breath contains about 16 percent oxygen, and this percentage is even higher during intense exercise because the respiratory muscles are capable of causing very large increases in the rate and depth of breathing during intense exercise. Therefore, the body does not use a lot of the inhaled oxygen.

© Human Kinetics

By increasing neuromuscular efficiency and reducing nonessential movement, resistance training improves running economy.

87

Why does resistance training of the respiratory muscles improve endurance performance? Probably because stronger respiratory muscles are more efficient, require less oxygen at a given level of effort, and reduce perceived exertion during exercise. Many people stop exercising because they feel out of breath or that their lungs are bursting, despite the fact that their lung capacity does not actually limit their performance. Strengthening the respiratory muscles reduces the sensation of effort associated with breathing and improves performance.

You can train your respiratory muscles using a relatively inexpensive handheld device called POWERbreathe (www.powerbreathe.com). Research studies have used respiratory training protocols involving two sets of 30 repetitions each day for six weeks. While this appears to improve endurance performance, it is unclear whether this is the optimal training regimen and how effective long-term respiratory muscle training is in maintaining improvements in performance. Still, respiratory muscle training is emerging as a useful form of upper-body resistance training that serious runners looking for new and innovative ways to improve performance may want to consider.

Designing Your Program

There are several important variables to consider when designing a resistance-training program: needs analysis, exercise selection, training frequency, exercise order, repetitions, loads, rest periods, and number of sets.

Analyzing Your Needs

A needs analysis looks at the requirements of the sport and assesses the fitness of the athlete undertaking the program. It is difficult to outline a generic needs analysis for upper-body resistance training for runners because every runner is different and the purpose of the needs analysis is to ensure that the program is tailored to the individual's specific requirements. The needs analysis need not be a formal process, but it is important to consider your own requirements rather than simply following a ready-made program. Some questions to ask include the following:

- What movement patterns are involved in running? For example, what is the speed of movement? What muscle groups are used? What are the relative forces exerted by the upper body?

- What are the common injury sites? What is your own history of injuries? What are common injuries experienced by runners?

- How important is muscular endurance versus muscle size versus strength versus power?

- What is your training history? Are you a beginner, intermediate, or advanced resistance trainer?

- What are your strengths and weaknesses?

The answers to these questions will help you determine which muscles or muscle groups to focus on, how quickly to increase the workload, and whether muscle hypertrophy is a major concern.

Selecting Exercises

The next step is to select the best exercises for your program, keeping in mind the principle of specificity. Structural exercises that stabilize posture are likely to be the most appropriate in an upper-body training program for runners. An example of an upper-body structural exercise is the alternate standing shoulder press; here, the muscles of the core stabilize the body while you lift the weights over your head. Isolated single-joint exercises of the upper limb, such as biceps curls, are unlikely to provide much benefit, because these muscles are rarely used in isolation during running (except, perhaps when passing a drink station).

Consider also muscle balance when selecting exercises. For example, many back exercises are useful to runners because the muscles in the back help maintain posture and stabilize the upper body, thus enabling better running economy. To balance the strengthening of the back, however, it is important to also include exercises for the muscles in the chest and shoulders, which provide opposite or antagonistic actions to the actions of the back. Including both types of exercises limits muscle imbalances that can lead to injury. In addition to selecting exercises that balance musculature, consider administrative concerns, such as the availability of time, space, and equipment when selecting exercises.

Deciding on Training Frequency

Training frequency refers to the number of training sessions performed in a given time period. Most runners should perform upper-body resistance training twice a week. This leaves plenty of time for other primary forms of running training such as aerobic conditioning.

Some research suggests that performing strength and endurance training concurrently can inhibit the development of one component of fitness; however, this appears to be the case only when strength athletes add endurance training to their normal resistance-training program. Endurance athletes adding strength training to their normal endurance-training program, on the other hand, show no negative effects in their endurance performance.

Determining Sequence, Load, and Volume

Exercise order is the sequence in which you perform the exercises within a training session. As a general rule, perform large muscle–group exercises before small muscle–group exercises, and do compound exercises involving the concurrent movement of several joints before doing single-joint isolation exercises. For example, it is advisable to perform bench presses before undertaking bicep curls. A good strategy for decreasing the amount of time per training sessions is to perform "supersets"—alternate sets of two different exercises that train opposing muscle groups. For example, in a superset of lat pull-downs and bench presses an athlete performs a set of lat pull-downs (which work the latissimus dorsi of the back) followed by a set of bench presses (which work the pectorals of the chest), and then repeats this until completing the desired number of sets of each exercise. This enables the back muscles to rest while the chest muscles are working and vice versa. It also guards against creating muscle imbalances.

Once you've selected the exercises and their order, you can determine the repetitions, loads, rest periods, and number of sets. Resistance training loads are usually determined as percentages of a one-repetition maximum (1RM)—the greatest amount of weight that can be lifted once for a particular exercise. Loads may also be expressed as a weight that can be lifted for a specified number of repetitions (repetition maximum or RM). For example, 8RM is the weight that can be lifted for eight repetitions during a specific exercise.

Resistance training is a unique form of training because you can elicit a wide variety of adaptations by carefully manipulating the repetitions, loads, rest periods, and number of sets. A slightly different type of resistance-training program is required to achieve each different resistance-training goal: increasing muscular endurance, increasing muscle size, increasing muscle strength, and increasing muscle power (see figure 5.1).

Muscular endurance refers to the ability of a muscle to repeatedly generate high-force contractions or sustain prolonged high-force contractions. Resistance-training programs that emphasize muscular endurance include a high number of repetitions per set, relatively low loads, short rest periods between sets, and a moderate number of sets per exercise. For example, a muscle-endurance program consists of 12 or more repetitions per set, a load of less than 70 percent of 1RM, 30 to 45 seconds of rest between sets, and two or three sets per exercise.

RM	≤2	3	4	5	6	7	8	9	10	11	12	13	14	15	16	17	18	19	≥20
Training goal	Strength						Strength				Strength				Strength				
	*Power					Power				Power					Power				
	Hypertrophy			Hypertrophy				Hypertrophy				Hypertrophy							
	Muscular endurance			Muscular endurance				Muscular endurance											

Figure 5.1 The repetitions, loads, rest periods, and number of sets for a resistance training program depend on the desired goal.

Reprinted, by permission, from D. Wathen, 2000, Resistance training. In *Essentials of strength training and conditioning,* 2nd ed., edited by T.R. Baechle and R.W. Earle (Champaign, IL: Human Kinetics), 414.

Resistance-training programs specifically designed to increase muscle size typically use a moderate number of repetitions per set, moderate to heavy loads, short to moderate rest periods between sets, and a high number of sets for each exercise. A high training volume has been shown to result in the greatest increases in muscle size. Therefore, muscle-hypertrophy training keeps the muscle under high tension for long periods of time. A typical muscle-hypertrophy program consists of 8 to 12 repetitions per set, a load of 70 to 85 percent of 1RM or 8RM to 12RM, 30 to 90 seconds of rest between sets, three to six sets per exercise, and several different exercises for each muscle group.

Muscle strength is the maximal force produced under a given set of conditions. Therefore, training programs that increase maximal strength include a low number of repetitions per set, heavy loads, long rest periods between sets, and a moderate to high number of sets per exercise. The most important aspect of maximal strength training is to provide enough rest between sets for the muscle to produce maximal or near-maximal forces during each set. A maximal-strength training set might be two to six repetitions per set, loads greater than 85 percent 1RM or 2RM to 6RM, three to five minutes of rest between sets, and two to six exercises per set. *sets per exercise.*

Power—defined mathematically as the product of strength and speed of movement—is the explosive aspect of strength. Typically, power-training programs consist of a low number of repetitions per set, light to moderate loads that can be moved at high speed, long rest periods between sets, and a moderate number of sets per exercise. A power-training program might include three to five repetitions per set, loads of 50 percent 1RM, three to five minutes of rest between sets, and three to five sets per exercise.

Most runners want to select appropriate repetitions, loads, rest periods, and number of sets for their upper-body resistance training to ensure that they develop strength with minimal hypertrophy. As figure 5.1 shows, an individual will experience a continuum of adaptation and some degree of hypertrophy after undertaking muscular endurance, maximal-strength training, or power training; however, the muscle-hypertrophy training program will result in the greatest increases in muscle size. Most runners will benefit most from a strengthening program that emphasizes muscular endurance with occasional training in the maximal-strength or power ranges to provide variety or to work on specific weaknesses.

Sample Upper-Body Program

Table 5.1 presents a sample 20- to 30-minute upper-body resistance-training program for a distance runner to perform twice a week. The program is designed for people with some, but limited, experience with resistance training and focuses on improving muscular endurance. More advanced individuals may want to incorporate variations to the listed exercises, such as performing the alternate

91

dumbbell chest press on a stability ball rather than on a bench. This is a more challenging form of this exercise because it calls on the core musculature to stabilize the body. This enhances the benefit of this exercise, and most runners should aim to progress to a stage where more challenging variations of these exercises can be incorporated. More advanced variations of each exercise are listed in the last column of table 5.1.

The exercises work primarily the back, chest, and shoulders with assistance from the biceps and triceps. Where possible, the exercises are specific to running—they involve alternate movements of limbs and can be performed in a standing or upright position. It is important to also adhere to specificity of movement speed by performing each exercise at the same tempo as your normal stride rate during running. Loads are set as repetition maximum. Increase weight regularly as you become able to perform more repetitions at a particular weight. I also suggest that you perform daily respiratory muscle training using the POWERbreathe device. This program is by no means definitive; many variations are possible to meet the needs of different individuals. The key is to perform your own needs analysis and adhere to the training principles when designing your program.

Table 5.1 Upper–Body Strengthening Program

Exercise	Sets × reps	Load (RM)	Rest (sec)	Advanced variation
Lat pull-downs	3 × 12	12	45	Wide-grip pull-up
Alternate dumbbell chest presses	3 × 12	12	45	Perform on stability ball
Cable seated rows	3 × 12	12	45	Perform using one hand
Alternate standing shoulder presses	3 × 12	12	45	Perform on stability ball
Dumbbell side delt abduction	2 × 15	15	30	Perform in lunge position with knee 15 cm (6 in) above floor
Dumbbell one-arm lat rows	2 × 15	15	30	Perform on stability ball
Cable shoulder internal rotation	2 × 15	15	30	Perform using dumbbells
Cable shoulder external rotation	2 × 15	15	30	Perform using dumbbells

Lat Pull-Downs

To perform an advanced version of this exercise, grip an immoveable bar and raise the body up using the movement described in the steps listed.

1. Place hands on the bar in a grip wider than shoulder width.
2. With knees under the pad, bend the elbows and pull the arms out and down until the upper arms are parallel to the floor.
3. Let arms extend back up to the starting position.

Alternate Dumbbell Chest Presses

To perform an advanced version of this exercise, complete the steps listed while lying on a stability ball instead of a bench.

1. Lie flat on your back on a bench. Begin this exercise holding a dumbbell in each hand, with one arm extended straight up from the shoulder and the other arm bent at the elbow to 90 degrees.

2. Bend the elbow to bring the dumbbell in the hand of the straight arm down until that elbow is bent 90 degrees. At the same time, contract the chest and straighten the other arm so that it extends straight up from the shoulder.

Cable Seated Rows

To perform an advanced version of this exercise, perform the movement described in the steps listed using only one arm at a time.

1. From a seated position, with the hips and knees slightly flexed, grasp the pulley handles with both hands.
2. Bring the handles toward the trunk while squeezing the shoulder blades together and down. Keep arms close to the body during the movement.
3. Return the pulley handles back to the starting position.

Alternate Standing Shoulder Presses

To perform an advanced version of this exercise, follow the steps listed while sitting on a stability ball.

1. From a standing position, begin this exercise with one arm extended straight up from the shoulders and the other arm with the elbow bent at 90 degrees.

2. Bring the dumbbell in the hand of the straight arm downward until the elbow is bent at 90 degrees. At the same time, straighten the other arm so that it extends straight up from the shoulders.

3. Maintain tension in the trunk musculature to stabilize the body throughout this exercise.

Dumbbell Side Delt Abduction

To perform an advanced version of this exercise, maintain a lunge position with the knee approximately 15 centimeters (6 inches) above the floor.

1. From a standing position, lean forward slightly while holding a dumbbell in each hand, with arms extended straight downward from the shoulders and elbows slightly bent.
2. Bring the arms outward and upward with elbows only slightly bent until the arms are outstretched and parallel to the floor.
3. Return hands to the starting position.

Dumbbell One-Arm Lat Rows

To perform an advanced version of this exercise, place the knee on a stability ball instead of a bench.

1. Place the left knee on a bench with the shin along the length of the bench.
2. Bend forward at the hip so that the spine is almost parallel with the bench.
3. Hold a dumbbell in the right hand with the right arm extended straight downward from the shoulder.
4. Raise the dumbbell while bending the elbow until the upper arm is parallel with the floor, keeping the arm close to the body.
5. Lower the dumbbell to the starting position. Repeat on the other side.

Cable Shoulder Internal Rotation

To perform an advanced version of this exercise, use a dumbbell while lying on one side.

1. Stand upright with your right side facing a cable machine.
2. Grasp the pulley handle with the right hand. Hold the hand away from the body with the elbow flexed to 90 degrees. The elbow should be next to the body but slightly outside the line of the shoulder. (Pressing the upper arm against a rolled-up towel placed between the elbow and the side of the body can help to maintain the proper position.)
3. Pull the cable in front of and across the body as far as possible without lifting the elbow away from the side of the body.
4. Return to the starting position. Repeat on the other side.

Cable Shoulder External Rotation

To perform an advanced version of this exercise, use a dumbbell while lying on one side.

1. Stand upright with your right side facing a cable machine,
2. Grasp the pulley handle with the left hand and hold it in front of the body while flexing the left elbow to 90 degrees. The elbow should be next to the body but slightly outside the line of the shoulder.
3. Pull the cable across and away from the body as far as possible without lifting the left elbow away from the side of the body.
4. Return to the starting position. Repeat on the other side.

Strength training for the upper body is an important training component often overlooked by many runners. However, a stronger upper body can improve performance by enhancing respiratory efficiency, core stability, and running economy. When designing resistance-training programs, take into account the training principles of specificity, progressive overload, reversibility, and individuality. A key aspect of upper-body resistance training for runners is to increase strength with only minimal increases in muscle size. You can accomplish this through carefully manipulating the training sets, loads, and rests.

Finally, recognize that training the entire body is essential to your development as a runner. To complement the benefits derived from upper-body strength training, be sure to implement the lower-body exercises described in chapter 6.

CHAPTER 6

Boosting Economy Through Lower-Body Strength

COLLEEN GLYDE JULIAN, MS

Not surprisingly, the primary element for optimizing distance-running performance is a solid, individualized running program. Still, you can complement your running fitness, reduce your risk of injury, and improve your speed greatly by incorporating additional modes of training. One of the best ways to expand your training is to develop your lower-body strength through strength training and other exercises to counteract running stress.

At the mention of the words "strength training," many people envision leather weight belts and straining voices above stacks of iron. Although this stereotypical notion of strength training is applicable for athletes who engage in sports such as football, sprinting, or the shot put—all of which rely on coordinated, explosive movements or "raw strength"—it is not of primary importance to distance runners. Endurance sports such as running and cycling rely primarily on strength-endurance, the ability to exert a submaximal force for a longer duration or to repeat dynamic movements rather than execute a single ballistic movement.

"Don't cut corners with your training," advises Nike Farm Team coach Frank Gagliano. "Make sure you do it all and don't think running only will make you a champion. You need to do drills, weights, stretching, et cetera."

So cardiovascular fitness, while obviously vital to a distance runner's development, is not in itself sufficient; building muscular strength-endurance is also critical because certain muscles and muscle groups are asked to contract a tremendous number of times in the course of a long race. Furthermore, the ability to generate power (defined as the rate of work over time, it is of paramount importance in the "explosive" disciplines) is something distance runners must address. Rough terrain, hills, and the need for a fast finish—all of which rely to some extent on power—are elements that competitive runners inevitably face.

To sustain their strength over the duration of a run, distance runners require not only aerobic development but also the development of neuromuscular characteristics related to voluntary and reflexive neural activation of the muscles, muscle force, and muscle elasticity (Häkkinen 1994). Strength training can help develop these neuromuscular characteristics, which include increased efficiency of motor-unit recruitment, heightened neuromuscular coordination between muscles, increased neural drive to muscles, and enhanced motor skills. Because of the dynamic nature of racing, endurance athletes must be able to react to brisk changes in tempo; this requires the rapid generation of power. Therefore, distance runners must find a balance between efficiency, or economy, of motion (described later in this chapter and also in chapters 1 and 5) and strength. Efficiency, in short, refers to the amount of energy used to perform a given workload. Being inefficient as a runner means wasting precious energy on excessive movement, leaving less residual energy for responding to changes in pace. Without the power necessary for shifting gears and running at higher velocities, you will likely be left watching your competitors finish in front of you.

Running events vary in terms of their relative requirements for endurance and power, a fact that athletes must apply to their individual training regimens. For example, marathoners must spend the majority of their training time focusing on training volume and marathon-pace, interval, and tempo workouts and spend a smaller portion of time on power-oriented strength and speed exercises. Sprinters, on the other hand, must generate huge bursts of power, both to propel them from the blocks and to maintain maximal velocity and form for the duration of their races. Both kinds of runners can benefit from lower-body strength training that is specifically geared toward their needs. All distance runners can increase their speed and their ability to generate power. And by maintaining proper posture, stabilizing joints, and preventing excessive movement while running, strength training can help runners decrease the likelihood of overuse injuries.

"The primary reason for strength training, I believe, is to prevent muscular-imbalance injuries," says Brad Hauser, 2000 Olympian in the 5,000 meters. "I use lifting mostly as a preventive measure during marathon training. However, the 5,000 meters, 1,500 meters, and under rely so much on speed and power—it comes down to changing gears—so in these cases lower-body strength is important to develop that power."

As with any type of training, some athletes benefit more than others. Incorporating strength training may be particularly advantageous for women, older athletes, and those who tend to be injury prone owing to specific weaknesses.

Strength Differences Between Men and Women

Contrary to popular belief, "female muscles" themselves are not quantitatively different in terms of strength as compared to those of men. The strength discrepancy is more a result of the women having less muscle mass than men. Research has shown that women's strength is approximately 60 percent of that of men. However, when this data is corrected for differences in muscle mass, muscle-tissue strength is approximately equal. Additionally, on average, women have approximately 8 to 10 percent more body fat than men. In weight-bearing activities such as running, this increases energy costs (Fahey 1994) and decreases efficiency. To decrease the energy cost of running, women can improve overall strength, decrease body fat, and improve performance through resistance or weight training. Interestingly, weight training, when combined with aerobic exercise, has been shown to improve aerobic capacity in women more than aerobic training alone (Kraemer and Evans 1996). Therefore, it is advantageous for women to improve strength to increase power generation, endurance, overall strength, and work economy, and to decrease the incidence of injury.

A study incorporating cyclists and runners illustrates that the benefits of strength training are particularly evident in activities that recruit fast-twitch muscle fibers (Hickson et al. 1988). Fast-twitch muscle fibers (those that use primarily nonoxidative, or glycolytic, pathways to generate energy) are recruited during activities of high intensity and short duration, such as the 800 meters, 1,500 meters, and even the last 400 meters of a marathon. In this investigation, subjects performed strength training three days a week for 10 weeks; their endurance-oriented training remained constant. After 10 weeks, subjects' leg strength increased by an average of 30 percent, but thigh girth, the areas of both fast- and slow-twitch muscle fibers in the vastus lateralis, and activity levels of citrate synthase (an enzyme critical to anaerobic metabolism) within the muscles were unchanged; short-term (four- to eight- minute) running endurance improved by 13 percent. These data demonstrate the benefit of strength training for runners competing in race distances ranging from 800 meters to 3,000 meters.

Although short-term endurance does not by itself dictate performance in a longer event such as the 10,000 meters, it is still necessary. Many 10,000-meter track specialists describe the event as a 3,000-meter race with a 7,000-meter tempo run as an appetizer. So the final 3,000 meters of the 10,000 meters demands short-term endurance to maintain near-maximal velocity for the final eight-plus minutes of the race. Strength at this point means two things: maintaining velocity and maintaining composure. Both depend heavily on lower-body strength.

Additional adaptations to resistance training may potentially improve performance, muscle function, or both. Low-intensity, high-volume resistance training increases capillary density—the number of capillaries per unit area and per muscle fiber. Increased capillary density increases blood supply to the active muscle, which may improve the ability to remove lactate, a waste product of anaerobic metabolism. Neural adaptations to strength training appear to be the primary instigator of improved muscular strength within the first stages of a resistance-training program. These adaptations include increased neural drive to muscle, increased synchronization of motor units, increased activation of contractile apparatus, and inhibition of the protective mechanisms of the muscle. Several modes of strength training can accomplish these goals. Before we discuss each mode, however, let's look more closely at how running stresses the lower body.

Stress of Running

Running places a large amount of stress on joints, muscles, and connective tissues (bone, ligament, tendon, and cartilage) through impact stresses and repetitive movements. Depending on running pace, the body must absorb an impact of approximately two to four times its own weight with each footstrike. For a 135-pound person, this equates to approximately 350 to 700 tons per foot over the course of a 10-mile run. Clearly you need architecture with great integrity to support this force.

Attachment sites of muscles, tendons, and ligaments are frequent sites of injury because of force and muscle imbalances. Endurance training itself can increase the durability of these sites (ACSM 2001). Just as the cardiovascular system adapts to aerobic training stimuli, connective tissue adapts to bear the greater forces generated by skeletal muscles, and the muscles themselves adapt to more effectively bear the weight. You accomplish this incrementally, mostly by the act of running itself; that is, when running is continued over time and the workload is increased sensibly, the relevant support structures naturally become more resilient. However, you can also enhance these adaptations with supplementary strength training. Without muscular strength, the surrounding structure's ability to absorb shock decreases, causing bony structures to bear a higher proportion of impact. This often results in injury. Research has indicated that lifting regimens of moderate to high intensity and volume stimulate connective tissue growth most effectively and therefore decrease injury risk by increasing the amount of energy a given tissue can absorb before failure and by increasing the maximum tensile strength of the tissue (Stone 1988). Articular cartilage, which provides cushion within the bony structures of joints, has been shown to thicken with weight-bearing exercise (Barneveld and van Weeren 1999), thereby reducing injury risk. Strength training using antigravity musculature, the muscles responsible for maintaining erect posture such as the extensor muscles of the back, also enhances cartilage growth (ACSM 2001).

Support-system durability describes an underlying muscular foundation that provides an appropriate method to deal with a particular stress. For the purposes of this chapter, I use this term to mean support systems that should be developed specifically to handle the stress—overuse strain and connective tissue stresses—presented by running. Adequate support-system durability requires strength in both large and small muscle groups, which together maintain appropriate posture and stabilization during running; the exercises listed later in this chapter are aimed specifically at this integrated, or dynamic, stabilization.

Running Movement

Running involves a unique balance of directed power and efficiency and requires substantial lower-body strength. In terms of running, efficiency means using less energy to generate or maintain a given velocity over a given distance. Generally, as a runner progresses in fitness and experience, he or she becomes more biomechanically efficient because of increased balance and coordination, the elimination of excess movement, and fine-tuning within and increased coordination among agonistic, antagonistic, and synergistic muscles (Martin and Coe 1997).

Because it is free of excess movement, the unusual running form of Paula Radcliffe, world-record holder in the marathon, serves her well.

105

Agonistic muscles initiate a particular movement, while antagonistic muscles oppose the action of agonists; therefore, agonists and antagonists are found in pairs and work accordingly (see figure 6.1). A good example of this relationship can be seen when flexing the knee joint. Here, the biceps femoris (hamstrings)

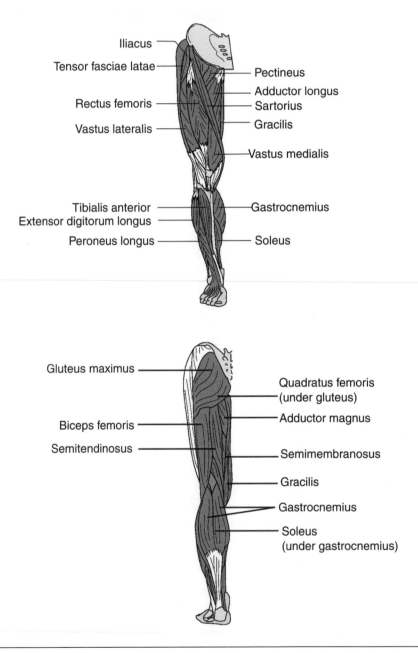

Figure 6.1 Agonistic, antagonistic, and synergistic muscles of the lower body act in concert to produce the multiple actions that make up the running motion.

group acts as the agonist while flexing the leg (bending the knee), and the quadriceps group acts as the antagonist. During extension of the knee joint (i.e., as the leg is straightened), these agonist-antagonist roles are reversed. Synergistic muscles, on the other hand, assist the primary muscles involved in a particular movement. In the example of bending the knee, the individual muscles of the quadriceps group—the vastus medialis, vastus lateralis, vastus intermedius, and rectus femoris—produce a synergistic action at the knee joint. Without coordinated and balanced relationships among these muscles, injuries and ineffective movement are likely results. For example, if a synergistic muscle lacks appropriate strength, the muscle it supports is prone to injury because it must bear an increased workload. Therefore, without *underlying* support, your muscles cannot optimally accomplish the primary task of running.

As you recall from chapter 1, if you watch a runner in slow motion, you see two basic positions of the lower body during a single running cycle (a series of two footstrikes): bearing weight on a single leg and driving the rear leg forward. Bearing weight on a single leg, or the *stance phase*, is made up of three primary stages: footstrike, midstance, and propulsion.

During footstrike, the lower body must absorb a tremendous amount of impact stress. When the foot strikes the ground, the quadriceps muscles allow the knee to flex to aid in shock absorption. Internal rotation of the lower extremity in this phase is elicited by eccentric and synergistic tension of the posterior tibialis, soleus, and gastrocnemius muscles, or calf muscles. In midstance, the body must stabilize promptly before propulsion. Small stabilizing muscles provide the strength necessary for a smooth and efficient transition. The propulsive phase is initiated by hip, knee, and ankle plantar extension; these movements require the use of the gluteals and hamstrings, quadriceps, soleus, and gastrocnemius. Shifting the direction of momentum from propulsion to driving requires hip flexion via the iliacus and psoas muscles and forward rotation of the pelvis.

All of these movements require adequate strength in the large muscle groups and the smaller muscles that support them. Weaknesses in small muscle groups contribute heavily to the incidence of running injuries involving both soft tissue and connective tissue (bones and ligaments). The key is to recognize the confluence of the multiple muscular actions required in a single stride cycle; a solitary weak point can unravel the entire process and literally stop runners in their tracks.

Muscle Imbalances or Weaknesses

An examination of several common running ailments—hamstring injury, patellofemoral pain, and iliotibial band (ITB) syndrome—illustrates the contribution of muscle weakness and imbalances to the prevalence of running-related injuries.

Hamstring strains, tears, and pain are common in both short- and long-distance runners. Hamstring injuries in distance runners are often the result of poor core-muscle strength, which allows the top of the pelvis to rotate anteriorly—that is, toward the belly button—thereby adding tension to the hamstring insertion at the base of the buttocks. During the extension phase of the stride (when the knee drives forward and the lower leg is extended), the hamstring must contract eccentrically (the muscle lengthens) to control the movement of the tibia, or lower leg (Fredericson 1999). Together, these factors place a tremendous amount of stress on the hamstring muscle tissue itself and the connective tissue insertions at either end of the muscle.

Along with stretching (see chapter 4) at appropriate volume and intensity levels, certain strengthening exercises—among them eccentric and core-strengthening exercises—can, through stabilization, prevent or alleviate hamstring pain. Similarly, strengthening the small muscle groups surrounding the pelvis and low back (internal obliques, external obliques, transversus abdominis, and erector spinae) supports the pelvis in a neutral position, preventing it from tilting forward; this allows the muscle groups to perform in a synergistic or assistive manner and function properly, thereby reducing the incidence of injury.

Specific muscle imbalances or weaknesses contribute to the development of patellofemoral pain, often described as pain behind the kneecap. According to Fredericson (1999), the primary functional contributor to this injury is insufficient patellar stabilization as a result of an imbalance between the medial and lateral quadriceps muscles. Often, the vastus medialis oblique, the solitary medial stabilizer of the patella, is weaker than the lateral stabilizers, including the vastus lateralis and the iliotibial band (McConnell 1991). Specifically strengthening the quadriceps and the gluteus medius stabilizes the lateral pelvis and aids in injury treatment. This again illustrates the contribution of balanced muscle strength in preventing injury.

Iliotibial band (ITB) syndrome presents as pain at the bony protuberance on the outside of the knee. A careful study of 24 distance runners with ITB syndrome showed marked weakness in the gluteus medius on the affected side using both the asymptomatic side and noninjured counterparts as control groups (Fredericson 1999). Following a six-week rehabilitation period of gluteus medius–strengthening exercises, all 24 of these runners were without pain. The study investigators concluded that hip adductor weakness might precede the onset of ITB syndrome by allowing excessive internal rotation and therefore placing undue tension on the ITB.

Clearly, muscle weakness or fatigue may lead to injuries that can be prevented by performing lower-body strengthening exercises. In addition to keeping athletes running pain free, strength is a requirement for optimal performance. It is particularly important for novice runners, whose bodies and joints are not accustomed to the high impact that running presents, to engage in regular strength training primarily to prevent injury. See chapter 7 for a thorough discussion on a related and important topic—the role of muscle balance and skeletal alignment in forestalling and alleviating running injuries.

Top athletes and coaches believe that no competitive runner can afford to neglect focused strength work. "To me, the most important muscle groups for distance runners are in the trunk: abdominals and back. Everything of importance works from that basic foundation," says Jack Daniels, PhD, an exercise physiologist and cross country coach at State University of New York at Cortland. "Relative to the legs, it seems that light (especially uphill) bounding works well in the strengthening of calves and quads, as well as gluteals. Deep-water running (see chapters 7, 11, and 12) is a good, nonimpact technique to strengthen hip flexors and extensors—groups that normal running tends to ignore somewhat."

How to Get Stronger

Several strength-training methods can be applied to specific sport performance: isometric, isokinetic, eccentric, dynamic, and plyometric. Isometric exercises are those performed without a change in muscle length, such as pushing against a wall. Isokinetic exercises are those performed at a constant speed against resistance that increases or decreases in proportion to applied strength; an example is a programmable stationary bicycle set at a certain number of pedal revolutions per minute. Eccentric training emphasizes the muscle-lengthening stage of a movement (the concurrent lengthening and tensing of the quadriceps during downhill running); unfortunately, this often results in excessive tissue damage. Although improvements in strength have been observed following these three strengthening methods, the usefulness of static movements and those that often induce excessive tissue damage is limited in application to most athletic endeavors. The goal in using resistance training to improve running is to support *movement* and decrease injury, not to create it. Therefore, both dynamic and plyometric methods of strength training are more useful for runners and other endurance athletes in developing strength and reducing injury potential. These are the methods I focus on in this chapter.

Dynamic strength training requires movement, thereby improving strength throughout a given range of motion. Concentric (muscle-shortening) and eccentric (muscle-lengthening) contractions are both used in dynamic exercise. Typical strength-training programs revolve around dynamic exercises that use either free weights or controlled-movement machines, with basic preference determining which type a given athlete uses. Although it may seem obvious, the most beneficial dynamic lifts are those that use a range of motion that is similar to or that complements the running movement. These exercises result in increased functional strength.

Several methods of dynamic training can accomplish this: body-weight exercises, core strengthening, and the use of elastic tubing to create resistance. For example, the hamstring curl emphasizes strength from a relaxed muscle position to a shortened one. Although this is useful for the kick-back phase of the

Retaining Strength With Age

No one wants to stop running at the ripe old age of 35. However, physiologically speaking, peak muscle mass occurs somewhere between the ages of 25 and 30 and declines approximately 8 percent every 10 years (Brooks, Fahey, and White 1996). This means that before athletes even reach the masters (40-and-over) category, their muscle mass has decreased by 8 to 12 percent. Likewise, there is an approximately 1 percent loss of bone mass per year after age 35 (WHO 1994). Inevitably, aging entails a loss of muscular strength and endurance, which eventually affects not only everyday activity but also athletic performance, and increases the risk of injury with exercise. Although the mechanisms of these changes are not fully understood, they are intrinsic to muscle tissue and its components (Brooks, Fahey, and White 1996). In addition, there is a preferential atrophy of fast-twitch muscle fibers and a decrease in motor-unit number (Porter et al. 1995) that, by decreasing the precision of muscle movements, can lead to injury. However, strength training can delay these changes (Hurley and Roth 2000). This is an essential piece of information for athletes who want to continue competing and maintain a semblance of speed.

A prevailing notion is that as athletes age, they must increase their training volume to compensate for the loss of muscle mass and fast-twitch fibers. However, the key element in optimizing running performance as you age is maintaining not only cardiovascular fitness, but also muscle strength. The key to improving performance in any sport is to develop those areas that present the weakest link. Because strength naturally comes to occupy this role with increasing age, it may be necessary to increase the proportion of training devoted to strength and fast-twitch fiber activity to maintain performance. This idea is supported by a study that followed 24 track athletes, ages 50 to 84, for 10 years to observe temporal changes in body composition and cardiovascular fitness. The study showed that cardiovascular fitness remained constant; however, percentage of body fat increased as a result of decreased muscle mass and *not* from adipose accumulation. Those athletes participating in regular strength training or cross-training were able to maintain upper-body muscle mass throughout the duration of the study. Resistance training can benefit older athletes further by increasing muscle size, strength, power, and basal (or resting) metabolic rate, and by decreasing blood pressure and increasing bone density (ACSM 2001). Strength training therefore preserves supporting and major muscle groups in masters athletes, which aids in maintaining a higher basal metabolic rate, lower body fat, and reduced injury risk.

In particular, running's repetitive stress on the joints may be partially alleviated or reduced with improved musculature. Even folks 86 to 96 years old showed a 174 percent increase in quadriceps strength after an eight-week high-intensity strength-training regimen (Fiatarone, Marks, and Ryan 1990). The bottom line is that resistance training, regardless of age, aids in keeping injuries to a minimum, thereby enabling you to continue your healthy habit of running well into your golden years.

stride, it ignores the movement of the hamstring in the stride-out and pull-back phases; adding resistance exercises using elastic tubing and plyometric exercises can address the latter concern.

Plyometric exercises focus primarily on developing power by coupling eccentric and concentric motion. Bounding exercises are a good example. Martin and Coe (1997, 266) provide the following mechanical explanation of strength generation through eccentric–concentric coupling using bounding exercise as an illustration, "a period of eccentric tension generation occurs as the landing legs absorb the impact effects of the body weight and gravity . . . a split second later, this is followed by concentric tension generation. During concentric tension, forward and upward movement then occurs."

Plyometrics increases concentric power through the use of eccentric tension. This type of power generation teaches the body to respond to changes in race tempo and to shift gears by strengthening the muscles (hip and leg extensors) necessary for these actions that are not normally trained by running alone (Martin and Coe 1997).

Incorporating Strength Training Into Your Program

How to best combine classic strength-training routines with plyometrics, drills, and core-strengthening techniques is a highly individual consideration; however, any regimen needs to accentuate particular areas you want to improve as well as include a general program for overall conditioning. High-intensity, low-repetition programs emphasize improvements in strength, whereas low-intensity, high-repetition regimens primarily improve endurance.

Periodization refers to the practice of correlating specific types of training with specific goals at different points in a training cycle—for example, adding sharpening work (usually short, fast intervals) toward the end of a competitive season to help effect a speed peak. Typically, distance runners dedicate the beginning of the season, or preseason, to developing the basic cardiovascular fitness and muscular strength needed to support future training intensity and volume. This type of training serves as preventive and preparative medicine. This period is generally followed by a gradual acclimation to short-term endurance and speed. Should an athlete attempt to go about this in the opposite sequence, the likelihood of injury and suboptimal performance increases. Similarly, attempting to increase intensity, duration, and strength simultaneously increases injury risk. The classic example we all know too well is the excited high school runner who enters cross country season having not run all summer, jumps into interval sessions, and just as quickly, ends up cheering on her teammates with ice bags strapped to her knees. This illustrates the need to *sequentially* increase training volume and intensity to reach peak fitness at the appropriate time while reducing the occurrence of injury. Periodization allows time for the body to adjust to a specific workload before adding intensity or duration.

One way to set up a periodized plan is to break a training year into phases: for example, a preseason phase, in-season phase, and a postseason phase. During the preseason, runners gradually build up training volume while keeping intensity at a minimum. This stage of training develops basic cardiovascular and muscular strength, so it follows that this developmental time frame should be dedicated to forming a foundation of strong overall musculature to support increasing training volume and to prepare for future increases in intensity. The bulk of strength training should be done during this preseason stage, before the more intense interval training sessions begin. As with running volume, strength-training volume during this period should be relatively high.

Start the preseason strength training at a low intensity and volume (one or two sets of 8 to 10 repetitions of each exercise, twice per week) and gradually reach higher intensities (three sets of 8 to 10 repetitions of each exercise, three times per week). Again, the time you devote to strength training is event specific and highly dependent on your individual athletic needs. For example, middle-distance runners require greater strength and power than 10,000-meter runners or marathoners. Therefore, training should reflect this need in both quantity and quality. For example, in comparison to an 800-meter specialist, a 10,000-meter runner would spend less time in the weight room and focus on the less explosive exercises.

The in-season is typically the longest phase and the most intense in terms of racing and preparatory running workouts. The goal for this time period is to perform at an optimal level by maintaining fitness gained throughout the season while recovering adequately. Toward the end of the in-season segment, the focus shifts from developing speed and strength to cutting the overall workload while still maintaining optimal fitness. Typically, total running volume decreases, but intensity increases. The same applies to strength training. Therefore, it is particularly important to be aware that concurrently engaging in intense interval sessions and supplementary exercises can lead to excessive muscle fatigue, increased incidence of injury, and poor racing performance. This means that the in-season period requires less frequent strength-training sessions (decreasing from three per week to one or two) and a decrease in volume (from three sets to one or two) during the heart of the season. Studies indicate that as with running fitness, strength can be maintained with even one session per week (Taaffe et al. 1999).

It is a good idea to avoid strength training the day before a hard running workout and to plan time after workouts for supplementary training. As mentioned earlier, consistent running, quality workouts, and avoidance of injury form the cornerstone of peak running performance; be diligent in the timing of your strength-training sessions to avoid incurring muscle fatigue before hard efforts because this can put you at risk for injury. Before the final weeks of the competitive season, abstain from strength training altogether and focus on the task at hand—racing well. All the benefits to running performance have been reaped by this point, and it is simply time to perform. During the racing season, think of strength training as the antithesis of racing: Start strong and then taper off completely.

The remainder of the training cycle is the postseason. This heralds a time of rest and rejuvenation. However, it is beneficial to maintain some level of fitness to prepare once again for the upcoming season. Therefore, following a month or six weeks of complete rest, slowly incorporate a moderate strength-training schedule.

Strength training is an established method of injury prevention, but it is not uncommon for injuries to occur at the onset of strength-training regimens. For this reason it is essential to periodize training and recognize your fatigue level in response to intense running or strength-training sessions. To avoid injury, incorporate recovery periods into your running and strength-training regimen. As running intensity increases, supplementary training should decrease in quantity and quality. Similarly, as the intensity of the training and the stress on the body increases, runners should be extremely cautious in performing ballistic exercises. This applies especially to plyometric exercise, which involves a significant amount of stress on the joints, connective tissue, and muscles.

Primary Strengthening Exercises

In addition to standard weightlifting exercises aimed at increasing strength, several body-weight exercises can enhance performance indirectly by reducing the incidence of injury. The exercises described here benefit all runners, particularly novice or injury-prone athletes. These exercises develop support-system durability as defined previously. Therefore, the best strategy is to incorporate these exercises into the beginning (preseason) of your running plan using low reps and low frequency just as you would traditional strengthening exercises, gradually increase to higher reps and higher frequency as you enter the in-season, and reduce your effort to low reps and low frequency late in the season. When incorporated into a year-round cycle that includes a period of rest from running, these exercises are a useful tool for reducing the potential of injury.

Leg Raises

Primary muscles used: Iliacus, psoas, abdominals, and sartorius

1. Hang with the arms from a single horizontal bar (such as a chin-up bar).
2. Slowly lift both feet (keeping the legs straight) simultaneously toward the ceiling until the legs are parallel to the floor.
3. Slowly lower the legs back to the starting position and repeat. Avoid the tendency to swing your legs as you transition from one repeat to the next, as this introduces the unwanted element of passive momentum into the exercise.

Calf Raises

Primary muscles used: Soleus and gastrocnemius

1. Stand with the ball of one foot on a raised surface such as a stair with the sole of the foot parallel to the floor.
2. Slowly raise yourself onto the toes and then slowly back down. Do not let the heel drop below the level of the forefoot. You may perform this exercise with handheld dumbbells, a shoulder barbell, or without added weight.

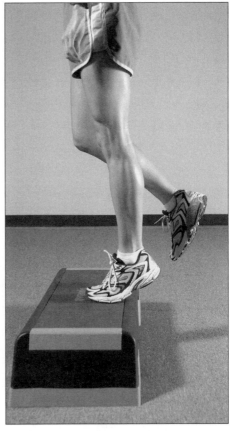

Lunges

Primary muscles used: Gluteals, hamstring group (biceps femoris, semitendinosus, and semimembranosus), and quadriceps group (rectus femoris, vastus lateralis, vastus medialis, and vastus intermedius)

1. Start the exercise standing upright. You may use handheld dumbbells or a shoulder barbell for extra weight or use no weight.

2. While keeping the back straight, lift one leg and lunge forward as if taking a large step.

3. Bend the knee until the quadriceps muscles are parallel to the floor. Be sure to keep the quadriceps and the lower leg at a right angle to minimize stress on the knee.

4. Gently return to the upright position and repeat the exercise with the other leg.

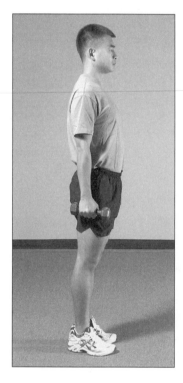 

Drills may take the place of or accompany lunges (particularly the walking lunge, an important exercise introduced in chapter 4). Using your arms in a running motion (opposite arm, opposite leg), take large lunging steps, keeping in mind the proper position of the front knee. With each step, squat slightly and bring the rear knee close to the ground. See chapter 1 for instructions on performing additional drills for strengthening the muscles you use in your stride.

Hamstring Curls

Primary muscles used: Gluteals and hamstring group

1. This exercise is best accomplished lying facedown on standard, controlled-strength training equipment.
2. Keeping your hips flat and without raising your buttocks, slowly bring your feet toward your gluteals. If possible, use a machine, which allows you to work one leg a time.
3. Slowly return to the starting position.

Step-Ups

Primary muscles used: Gluteals and quadriceps group

1. Facing a stable chair, box, or step 12 to 18 inches (30 to 40 centimeters) high with your hands on your hips, step up onto the raised surface one foot at a time so that you are standing on top of it. You may add resistance by holding dumbbells in each hand.

2. Proceed by stepping down backward, one foot at a time, to the starting position.

3. Repeat the exercise starting with the opposite foot.

Secondary Strengthening Exercises

To support the larger lower-body muscle groups, it is essential to strengthen smaller muscle groups as well. The following circuit of exercises has been developed and provided by Sports Medicine Institute International (SMI) of Palo Alto, California. With the permission of SMI, I've included this section to illustrate a series of exercises that helps prevent and treat injuries of elite and novice runners alike by strengthening core musculature.

The program is broken into four phases of four weeks each. For the first three phases, complete the circuit twice a week for each of the four weeks. For the last phase, complete the circuit just once per week.

The most effective way to use this program is to begin the first phase four months before your goal event. Phase I corresponds with the preseason, phase II corresponds with the in-season, phase III is the time for general maintenance, and phase IV begins toward the end of the season. Following the description of each exercise for which the number varies by phase is the number of reps to be performed in each particular four-week phase. Do one set of each exercise in order with a 15-second break between each exercise. After performing all of the exercises, you will have completed one full circuit. Take a three- to four-minute rest and repeat the circuit once or twice. Focus on achieving proper form for each repetition for maximal benefit.

Heel Walking

Benefits the muscles in the shins (tibialis anterior)

1. Keep the upper body erect with the eyes looking forward as you walk for 15 meters on the heels, with the toes pointed straight ahead. The toes should never touch the ground.

2. Repeat with the toes pointed out and again with the toes pointed in for a total of three times (that is, do three repetitions of 15 meters).

Toe Walking

Benefits the calf muscles (gastrocnemius, soleus)

1. Keep the upper body in the same position as with heel walking. Walk for 15 meters with the toes pointed straight ahead.
2. As each foot lands, let that heel come as close to the ground as possible without touching it and then come as high onto your toes as possible before pushing off the ground.
3. Repeat with your toes pointed in and your toes pointed out. Do three repetitions of 15 meters each.

Single-Leg Balance Drill

Assists in coordinating movements of the lower limb

1. Stand, balancing on the right leg with the left knee bent approximately 30 degrees and the left leg extended behind you.
2. Bring the left knee forward and up while bringing the right arm forward and the left arm back.
3. Straighten the right leg. For added difficulty, rise up on the toes.
4. When the left thigh becomes parallel to the ground, bring the leg back in the opposite direction. Be sure that the left leg goes straight back and does not come across the body to the right.

Phase I: 12 reps, phase II: 20 reps, phase III: 12 reps, phase IV: 8 reps

Squats

Benefits the hamstrings, gluteals, quads, calf muscles, and low back muscles

1. Start with the feet shoulder-width apart. Focus the eyes upward. Hold the arms straight or folded in front of you.
2. Sit back as if you were going to sit in a chair. Keep the back straight and the knees stable over the feet. Your weight should remain on the heels.
3. Bend the knees until the thighs are parallel to the floor.
4. Straighten.

For added difficulty, perform a squat hop. The only change is that you hop as you straighten the legs. When you land, make sure that the knees are bent.

Phase I: 10 reps, phase II: 15 reps, phase III: 10 reps, phase IV: 8 reps

Strengthening the core, or central trunk, musculature is vital to proper form and therefore important in injury prevention. The following exercises focus on core strength (see also chapter 7).

Supine Core Stabilization Drill

1. Lying on the back, balance all of your weight on the forearms and heels. Keep the back, hips, and legs as straight as possible during the entire exercise.
2. Lift the right leg four inches off the ground.
3. Hold this position for two seconds and return the leg to the starting position.
4. Repeat with the left leg.

With each leg—Phase I: 6 reps, phase II: 12 reps, phase III: 10 reps, phase IV: 6 reps

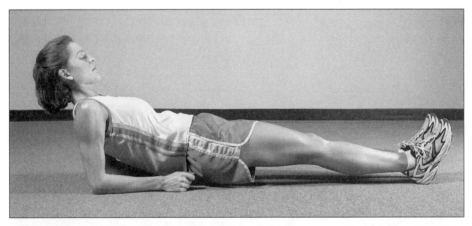

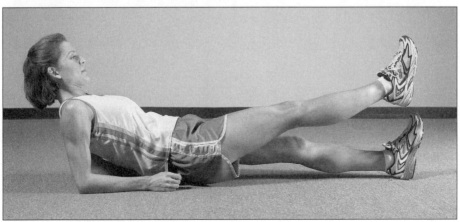

Fire Hydrants

Strengthens the pelvic girdle by working the adductor muscles of the hip

1. Start on the hands and knees.
2. Extend the right hip while keeping the knee bent.
3. Push the right foot up toward the ceiling without arching the back; all of the movement should come from the hip.
4. Repeat by adducting the knee away from the body and again by abducting the knee across the body. For added difficulty, lift the left arm off the ground. Moving through all three directions constitutes one repetition.

Phase I: 4 reps, phase II: 7 reps, phase III: 5 reps, phase IV: 3 reps

Side-Lying Core Stabilization Drill

1. Start by lying on your side with your knees bent and your arm bent under you. Push up with your arm and lift the hips so that your weight is balanced on the forearm and the side of the knee.

2. Maintain a posterior pelvic tilt by pushing the bottom of the pelvis forward and the top of the pelvis back. Keep the body as straight as possible. Do not let the hips sag toward the ground.

3. For added difficulty, come up onto the side of the foot. Then move your top leg through a running motion. Repeat on the other side.

Phase I: 30 seconds, phase II: 45 seconds, phase III: 60 seconds, phase IV: 30 seconds

Bridges

1. Start on the back with the arms lifted above the head and your weight balanced on the shoulders and heels.
2. Straighten the right knee and raise the right leg.
3. Hold this position for two seconds and then switch legs.
4. After both legs have been in the air you have completed one rep.

Phase I: 16 reps, phase II: 22 reps, phase III: 18 reps, phase IV: 14 reps

Bicycles

1. Lying on your back, start with the knees and hips bent at 90-degree angles.
2. Place one hand beneath the low back. The low back should not lift off nor push down onto the hand.
3. Slowly bring the left foot down toward the ground while keeping the left knee bent. When the left foot is approximately one inch off the ground, stop and hold this position for two seconds before bringing the left leg back to the starting position.
4. Repeat the exercise with the right leg.
5. To make the exercise more difficult, straighten the left leg as you bring the foot toward the ground and hold the leg approximately four inches (10 centimeters) off the ground before bringing it back to the starting position.

With each leg—Phase I: 12 reps, phase II: 20 reps, phase III: 15 reps, phase IV: 10 reps

Prone Core Stabilization Drill

1. Balance all your weight on the knees and forearms.
2. Keep the back as straight as possible.
3. Maintain this position while slowly lifting the right knee four inches off the ground.
4. Hold for two seconds and return the knee to the ground. Repeat the exercise with the left leg.
5. For added difficulty, balance on the toes and forearms.

Phase I: 20 to 30 seconds; phase II: 45 seconds; phase III: 60 seconds; phase IV: 30 seconds.

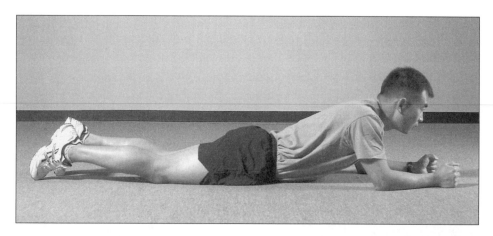

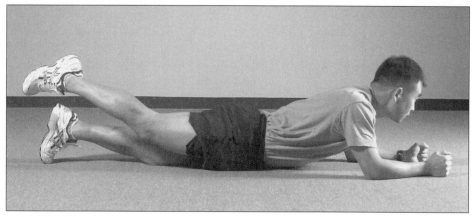

The following exercises are designed to strengthen the calf–Achilles tendon complex.

Heel Drops

1. Stand on the toes with both heels over the edge of a stair or ledge. Slightly bend the knees throughout the entire exercise.
2. Lift the right foot off the stair and slowly drop the heel of the left foot down as far as you can; this should take five seconds.
3. Hold the position for two seconds, then put both feet back on the stair and push up onto the toes again.
4. Repeat for 10 reps each with the right foot pointed 30 degrees to the right and the left foot pointed 30 degrees to the left. Try to keep most of the weight on the feet and use the fingertips against a wall to keep your balance.

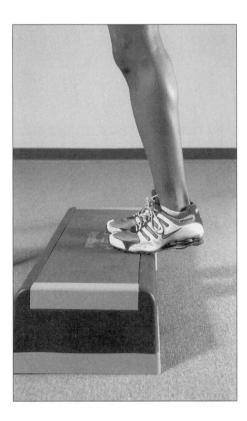 

Single-Leg Knee Pointers

1. Stand facing a wall, with the toes two to three inches away from the wall.

2. Balance on the left foot and slowly bend the left knee until it touches the wall. It should take five seconds to bend down to the wall. Keep your body weight on the heel and not the toes.

3. Hold this position for two seconds without resting the knee against the wall.

4. Repeat by moving your knee 30 degrees to the left and again 30 degrees to the right. Make sure the movement occurs at the ankle and not from rolling your foot or twisting your hips.

5. For added difficulty, do the same exercises with a Dynadisc. Do two sets of 10 reps.

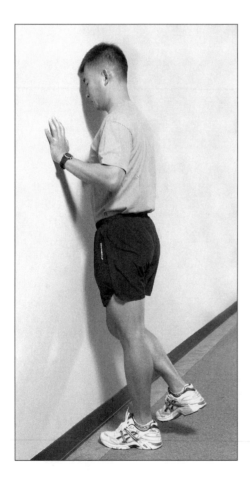
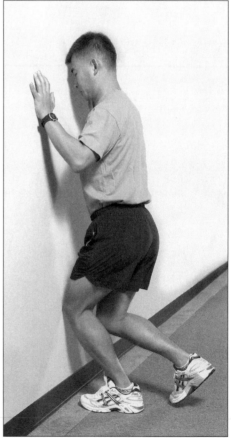

Toe Pointers

1. Stand approximately two feet away from a wall.
2. Balance on the left foot with the right leg extended in front of you.
3. Bend the left knee and bring the right foot straight ahead until the toe touches the wall.
4. Hold this position for two seconds before returning to the starting position.
5. Repeat by angling the right foot and left knee 30 degrees to the right and again 30 degrees to the left. Make sure that the movement comes from the ankle and not from rolling the foot or twisting the hips. Do two sets of 10 reps.
6. For added difficulty, do the same exercises using a Dynadisc.

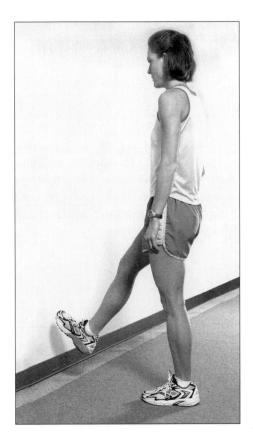
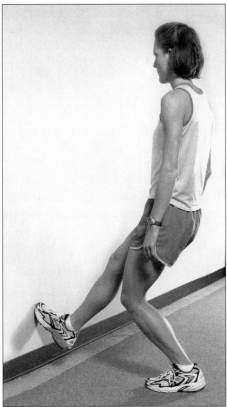

The "hopping" exercises noted here are of the plyometric family mentioned earlier. For further details, see chapter 1.

Toe Hops

1. Hop in place on one leg. The leg should act like a spring. Do not pause when the foot hits the ground. The heel should not touch the ground during the exercise.
2. Start out with short hops and progress to higher hops. Do two sets of 8 to 12 reps.

Low Box Hops

1. This exercise is similar to toe hopping, except this time, hop up and down from a six-inch-high (15-centimeter-high) box or stair.
2. Let your heels drop below the edge of the box before jumping off the box.
3. Do two sets of 8 to 12 reps.

Running itself is clearly the most essential element to optimal running performance; you should not replace or forgo interval sessions to incorporate strength training. However, incorporating running-specific strength exercises in addition to other supplementary training such as stretching and rest can complement running and improve performance.

CHAPTER 7

Aligning and Balancing the Body

CHRIS CHORAK, PT, ATC

My earliest memory of running is as a little girl when my dad whistled up toward my bedroom window as he finished his evening run around the neighborhood. I dreamed of the day that I too would run the nightly neighborhood loop. After my day finally arrived, I ran a loop around the block, and my dad dropped me off as he continued for a couple more miles. It wasn't long before I was able to join him for the full two miles that wound through our neighborhood.

Some of my fondest moments while growing up were those times with my dad, just the two of us running year-round, season to season. Most of the time, we didn't talk—we just shared the rhythm of our feet as they struck the ground. By the time I was in college, *I* was the one who was convincing *him* to join me for a run. He always did, but after our two-mile loop, I dropped him off at home and continued for longer runs. He was my inspiration then and continues to be now. He was the one who introduced me to running, and I am forever grateful.

Why do people run? Different runners offer different reasons: the feeling of freedom, the love of a quick workout, the promise of solitary time to think, the opportunity to challenge the body, a way to control weight gain, enjoyment of the sense of speed, or maybe just a desire to complete the third leg of a triathlon. There are probably as many reasons for running as there are runners. However, a commonality among all runners is that they want to run injury free, and most would be happy if they could run faster.

Over the past 20 years, I have served the running community, working first as an athletic trainer at Purdue University and now as a physical therapist. For the past seventeen years, I have focused my professional career—in collaboration

133

with my colleagues—on developing sound athletic principles to help prevent injuries and improve running performance. In this chapter I share these basic concepts.

For many runners, running faster while remaining injury free is as elusive as the Holy Grail. But fortunately you can accomplish this goal by simply applying a few principles: achieving symmetry between the extremities on each side of the body, developing proper body alignment, using correct running form, conditioning the muscles specifically used for running, and building core strength.

Striving for Symmetry

To be able to run successfully for many years, you must be efficient and stable, and must recognize that your form is also determined by your own mobility. Mobility, also known as range of motion, determines the safe distance of movement for the muscles, tendons, and joints (see chapter 4). The body must have a stable base to generate power to move the extremities through a symmetrical range of motion.

Finding symmetry between the extremities of each side of the body refers to achieving a balance of strength, flexibility, and coordination on each side and in each muscle. If the right quad (thigh muscle) is ready for a 20-mile run but the left quad fatigues at mile 10, you could be inviting injury.

Visually compare your legs in a mirror, specifically the thigh muscles. Muscle size is a good indicator of muscle development. When a muscle group is larger on one leg than on the other, problems may arise.

Another way to check for symmetry is to compare the length of each of your hamstrings to one another. You can do this by lying on your back with your legs straight in front of you. Lift your right leg while keeping it straight (see figure 7.1), and note (or have a friend note) the angle you are able to achieve between your leg and the floor (the ideal is 80 to 90 degrees). Now perform the same exercise with the left leg. Are the angles equal? Different ranges could create different stride lengths in each leg. Over a long distance, this difference in stride length could create torque, or an unbalanced force, in the pelvis and low back; this imbalance could extend through one side of the pelvis, causing injury to the hip flexors or low back. Form determines function, and an athlete's individual flexibility, strength, and joint mobility define his or her running form. The exercises detailed later in this chapter focus on helping you maintain your best form.

How do we test for coordination and balance, the final components of symmetry? To test for balance, pay attention to how the bottom of each foot feels while running. As you roll through your stride, does the bottom of your right foot feel the same as the bottom of your left? Often a runner favors one side over another, shifting his or her weight to that side when landing. Careful attention to the physical sensations while running—including the sound of your footfalls might uncover this habit. Another test is to check your balance when barefoot

Figure 7.1 Compare the length of the hamstring muscles on one side of the body with that on the other side. A significant difference can affect your stride length and make you vulnerable to injury.

and performing a very light activity, like brushing your teeth. Stand on your right foot for 30 seconds, then test your left foot. Are you more balanced on the right or left?

Coordination, or "balance in motion," is a little tougher to test. Cyclists do a drill called single-leg cycling on a stationary trainer. They cycle first with one leg for about a minute and then with the other for about a minute. This is an excellent method for testing strength, endurance, and coordination. Runners can test their coordination in the water, mentally isolating each leg while simulating running form, right-left-right-left, while suspended by the water. (I address water running later in this chapter.)

Developing Proper Alignment

Alignment refers to keeping the parts of any mechanical entity—in this case, a runner's body—in relative position for optimal power output. Proper alignment enhances running form; it allows minimal energy expenditure and maximal joint stability. Think of the alignment of a car. You might suspect that a car is out of alignment if the tires on one side become bald. Similarly, an injury such as iliotibial band (ITB) syndrome or hip pain can indicate that a runner's form is out of alignment. Possible reasons for a runner's misalignment include joint stiffness that limits ranges of motion, scar tissue lesions that restrict muscle length, or other problems with symmetry discussed previously.

Perfecting Running Form

As a physical therapist, I am often asked how the body *should* look while running. There are many biomechanical interpretations of proper running form. Most physical therapists' stand is that an athlete's individual flexibility, strength, and joint mobility define his or her form, so there is no one correct answer; however, a runner's knowledge of what constitutes basic proper form is important.

As detailed in chapter 1, running is broken into phases based on the positioning and movement of the foot:

Footstrike. The initial contact between the ground and the foot

Midstance. Composed of two subcomponents:

- **Foot-flat.** Body completely over the stable foot contacting the ground
- **Heel rise.** Beginning of the propulsion forward as the heel begins to leave the ground

Toe-off. Final propulsion and last contact between the foot and the ground

© Sport the Library

Once you're familiar with the feel of your best form, you can implement it more easily.

Swing-through phase. The leg swinging under the body getting into position for the next footstrike

To get a feel for optimal running form, try going through the following movements in slow motion while standing in front of a mirror. Balance on one leg and strike the ground approximately six inches (15 centimeters) in front of the body with the other foot, either at the heel or the midsole. Be sure to flex the knee of the moving leg 10 to 20 degrees and the hip 20 to 25 degrees and lean forward slightly at the trunk. As the body weight completely transfers to this foot, keep the knee bent, letting it cushion the joints at the foot-flat phase. The body continues to move forward, and the hip extends (straightens), the knee extends, and the heel lifts. This is followed by the toe-off phase. As the foot leaves the ground, the thigh swings backward maximally. The direction of the leg changes as the thigh drives forward, with the knee bending in the swing-through phase. Try this with each leg; a few rehearsals should give you a feel for the optimal relative positioning of each part of your body during an actual run.

That takes care of proper lower-body mechanics, but what should the rest of the body do during this movement? The following list describes upper-body movements and how they coordinate with lower-body movements.

- Maintain an upright body position while relaxing the shoulders and face. Less tension in these areas helps promote more relaxed, free-flowing movement throughout the body as a whole.

- Hold the sternum high. This allows the chest to expand and increases lung ventilation.

- Swing the arms from the shoulder joint forward and backward, maintaining a relatively fixed elbow bend at 90 degrees. The shoulder is a pendulum; allowing the arms to passively swing as a result of momentum imparted by gravity rather than actively "flailing" or pumping them minimizes energy wasted through excessive body movements.

- Synchronize the arms with the legs, mimicking the same rhythm. The arms are used for balance, momentum, and to assist with forward propulsion.

- Engage the trunk muscles with a slight lean forward to help support the upper body over a moving lower body. Think of a long spine and visualize space between each lumbar vertebra.

- Rotate the pelvis slightly forward. If you put your hands on your hips, under your fingers is the portion of the iliac crest called the ASIS (anterior superior iliac spine). These points of the hip move slightly forward as the leg swings through and prepares for the footstrike. This hip drive provides propulsion and forward momentum while wasting little energy.

- Let the knee drive the leg forward with the footstrike about six inches (15 centimeters) in front of the body. The feet stay under the hips and the hips under the trunk, which helps maintain the body's center of balance.

- Transfer your body weight evenly from one foot to another, making sure only one foot is on the ground at a time. If both feet are on the ground at the same time, you may not be propelling yourself forward efficiently during the toe-off phase.

- During toe-off and in the beginning of the swing-through phase, the leg must go past the front-to-back midline and behind the opposite leg. This creates propulsion.

Strong supporting muscles help you maintain efficient running form. When these muscles fatigue, your form deteriorates. Being aware of your running form and consciously trying to maintain form during the latter stages of a run are important means of preventing injuries. Of course, conditioning can help you avoid muscle fatigue and the muscles' failure to function. However, muscles will fatigue, especially in long events such as the half-marathon and marathon, so it's important to think about maintaining proper form. Although it is difficult to think of your form for the duration of a long race, reminding yourself of the basics when you start to fatigue centers your focus on the running motion and helps you optimize your performance. The visualization exercise at the end of the chapter emphasizes conscious awareness of proper head-to-toe form. Conditioning and form drills, detailed in chapters 1, 4, 5, and 6 will strengthen your body and enable you to put this visualization process into practice.

Conditioning Specifically for Running

It is essential to train your muscles specifically for proper running alignment and symmetry. Different sports use muscles differently. For example, in cycling, the muscles of the legs contract in a concentric, or shortened, position. Weight-lifting incorporates both concentric (shortening) and eccentric (lengthening) contractions. Imagine doing a biceps curl with a weight in your hand. As you lift the weight up, the biceps concentrically contracts. As you lower the weight in a controlled motion, the muscle eccentrically contracts. Running also involves a combination of eccentric and concentric muscle contractions. The eccentric contractions help absorb body weight as the foot strikes the ground, while concentric muscle contractions propel the body forward (as when the foot pushes from the ground). This sequence of lengthening and shortening preloads the muscle, or applies stress before contraction, and has been shown to enhance force output (Cavanaugh 1990).

Running uses many muscles (see figure 6.1 on page 108), so be sure your strengthening program focuses on the following.

Anterior tibialis. This muscle is located at the front of the shin and decelerates the body during the footstrike to foot-flat phase. It is also active during the swing-through phase, bringing the toe and ankle up so that they clear the ground as the foot prepares for footstrike. "Foot-slapping" indicates weakness, which occasionally leads to shinsplints. The heel-walking and toe-walking exercises listed in chapter 6 are a great way to strengthen this muscle.

Gastrocnemius and soleus. These two muscles make up the calf and decelerate the shinbone during the foot-flat phase, keeping it from moving forward. Then they shorten to assist in the toe-off phase. These muscles travel down the back of the shinbone and merge with the Achilles tendon, which attaches to the back of the calcaneus (heel bone). Eccentric weakness in the calf can contribute to Achilles tendinitis; exercises to help forestall this involve eccentrically loading the Achilles, such as the heel drops described in chapter 6. (*Note:* If you have a previous or existing Achilles injury, do these exercises only if there is no current inflammation and you are well into the healing stage.)

Quadriceps. The quadriceps are made up of four muscles that travel down the thigh and dovetail into the patellar tendon, pass over the patella (kneecap) and attach to the tibia (shinbone). They absorb shock and eccentrically contract as the body moves forward from the footstrike to foot-flat phase. Kneecap pain indicates possible weakness of this group of muscles. To strengthen them, try the squat exercises recommended in chapter 6; these may be done on one leg at a time to add specificity.

Hamstrings. These muscles span the hip and knee joints, starting at the back of the hip (ischial tuberosity) and attaching behind the knee, both on the inside and on the outside. During the last part of swing-through phase, as the leg moves under the body and forward, the hamstring eccentrically contracts to slow the forward motion of the leg and helps to stabilize the knee as footstrike begins. Once the foot is on the ground, the hamstring starts to concentrically contract to propel the leg backward. Occasionally, a runner has a shorter stride with one leg than with the other. A previous hamstring injury that resulted in scar tissue can keep the hamstring from lengthening normally during the footstrike phase and result in a loss of power when trying to propel the body forward. This imbalance is usually associated with pain or stiffness in the hamstring.

Exercises that help correct this imbalance include single- and double-leg bridging. For the double-leg bridge lie on your back and bend your knees at 90 degrees. Pressing through the heels, slowly raise your hips and low back off the floor as high as you can, keeping the abdominals tight. Hold briefly, then slowly lower your back and hips to the starting position. Repeat 10 times. The single-leg bridge is performed just as the double-leg bridge, except that one leg is fully extended throughout the exercise.

Gluteus maximus. The muscles of the main muscle group of the rear end, the glutes, eccentrically contract as the leg swings forward in front of the body to slow the thigh and help to stabilize the trunk over the opposite leg at the footstrike to foot-flat phase. The glutes also help propel the body forward and provide power in uphill running. Weakness in the glutes causes you to overcompensate by using other muscles. For example, when the glutes are weak, other muscles of the back of the hip must help stabilize the body or propel it forward while running. If this is not the primary action of these muscles, over time they can become injured. For example, you could end up with piriformis syndrome, or rear-end pain, in which the muscles of the hips become painful and even spasm. The single- and double-leg bridging exercises described earlier are an excellent means of strengthening the glutes.

Gluteus medius. Recalling workout videotapes of yore, think of this one as the "Jane Fonda" muscle. It is located behind and outside the hip. This muscle helps maintain hip symmetry, preventing a lateral pelvic tilt. This muscle eccentrically contracts during the late swing-through phase, through the footstrike, and at the beginning of foot-flat phase. Sloppy pelvis syndrome (SPS), where one side of the hip drops down, indicates weakness. To strengthen the gluteus medius, try the side-lying core stabilization exercise described in chapter 6.

Adductors. The inner thigh muscles are the only muscles engaged throughout the entire gait cycle. The adductors stabilize the trunk on a fixed leg and keep the thigh under the body during the swing-through phase. Weakness in the adductors often results injury to this and other muscle groups. For example, soccer players incur groin strains from the lateral, or side-to-side, motion needed on the soccer field. This strain results in pain upon footstrike as they attempt to propel the body forward, causing them to alter their running form, and possibly leading to secondary injuries. Groin injuries are less common in distance runners; however, beginners may experience soreness in their inner thighs. It is important to note the significant role this muscle group plays in maintaining pelvic symmetry; endurance in these muscles is necessary for maintaining proper leg and pelvis alignment. Strength in these muscles generally develops naturally as the runner progresses.

Because many of these muscles lengthen and shorten to control the body and leg position during running, strengthening them is critical for preventing injury. I often see runners with pain in the front of the knee, and after evaluation, determine that part of the problem is weakness of the quadriceps muscles. Many athletes try to solve this problem by using the leg extension machine in the gym, but this is the wrong approach. It is more effective to retrain the quads using a movement similar to the running motion. To strengthen the quads, stand on one leg with your weight distributed equally over the ball and heel of your foot. Perform a quarter-squat by bending the knee two to three inches, then rising up. The knee must stay aligned under the body and hip, and over the ankle. Don't allow the knee to fall inward. Repeat this quarter-squat 40 to 50 times. Repeat with the other leg. While running you perform this same movement 450 to 500 times per mile, so this exercise is very sport-specific. Perfect form and eccentric control are the keys to protecting the knee joint. (See also the squat exercise detailed in chapter 6.)

Building Core Strength

Building and maintaining core strength is also critical for proper running form and staying injury free. The core muscles include the abdominal and low back muscles, which support the body during movement. Being aware of these muscles and how to recruit them can provide a stable foundation for more efficient running form. These muscles also provide balance when moving the extremities; this is known as "dynamic stability." To illustrate their function, imagine an earthquake hitting a city. The houses built on sand sustain extensive damage compared to those built on bedrock. A strong core foundation stabilizes the trunk, which means it does not absorb the energy needed for propulsion. Improved core strength allows the athlete to achieve a better sense of balance and to generate greater power.

I divide the core muscles into three categories: The deepest abdominal muscles (transverse abdominals, internal and external obliques); the deepest spinal muscles such as the multifidi, as well as the spinal extensors and the long superficial spinal muscles; and the pelvic-floor muscles.

Deep Abdominal Muscles

Running is an endurance sport, so the muscles that enable proper alignment of the trunk must have adequate muscle endurance, especially for the long-distance races. Athletes often train with crunches. However, a more sport-specific and therefore more directly beneficial option is to strengthen your core muscles in the neutral-spine position. The neutral-spine position is determined by the amount of curve in the low back during standing or running. Runners should strengthen their abdominals in a long and stabilized position rather than in a shortened, or crunched, position. This optimizes the full potential for power and stability when the spine is in a neutral position during running.

Runner–Specific Transverse Abdominal Exercise

For most people contracting the abdominals with the spine in a neutral position is a new movement, and it may take a few sessions before you can properly recruit the targeted muscles.

1. Lie on your back with the legs straight.
2. Concentrate on bringing your belly button toward your spine and lowering your ribs toward the pelvis. Maintain a normal low back curve; avoid pressing it flat onto the floor.
3. Place your hands behind your neck for support and lift your head and shoulders from the floor, similar to a crunch but with a neutral-spine position. The abdominal muscles should not push out, but rather maintain a flat position.

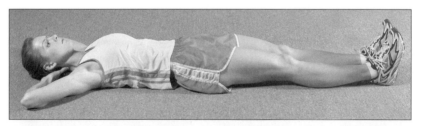

141

Deep Spinal Muscles

The multifidi are the innermost spinal muscles. A healthy spine with no low back problems automatically recruits these spinal muscles to stabilize the spine vertebra to vertebra while the body is in motion. If an athlete has had spinal problems, a visit to a physical therapist can help to re-educate these muscles. The next layer of core or spinal-support muscles is the erector spinae. Developing isometric endurance of the back muscles is an excellent means of preventing low back troubles.

Low Back Extensor Exercise

This is a simple exercise that improves back extensor muscle endurance.

1. Lie facedown on a bench with the hips and legs resting on the bench, the abdomen and chest suspended over the floor; the hands may be clasped behind the neck.

2. Without recruiting the gluteal muscles, hold this position for 30 seconds.

3. This should be a pain-free activity. The goal is to progressively increase the exercise duration to 60 seconds. Once you have established basic muscle endurance, there are many ways to modify this exercise. For example, in this isometric position, begin with your arms at your sides, then extend them out from the shoulders, perpendicular to your body, and finally stretch them out past your head in a "Superman" position. You can also alternate lifting your arms to mimic the arm swing of running while holding this position.

Aligning: Rehabilitation and Rehearsal

Often, athletes returning to running after an injury find that their form is altered, or they complain of an awkward or stiff feeling. This is caused directly by the injury and indirectly by the body trying to protect itself by hindering the use of the surrounding muscles during the healing process. Part of the job of physical therapists is to rehabilitate the injury through muscle re-education. To do so, they incorporate exercises in a clinical environment; often this means placing the athlete in deep water with a vest or other flotation device so they can concentrate specifically on running form without impact. When running on land, the foot receives direct input from the ground; however in deep water, the foot loses this sensory input, so the brain must consciously tell the body how to move. Water allows the athlete to concentrate on the re-educated movement, kinesthetic awareness (a sense of where the body is in space), and muscle recruitment without risk from the compressive forces of gravity. Usually, with the aid of a floatation device, the body is fully suspended in water, and therefore the joints experience no compressive forces. The water itself creates a resistance for the muscles to work against during re-education, so that conditioning in an injury-free environment can begin.

When you recruit the right muscles and ensure that they are of equal length and strength on both sides of the body, you begin to approach your ideal running technique. With the essential biomechanics in place, you can strive for every runner's two-pronged goal: increased power and decreased risk of injury. Therefore water running is not only a useful tool for athletes returning from injury, but for those seeking to optimize their body alignment even when healthy.

Using proper technique during water running is one way to help maintain proper form outside the water. When practicing water running, keep in mind the following techniques:

- Keep the body in a vertical position, with relaxed shoulders and the sternum held high.
- Swing the arms forward and backward from the shoulder joint, maintaining a relatively fixed elbow bend at 90 degrees.
- Mimic with the arms the same rhythm as the legs: opposite arm, opposite leg.
- Engage the trunk muscles with a slight lean forward to help support the upper body over a moving lower body. Think of a long spine and visualize space between each lumbar vertebra.
- Use the knee to drive the leg forward. The footstrike is about six inches (15 centimeters) in front of the body; drop the ball of the foot, slightly bend the knee, and push the leg back.
- Make sure the leg goes past the front-to-back midline and behind the opposite leg.

Runners who are healthy but prone to injury might benefit from at least one water run a week; the day after a speed workout or a long training run would be the wisest choice. For specifics on water-running workouts, see pages 230 to 231 in chapter 12.

All of the therapists in my clinic are required to teach a water-running class to local YMCA members and to many of our patients. We usually have more than 30 people in the class, drawn from the full age spectrum and ranging athletically from marathon runners to triathletes to weekend hikers. As a teacher, my favorite part of the class is the last five minutes. This is where I lead class members through a visualization of running a marathon. Sometimes I lead them through the final miles of the marathon in the Hawaii Ironman, sometimes down the streets of Chicago, and sometimes along the cliffs of the Big Sur Marathon. Before the "marathon" starts, I describe the course, picturesque view, competition, and nature of the surrounding environment. Part of the participants' mental preparation is to visualize themselves as strong, fit athletes with perfect running form. This visualization tool is an excellent way to practice being conscious of form in the later miles of long runs.

So here we go: *It's 7:00 a.m., and the gun goes off! I start my marathon at a confident but conservative pace. I feel strong. I think of my form. My head is high, my sternum is up, and my shoulders and face are relaxed. My arms swing from my shoulders next to my trunk in an even rhythm. Opposite arm and opposite leg are balanced and symmetrical. I have a long spine and there is space between each vertebra, especially in the low back. The pelvis has a slight rotational drive forward—right hip then left hip. Neither side of my hip "hikes up" to indicate sloppy pelvis syndrome. My thigh drives my leg forward, leading with the knee, then the foot. My knee is extended as my foot "hits" six inches (15 centimeters) in front of my body; my knee slightly bends, I drop the ball of my foot, and I sweep my leg aggressively backward. Does the right leg feel like the left leg? Does each leg recruit muscles equally to move the leg?*

I am suddenly at mile 22. I am strong, and I feel good. (As athletes, we usually note to ourselves when we feel bad. Recognize your wins!) Suddenly I am at mile 24. What will get me over the finish line? I must think about my form. I'm tired, and my form is starting to fall apart, but I can run through my checklist and pull myself together. I'm starting at my toes . . . by the time I make it to my nose, I am successfully over the finish line. I have completed another water marathon!

This type of visualization applies all the topics discussed in this chapter. Learn to focus on proper form while running, even when you're not running in the sort of relaxed environment where you can easily visualize your running form from your nose to your toes. To achieve the best possible running form, work on the symmetry between extremities and range of motion, flexibility, strength, and muscle endurance. Finally, after establishing a symmetrical balance in your extremities, don't forget the foundation: Core strength helps you maintain form and generate power.

CHAPTER 8

Fortifying and Supplementing Your Energy Levels

KYLE D. HEFFNER, MS

Many athletes have more than a passing interest in proper nutrition. Their interest, typically motivated by a desire to optimize how they feel and perform as runners, helps fuel the rapidly growing nutritional supplement industry—today a $20 billion business in the United States alone. Although more is known now about nutrition than ever before, the industry is fraught with exaggerated claims aimed at boosting product sales.

The medical community has traditionally considered the use of nutritional supplements generally unnecessary, stressing that the primary goal of our diets should be balance. Of course, this assumes that the quality of our food is adequate. Many health professionals reason that because the U.S. Food and Drug Administration (FDA) does not regulate nutritional supplements, claims regarding their composition are unreliable, their purported benefits are questionable, and their intake is unsafe. Although this may often be the case, this generalization overlooks industry standards and testing conducted by independent labs (from professional associations) as well as pharmaceutical-grade quality control of the leading supplement producers; FDA regulation would likely provide no guarantee of safety or quality, given that these same issues currently plague the highly regulated U.S. pharmaceutical industry.

In this chapter I cover what is known about some of the more popular supplements, their usage, and their effects on endurance performance. Throughout the chapter, I distinguish between mere hype and actual supporting evidence that justifies the need for specific supplementation for either general health or athletic performance. Although general nutrition guidelines are an important way to communicate health-oriented dietary practices to the public, they often fall short in optimizing nutrition at the individual level.

145

Athletes, of course, are interested in access to safe, reliably labeled food supplements. The primary issue is whether a supplement can assist in substantially improving performance or training adaptations, or preventing illness or injury while maintaining or improving general health. This chapter cites examples of studies showing improved athletic performance following supplementation, presumably resulting from the correction of underlying—and often unknown—nutrient deficiencies. Food supplementation is not a simple issue; it is complicated by the myriad claims consumers face daily and the amazing complexity of human nutrition.

Specific nutritional deficiencies or imbalances, as well as supplements designed to enhance muscle development, are beyond the scope of this chapter. This discussion focuses instead on supplements that appear relevant to endurance athletes or that contribute to general well-being, with the latter indirectly affecting endurance performance.

Before taking a supplement, you should ask several questions:

- Is the supplement safe at recommended intake levels?
- Is the supplement from a reliable source or manufacturer with a history of quality control (e.g., their products are not contaminated with unidentified substances)?
- If the supplement is new, what research has been conducted, either in the United States or abroad?
- Has the research been peer reviewed and published in a reputable journal?
- If it has been used in the past, what has been the historical usage?
- Is the supplement worth taking for general health and therefore *indirectly* related to performance?
- What type of dietary supplements *might* improve performance in competition?
- What form of the supplement is best for this purpose, and what is the recommended method of use?

Online searches can help you uncover the answers to these questions and gather information on manufacturers' backgrounds. Generally, most nutritional supplements are well tolerated; however, you should always discuss any nutritional supplement you plan to take with your health care practitioner before using it.

Nutritional Principles for Endurance Athletes

What are the fundamental principles for achieving a balanced diet through appropriate supplemental nutrition? The assumption that a particular supplement will work for everyone is most likely false. Just as athletes differ in their physical characteristics and experience varying levels of training stresses, it seems logical that nutritional demands differ not only from person to person, but within each person over a period of time. *Bio-individuality*, a concept gaining acceptance in the scientific community, posits that people's nutrient needs are more unique than previously believed.

Endurance athletes should base their nutritional foundation on eating a variety of foods that are fresh, wholesome, and minimally processed and thus retain their inherent level of nutrition. Avoid overprocessed foods or packaged foods that include hydrogenated vegetable oils, which often contain potentially harmful *trans* fatty acids. Whole grains, nuts, and fish contain high quantities of dietary fiber as well as healthier types of fat, such as monounsaturated oils and omega-3 fatty acids, the latter a research-confirmed provider of health-related benefits.

Some sport nutritionists claim that "a vitamin is a vitamin," whether it developed naturally or is synthetically produced, because it is made up of the same chemical compound in each case. It is not that simple; the body uses a vitamin only in concert with its associated naturally occurring nutrients, or *phytonutrients*, and not as an *isolated* compound. For example, vitamin C, or ascorbic acid, is found in many fruits and may also be synthetically produced. However, the continual intake of this vitamin by itself in large amounts without naturally occurring bioflavonoids, such as rutin, may lead to nutritional imbalances or deficiencies of minerals such as copper. Apparently, loading up on one vitamin, such as vitamin C, may be somewhat counterproductive because of ascorbic acid's interference with the absorption of other important micronutrients. Thus, it is important to consume essential vitamins and nutrients from their naturally occurring source in foods.

You can further help your body absorb the vitamins it takes in by including yogurt culture or other sources of friendly bacteria, such as Lactobacillus acidophilus, in the diet. These bacteria provide a healthy microflora environment in the intestinal tract, which aids in the absorption of minerals and vitamins such as calcium and vitamin B_{12}. These friendly bacteria apparently also offer protection against toxins produced while digesting bacterially contaminated foods.

Caloric Intake

A fundamental tenet of sound nutrition, of course, is that the athlete's total calorie intake must be adequate for meeting the needs of training as well as activities of daily life. The American Dietetic Association (ADA) has suggested general caloric guidelines for the major nutrient categories. However, the actual caloric needs of any athlete depend on his or her total daily energy expenditure, type of sport performed, gender, environmental conditions, and whether or not he or she is trying to lose weight.

Caloric intake for many athletes will be between 3,000 to 5,000 calories per day or up to 50 calories per kilogram per day. At this intake level, if 50 percent of the energy in the diet comes from carbohydrate, it would provide 500 to 600 grams of carbohydrate, about seven to eight grams per kilogram for a 70-kilogram (154-pound) athlete, which is sufficient for maintaining and replenishing glycogen stores. Protein, on the other hand, could probably be adequate at 10 percent of the total calories, or 100 to 125 grams per day, close to the 1.2 to 1.7 grams per kilogram per day recommendation (see table 8.1).

Table 8.1 ADA-Suggested Athlete Dietary Intake

Macronutrient	% of total calories	Grams per kg of body weight per day
Protein	12-15	1.2-1.4 (endurance); 1.6-1.7 (strength)
Fat	20-30	No number given, but 20-30% of calories
Carbohydrate	50-60	6 to 10 During recovery from prolonged exercise: ~1.2 g per kg per h (0.55 g per lb per h) in 15-30 min intervals during the first 2-5 hours of recovery

Macronutrients

Let's briefly go into more detail about the specific nutrients your body needs every day to function and run at its best: We'll start with the macronutrients: water, protein, fat, and carbohydrate.

Water. Adequate hydration is necessary for supporting the body's processes, and there is no better way to stay hydrated than with water. General recommendations range from four to six eight-ounce helpings of water daily, but this should be adjusted to runners' individual needs. Too little (hypohydration) or even too much water intake during competition can be a serious matter. Drinking plain water alone can excessively dilute body fluids; adequate amounts of electrolytes, such as sodium, potassium, and others, may be helpful in preventing the potentially fatal condition known as hyponatremia.

Because hydration is critical to runners, some have suggested using *glycerol* to help retain water. Glycerol is a common alcohol in the body containing three hydroxyl groups. Also named glycerin, it has an affinity for water and has been researched as a way to potentially hyperhydrate athletes before or during competition. Initial studies suggested that glycerol improved cycling performance in a double-blind, crossover trial. Average heart rate response also was lower in the glycerol-supplemented subjects. Subsequent studies in triathletes, however, have not confirmed this finding, while animal studies

© Human Kinetics

Runners rely on water and drinks containing vital electrolytes to stay properly hydrated.

show mixed results. Until a scientific consensus is reached, it probably is premature to use glycerol to help endurance athletes retain water.

Protein. Quality proteins that are generally excellent sources of amino acids include whey protein, fish, eggs, rice protein, lean meats, soy, colostrums, blue-green algae (spirulina), and chlorella. Certain amino acids help build muscle protein, repair tissue, and even replenish muscle glycogen. Adequate protein also ensures that the body can rebuild itself following intense training. Recently, the weight-loss industry has emphasized an increase in protein intake. Unfortunately, too many people consume levels of dietary protein in excess of two grams per kilogram of body weight to their detriment rather than benefit. Prolonged and excess protein intake can burden the kidneys unnecessarily as well as increase the risk of serious health problems. However, protein intake is critical for optimizing athletic performance because it provides the building blocks for muscle tissue development and cell repair and participates in many other physiological functions, including energy production. Refer to table 8.1 to determine how much protein you should ingest daily.

Fat. Beneficial oil and fat sources include nuts, wheat germ oil, olive oil, avocado, flax seeds, borage seed, and fish oils. Fat provides a primary energy source during prolonged exercise. Fat and carbohydrate are both involved in the production of high-energy phosphates, ATP, in the muscle cells. In addition, the production of hormones, absorption of certain nutrients, and numerous bodily functions depend upon adequate fat intake. Generally, a variety of fat is available in foods that also contain considerable amounts of protein, such as meats and nuts. Many people have a negative view of dietary fat, especially those trying to lose weight. Although the quantity of fat consumed is a factor in one's overall energy balance and thus has an impact on weight loss, it is the *type* of fat—monounsaturated oils versus trans fatty acids from hydrogenated vegetable oils—that most directly influences general health.

Carbohydrate. Complex carbohydrate, as opposed to simple sugars, helps provide an energy source as well as adequate fiber, certain naturally occurring nutrients (phytonutrients), and B vitamins. Common examples of complex carbohydrate include pasta, whole grains (such as wheat and rice), and starchy vegetables (such as corn and potatoes). Other carbohydrate sources are discussed below.

Most studies have found improved performance in subjects who ingested 25 to 60 grams of carbohydrate during each hour of exercise (Coggan and Coyle 1991; Murray et al. 1991). It is generally accepted that exercising individuals should consume solutions that provide 30 to 60 grams of carbohydrate per hour in the form of glucose, sucrose, or starch (Coggan and Coyle 1991).

The forms of carbohydrate vary among commercially available products such as thirst quencher–type drinks, energy drinks, or sport gels. Typically, sport solutions contain simple sugars, such as glucose, high-fructose corn syrup, or sucrose, while sport gels may contain both simple sugars and maltodextrins—compounds containing multiple glucose molecules in a treelike structure closely resembling a starch or glycogen molecule. Research findings also indicate that carbohydrate should be consumed during recovery as well, and in quantities of about 1.2 grams per kilogram of body weight per hour (0.55 grams per pound per hour) in 15- to 30-minute intervals during the first two to five hours of recovery. Thus, a 70-kilogram (154-pound) athlete should try to ingest about 85 grams of carbohydrate per hour following intense exercise, with the amount dependent on the duration of the preceding workout.

Postexercise consumption of protein or specific amino acids further increases muscle-glycogen replenishment if too little carbohydrate is ingested. However, if the intake of carbohydrate is greater than 1.2 grams per kilogram of body weight, the addition of protein does not seem to accelerate glycogen resynthesis.

The glycemic index has been developed to provide an indication of the effects of food based on how fast and how much the blood glucose changes after eating. The effect of eating glucose alone is rated at 100. Foods that rate high on the glycemic index include starchy foods and refined sugars, while low glycemic–index foods include high-fiber foods and higher-protein foods such as whey protein or meats. Low-glycemic foods are good preworkout choices because they do not lead to a blood glucose "spike" but rather provide a steady supply of energy. High-glycemic foods, on the other hand, make good postworkout fare because they quickly replenish lost fuel stores. Remarkably, the diets of arguably the best distance runners in the world, the Kenyans, often contain foods that have glycemic indexes exceeding that of pure glucose! According to Owen Anderson, who writes the *Running Research Newsletter*, a common breakfast enjoyed by the Kenyans is maize-meal porridge, which has a glycemic index of 107. Another dietary staple is Kenyan rice (glycemic index of 112). It is important to note, however, the other components of the Kenyan diet, in particular, the "whole foods" consumed, such as ugali (cornmeal), whole-meal wheat flour, and chapati (flat bread). These probably contain more wholesome nutrients than the refined "fast foods" readily available to American runners, although formal studies comparing the nutrient intake of Kenyan runners to that of American distance runners are currently unavailable.

Fat Loading Versus Carbo Loading

Some have suggested and researched the use of fat intake as a method of carbohydrate depletion prior to carbo-loading phases. This method involves consuming a high-fat low-carbohydrate diet for five or more days prior to one day of carbo loading. Several studies have demonstrated that "fat-loaded" athletes use proportionally more fat during cycling exercise than those using the more typical carbo-loading diets. However, the differences in the utilization, or sparing, of carbohydrate and cycling performance were small and statistically insignificant. A high-fat diet might be impractical if the absence of carbohydrate for several days would impair training and cause potentially adverse health effects. However, researchers have theorized that ultraendurance athletes could potentially benefit more than other runners because of the lower intensities demanded of them during competition and their enhanced need for efficient fuel sources, such as fat, that could potentially conserve stored carbohydrate.

Medium-chain triglycerides (MCTs) are a type of fatty acid found only in small amounts in the diet, but they are more easily absorbed and used as energy sources than ordinary fat is. Because of this, some have investigated the potential of MCTs as an energy source while conserving carbohydrate. Unfortunately, initial research findings (using 30 to 45 grams over two to three hours) have failed to demonstrate measurable success in improving endurance performance. A different study found that use of a combination of carbohydrate and MCT in solution was actually linked to decreases in performance, likely a result of the gastrointestinal distress experienced by participating athletes.

Antioxidant Nutrients

Many runners are aware that the increased physical demands of athletic training and competition increase cellular oxidative stress. Antioxidants are compounds in our diet that help prevent oxidative free-radical damage. Evidence suggests that we must consume sufficient antioxidants in our diets to adequately support the body's defense against free radicals. To illustrate oxidation or free-radical damage and how nutrients help protect us, slice open an apple and expose the slices to the air for an hour or so. You may notice the slices becoming darker because of the oxidation. If you pour lemon or orange juice over the slices, however, they will not darken. The vitamin C in the juice buffers the free radicals.

Because we continually breathe oxygen, oxidation occurs within our bodies but is buffered by certain biochemical and enzymatic reactions that minimize the biodestructive properties of free radicals. The body requires a certain level of antioxidants to support its protective mechanisms.

There is growing support for the addition of antioxidants, or foods rich in antioxidants, to the diet. News reports seem to detail new findings daily regarding disease prevention or other benefits of compounds such as *lycopenes* in tomatoes, *polyphenols* in green tea, and *indoles* in brussels spouts, to list a few. Our bodies also benefit from other antioxidants such as vitamin A (carotenoids), vitamin E (mixed tocopherols and tocotrienols), and certain trace minerals such as selenium and polyphenols found in green tea. Other antioxidants include grape seed extract (GSE) and other sources of oligomeric proanthocyanindins, such as white pine bark, have a high affinity for free radicals.

The best dietary sources of antioxidants are fruits and vegetables. The average orange contains about 75 milligrams of vitamin C. An adequate intake of vitamin C for an endurance athlete in heavy training is probably several multiples of the average person's requirements, and may be in the range of 2,000 milligrams a day or more—the equivalent of 26 oranges! Obviously, consuming this much fruit in a day is unreasonable. So supplementation with antioxidants is not only practical, it is a necessity, particularly for athletes.

Although research on antioxidants is plentiful, numerous studies have reached conflicting conclusions; some show no change in free-radical activity, while others show effective reduction in free-radical levels. The majority of food supplements studied have, in terms of their antioxidant effectiveness, produced equivocal findings. This is probably the result of the complexity of nutrition, individuality of the human subjects, quality and form of the nutrient being studied and how it is administered, and the current nutrient status of the subjects.

Multivitamin and Mineral Complexes

Taking in multivitamin and mineral complexes helps the athlete replenish what the body uses during intense exercise as well as minerals lost through the skin in sweating. These nutrients may be supplied primarily through general diet, although certain herbs, whole grains, meats, or other protein may be more concentrated, easily assimilated food sources. It is important to carefully select a multivitamin or mineral supplement to avoid products containing poorly absorbed compounds. For example, many products are of poor quality and contain calcium predominately in the form of calcium carbonate (chalk) instead of calcium citrate or calcium lactate; the body is much less likely to effectively use the former. Manufacturers typically include the more economical and synthetic vitamin E as alpha-dL-tocopherol, which is a poor substitute for a more natural form of vitamin E, alpha d-tocopherol, or the even more nutritionally balanced form, mixed tocopherols. In many cases, the quality of a vitamin product is revealed by the inclusion of poorly absorbed versions of key compounds such as calcium or magnesium. Refer to table 8.2, which lists four sample ingredients with typical compounds often used in lower-quality and higher-quality supplements.

Solid evidence supports the contribution of the following supplements to general well-being: vitamins C, E, and A; bioflavonoids, B vitamins including niacin, thiamine, riboflavin, B_{12}, and folate; glutathione; alpha-lipoic acid, and coenzyme Q10. It may be necessary to supplement your diet to obtain optimal systemic levels, although what constitutes an optimal level is difficult to predict because of the variance in individual requirements for these nutrients. A few of these nutrients have been identified as important in normal metabolic processes; however, this list is by no means complete because new compounds are continually being recognized as important.

Table 8.2. Differences in Vitamin or Mineral Composition

Vitamin or mineral	Lower quality (less beneficial)	Higher quality (more beneficial)
Calcium	Calcium carbonate, oyster shell	Calcium citrate, calcium lactate, calcium hydroxyapetite
Copper	Cupric oxide	Copper sulfate, cupric acetate, alkaline copper carbonate
Magnesium	Magnesium oxide	Magnesium gluconate
Vitamin C	Ascorbic acid	Calcium ascorbate w/bioflavonoids, ascorbyl palmitate w/bioflavonoids, magnesium ascorbate w/bioflavonoids

Vitamins C, E (mixed tocopherols), and A (carotenoids) are generally considered the major role-players in antioxidant protection in the body. However, certain other compounds, such as bioflavonoids, should be consumed with them to maximize their benefits. Alpha-lipoic acid also plays an important role in the synergism of antioxidants because it may directly recycle and extend the metabolic life spans of vitamin C, glutathione, and coenzyme Q10, and may even indirectly renew vitamin E. Glutathione is referred to as the "master antioxidant" and is present in numerous critical processes in nearly all living cells. It is a nonprotein molecule composed of three amino acids: glutamic acid, cysteine, and glycine. Glutathione protects the body from free-radical damage, but also detoxifies external substances such as drugs, environmental pollutants, and carcinogens. It also helps regulate protein and DNA biosynthesis and cell growth.

Other important nutrients include various macro minerals, such as calcium, magnesium, potassium, phosphorus, iron, and trace minerals such as zinc, copper, selenium, chromium, vanadium, manganese, and molybdenum, to name a few. Although many trace minerals might not directly affect performance, the human body needs small amounts of a large number of trace minerals daily.

Zinc is important for the immune system and the production of collagen. Copper is important in the storage and usage of iron—hence, its relationship to anemia and the elasticity of collagen, connective tissues, and smooth muscle such as that in blood vessels. Animal studies inducing copper deficiencies in poultry have demonstrated high mortality rates due to aortic aneurysms, presumably because of a loss of elasticity in the aortic wall and the aorta's decreased tolerance of normal blood-pressure fluctuations. Nutrition is a balancing act because of the many nutrients competing for absorption by the body. For example, the more zinc that is absorbed, the less copper that can be concurrently absorbed; an appropriate supplemental zinc-to-copper ratio is 10:1. However, it is difficult to determine how much of a trace mineral you are consuming, nor is it practical. Many believe that the body is able to absorb and effectively balance the minerals' ratios through the elaborate biochemical processes within the body. This has been shown, for example, in the body's ability to balance sodium-to-potassium ratios if adequate amounts of these minerals and water are available as well as appropriate levels of the hormone aldosterone, which regulates the retention or loss of these minerals through normally functioning kidneys.

Other Supplements

A number of popular joint-support supplements contain glucosamine and chondroitin, compounds naturally found between cells and joint spaces in the body. The body produces these compounds, but when added to the diet in sufficient amounts, they can nourish the joints and cartilage, rebuilding or maintaining joint structures and lubrication. Studies have been limited, but recent funding of studies through the National Center for Complementary and Alternative Medicine has been directed toward investigating these supplements. European studies and considerable empirical evidence suggest that various glucosamine forms are helpful in reducing joint discomfort. Other popular compounds include methylsulfonylmethane (MSM), a source of sulfur, which is a requirement of joints, that can serve as a natural anti-inflammatory. Preliminary studies of MSM's ability to reduce inflammatory symptoms show promising results; MSM has been used successfully in this capacity in racehorses.

Ergogenic Aids

What are ergogenic aids and why use them? The term *ergogenic* is derived from the Greek word *ergon*, meaning work, and the suffix *-genic*, meaning producing. Work-producing aids include anything that can increase or improve physical work production, resulting in increased speed, endurance, or strength. Although some use this term for anabolic steroids and other pharmaceutical products (in particular, banned substances), I use the term here in a more general and traditional sense to refer to legal substances that are intended to improve endurance performance or recovery from endurance training.

Adaptogens

Considerable investigation and research was invested as early as the 1940s in Russia on finding botanicals to assist soldiers, athletes, and cosmonauts in physical and mental tasks. The breakthrough findings of Dr. Israel Brekhman during a period of approximately 30 years of secret development have recently been made available to the public. The research varied considerably in its approaches and designs, but its findings—although not conclusive—suggest significant benefits, including improved physical work capacity, reduction of illness, improved mental concentration, and numerous others. Popular adaptogens include Siberian (eleuthero) ginseng, Asian (panax) ginseng, ciwujia (pronounced soo-wah-ja), and schizandra.

To be considered an adaptogen, a plant must conform to the following criteria:

- It must be nontoxic and totally harmless to the body, allowing the continuing normal physiological functioning of the individual.
- It must be derived mostly from plants and normalize functions of the body, regardless of the direction of the pathological change. Adaptogens have been reported to enhance the immune response and to increase resistance to stress.

Proprietary formulations of adaptogenic herbs are commercially available from several major sources. Extensive, though often poorly designed, studies on adaptogens abound, many with conflicting findings, some of them supportive, and still others showing no effect. Two adaptogens that may have significant relevance to runners include ginseng and schizandra.

The ginseng family of herbs has been researched extensively across the world over the last 50 years. There are a variety of ginseng-related herbs, such as American ginseng and Asian ginseng (panax), as well as "cousins" of the ginsengs, e.g., Siberian ginseng and ciwujia (acanthopanax). However, research has yet to produce a consensus on the effects of ginseng on athletic performance. One large study reviewed the results of a number of clinical trials involving 2,100 healthy men and women ages 19 to 72. Subjects were given doses of Siberian ginseng ranging from 2 to 16 milliliters of fluid extract, 33 percent ethanol, one to three times daily for up to 60 days. Subjects demonstrated increased mental alertness and work output, enhanced athletic performance, and improved work quality. They also exhibited an improved ability to withstand adverse conditions, such as heat, noise, increased workload, and physical exertion (Farnsworth et al. 1985).

Another study on 140 male distance runners compared the effects of an illegal stimulant (phenamine) with that of schizandra. In a 3,000-meter time trial, 59 percent of the runners given the stimulant ran their fastest times, while 74 percent of the runners given schizandra had personal-best times—a 25 percent improvement over the group given the banned substance (Lebedev 1971, 170). It is unknown whether these findings have been confirmed by other researchers. Although there is little information available describing side effects of adaptogens, some reports of hypertensive responses in some individuals have been documented. At the time of this writing, adaptogens, including schizandra, are not included on any internationally recognized banned-substance list.

Cordyceps

Cordyceps, a small grass-like mushroom, has been used to provide energy, improve health, and treat many ailments for thousands of years in traditional Chinese herbal medicine. Interest in cordyceps as a supplement was sparked following several world-record performances in various distance events by Chinese women in the early 1990s. Cordyceps grows in isolated, severe habitats in certain regions of Sichuan, Tibet, and Qinghai in western China. It is also cultivated in Hong Kong and the Cameron Highlands in Malaysia.

A small study presented at the American College of Sports Medicine (ACSM) annual meeting in 1999 described that a cordyceps-based supplement taken for six weeks significantly increased $\dot{V}O_2$max and anaerobic threshold (AT) in older humans, which may lead to improved exercise capacity and resistance to fatigue. One other randomized, double-blind study found lower blood lactate and heart rate levels during a 60-minute submaximal run (70 percent of $\dot{V}O_2$max). Although confirmation of these findings is needed, these early data suggest potential benefits to performance associated with the use of cordyceps.

Bee Pollen

Bee pollen is a popular nutritional supplement that contains 35 percent protein, 55 percent carbohydrate, 2 percent fatty acids, and 3 percent minerals (including selenium) and vitamins (B-complex, beta-carotene, and A, C, D, and E). There is considerable interest in the ability of bee pollen and related products to assist the immune system and provide energy for the entire body. Although logically there is a place for bee pollen products in nutritional support for athletes, research is needed to demonstrate a clear or direct relationship between the intake of these supplements and athletic performance.

Caffeine and Other Stimulants

Caffeine is very popular in energy drinks. Since the 1990s, considerable research has been conducted on caffeine. Caffeine, when taken alone and not ingested in coffee, has been shown to provide benefit to endurance performance. Studies show that, metabolically, caffeine stimulates the utilization of fat, which inhibits the use of muscle glycogen, in turn improving performance. Running times to exhaustion have been extended by 44 percent in runners at intensities of 85 percent $\dot{V}O_2$max. Unfortunately, caffeine also stimulates smooth muscle and intestinal motility, which may result in increased bowel activity.

Depending on the aid, it may be used prior to, during, or after competition. An electrolyte solution during a road race is a classic example of a thirst quencher or electrolyte-replacement drink. Whereas some sport drinks—referred to later in the chapter as sport energy drinks or gels—are designed for a carbo-loading phase preceding competition, others are aimed at enhancing the recovery process. Substances in this category include sport energy drinks, sport gels, amino acids, and buffering agents.

High-energy drinks or supplements containing modest quantities of caffeine can be helpful to the endurance athlete in maintaining healthy joints, preventing injury, and tolerating the stresses of intense training. However, avoid supercharged energy products that contain multiple stimulants (usually xanthine derivatives such as caffeine) that are engineered to speed metabolism and weight loss. These products are generally designed for a quick sell and lack fundamental nutritional value, and may even be risky. Weight-loss products containing mild appetite suppressants that mildly stimulate metabolism, such as hydroxycitric acid, are less of a concern.

Amino Acids, Enzymes, and Other Compounds

Amino acids are the building blocks of muscle protein, but they affect a variety of functions in the body. Of particular interest are creatine, tyrosine, pyruvate, carnitine, arginine, cysteine, leucine, glutamine, methionine, and branched-chain amino acids (BCAAs); ancillary substances of interest include hydroxy-methylbutyrate (HMB), nicotinamide adenine dinucleotide (NADH), and coenzyme Q10; all are discussed below.

A substantial amount of research suggests that certain amino acids (e.g., arginine, histidine, lysine, methionine, ornithine, and phenylalanine) exert anabolic effects by stimulating the release of growth hormone, insulin, or glucocorticoids, but there is little evidence that supplementation with these amino acids directly enhances athletic performance. Certainly, continued investigation is needed to examine the long-term benefits of the amino acids on muscle development and tissue repair as well as indirect influence on athletic performance.

There may be some support, however, for the idea that ingesting amino acids with carbohydrate may reduce the breakdown of muscle tissue during intense exercise as well as promote the resynthesis of glycogen and thus enhance recovery. Continued controversy surrounds the issue of whether electrolyte drinks used during competitive events should contain amino acids, because these require digestion and supply only an estimated 10 percent of the energy used during the event.

Foods rich in amino acids include milk protein (whey and casein, or the water-soluble caseinates), lean meats, fish, eggs, rice protein, soy protein, colostrum, spirulina, and chlorella. A diet that includes ample amounts of these high-quality proteins will supply all of the amino acids necessary for health and athletic performance.

Creatine

Creatine is a naturally occurring compound in the body involved in the creatine phosphate reactions. These reactions anaerobically produce energy in the muscle without producing lactic acid. Creatine is derived from foods containing the amino acids glycine, arginine, and methionine. The body generally requires two to three grams of creatine per day; half comes from the diet, primarily from meats or fish, and the remainder is synthesized in the body.

Recently, studies have demonstrated that supplemental creatine can assist in recovery from repeated bouts of intense exercise. As a common dietary supplement, creatine appears to have the greatest ergogenic potential for athletes involved in more intense training. It has been used to increase muscle mass and performance as well as lower cholesterol and help in the treatment of heart failure resulting from creatine deficiencies. Creatine occurs in various forms, such as creatine citrate, creatine monohydrate, and creatine phosphate.

According to Owen Anderson, the recommended intake for an adult desiring to improve athletic recovery from intense or repetitious interval work begins at 20 grams a day for five to seven days, after which the requirement drops to 5 grams daily. General maintenance consumption of 2 to 5 grams per day increases muscle creatine and phosphocreatine levels, but more slowly than with an initial loading dose.

Creatine's role in endurance performance is probably not significant because of its limited impact upon the slower, aerobic energy–producing processes used in most endurance activities. It could be of some assistance, however, in permitting more rapid recovery cycles in intense repetitions. Excessive consumption of creatine has been associated with diarrhea and cramping. It is also recommended that anyone with kidney problems avoid using creatine.

Tyrosine

Tyrosine plays an important role in thyroid and adrenal function and can drop to critically low levels that may affect the body's metabolic rate. Tyrosine is a parent compound in the production of catecholamine hormones and neurotransmitters, including dopamine, dihydroxyphenylalanine (DOPA), norepinephrine, and epinephrine. Although the body can generate tyrosine from phenylalanine, dietary intake is important for ensuring that levels are sufficient for the body to produce adequate catecholamines (e.g., the neurotransmitter hormones—also called adrenaline—and dopamine), particularly in people under intense physical or mental stress. Initial signs of tyrosine depletion are depression during endurance performance, which can lead to total despair. Research has demonstrated improved tolerance for physical and mental stress, enhanced cognitive performance, and improved recuperation from workouts after tyrosine administration. Dairy products, meats, fish, wheat, oats, and most other protein-containing foods are good sources of tyrosine.

Pyruvate

Pyruvate (pyruvic acid) is a critical substrate in the body during the energy metabolism of carbohydrate and protein. It has been used as a supplement for a variety of purposes, including athletic performance and weight loss. For performance, it is generally recommended to consume 25 grams (as DHAP containing 75 percent of dihydroxyacetone and 25 percent of sodium pyruvate) orally each day in supplement form.

L-Carnitine

Although acetyl L-carnitine has been used for years in Europe to improve cognitive skills and to relieve depression, it also may be used to increase muscle mass, and when used in concert with alpha-lipoic acid, to boost energy levels. Mixed results have been published regarding the role of L-carnitine in improving fat metabolism. Early studies were unable to demonstrate evidence of increased fat oxidation or a reduction in fatigue postexercise; however, more recent studies have been more encouraging. Recent studies in athletes have shown that carnitine supplementation may benefit exercise performance through an increase in maximal oxygen consumption; a lowering of the respiratory quotient, which indicates that dietary carnitine has the potential to stimulate lipid metabolism; and a significant postexercise decrease in plasma lactate formed during fully aerobic conditions (Karlic and Lohninger 2004).

Data from preliminary studies have indicated that L-carnitine supplementation can lessen the harmful effects of altitude training and speed recovery from exercise stress. Recent data have indicated that L-carnitine plays a decisive role in the prevention of cellular damage and favorably affects recovery from exercise stress. Uptake of L-carnitine by blood cells may induce at least three mechanisms: (1) stimulation of hematopoiesis (the formation of new red blood cells), (2) a dose-dependent inhibition of collagen-induced platelet aggregation (which prevents unwanted blood clotting), and (3) the prevention of programmed cell death in immune cells. As recently shown, carnitine regulates gene expression (i.e., carnitine-acyltransferases) and may also exert effects via modulating intracellular fatty acid concentration. Thus there is evidence for a beneficial effect of L-carnitine supplementation in training, competition, and recovery from strenuous exercise.

Branched-Chain Amino Acids (BCAAs)

BCAAs include the amino acids leucine, isoleucine, and valine, which are broken down differently than most amino acids. Although evidence shows a preferable uptake of these amino acids by the muscles, there is no clear evidence that these changes directly improve performance.

However, there may be benefits in rebuilding muscle tissue and reducing fatigue. It has been theorized that tryptophan, which is involved in the biochemistry of sleep, plays a significant role in fatigue. During endurance exercise, BCAAs are oxidized in the muscle rather than the liver, ultimately reducing the blood concentration of BCAAs and raising the ratio of free tryptophan to BCAAs. An exercise-induced imbalance in the ratio of free tryptophan to BCAAs has been implicated as a possible cause of acute physiological and psychological fatigue (central fatigue). Athletes in high-volume training have reported signs and symptoms of the *overtraining syndrome*, such as postural hypotension (i.e, dizziness or lightheadedness upon standing), anemia, amenorrhea, immunosuppression, appetite suppression, weight loss, depression, and decreased performance; all of these may be related to the depletion of BCAAs and accompanying increases in tryptophan. Theoretically, adequate intake of BCAAs may delay the onset of fatigue as well as prevent other overtraining symptoms.

Hydroxymethylbutyrate (HMB) and Leucine

In humans, leucine infusion has been studied and appears to decrease protein degradation. In animal studies, approximately 5 percent of oxidized leucine is converted to HMB. Increased survival rates in animals as well as gains in lean body mass have been observed after leucine supplementation. Early investigation of the effects of HMB supplementation demonstrated strength and lean mass gains in proportion to the amount of HMB used during a regimen of training in previously *untrained* male volunteers ages 19 to 29 (Nissen et al. 1996). However, limited data are available on the effects of HMB supplementation on training adaptations in athletes. It may be effective in helping untrained people to gain both strength and lean mass when beginning a resistance exercise program, but more research is clearly needed in this area. Whey protein is probably the best food source of HMB.

Glutamine

The body uses significant quantities of glutamine during metabolic stress such as exercise, illness, or fasting. It is considered a nonessential amino acid from a general supplementation standpoint because various tissues, such as the skeletal muscles, liver, and adipose tissue, can readily synthesize it. Various cells within the immune system, such as the lymphocytes and macrophages, and other rapidly dividing cells, such as enterocytes in the small intestine, depend on plasma glutamine as a primary fuel source.

Numerous studies have examined the role of glutamine and its synthesis by the body. In research, the infusion of glutamine to increase the availability of free glutamine has been doubly beneficial in that it not only prevents the breakdown of muscle protein, but also supports muscle protein synthesis and the regeneration of muscle glycogen following exercise.

Glutamine is sold in the form of gel capsules and powders in major health and nutrition stores and may be an ingredient in other dietary supplements such as protein powders. Significant glutamine intake (0.1 to 0.3 grams per kilogram or about 14 to 42 grams for a 70-kilogram [154-pound] person) may help prevent overtraining symptoms. It is generally regarded as safe, but ingesting large quantities can have undesirable effects on the intestinal system such as abdominal pains and diarrhea because of the electrolytic properties of the amino acid. Additional research is needed to help establish its practicality as a sport nutrition supplement.

Nicotinamide Adenine Dinucleotide (NADH)

NADH is the active coenzyme form of vitamin B_3. It plays an essential role in the energy production of every human cell. Promising preliminary findings by Dr. J. Birkmayer (1996) suggest NADH may provide substantial improvements in work capacity and $\dot{V}O_2$max in trained cyclists. Five-milligram tablets of NADH were given daily for at least four weeks in the initial study. Double-blind, placebo-controlled studies are needed to help substantiate these findings.

Coenzyme Q10

Coenzyme Q10 (ubiquinone), discovered in the late 1950s, is involved in the energy production in every cell of the body. European and Japanese scientists among others have thoroughly studied its effects on cardiac failure and chronic fatigue. Clinical findings indicate support for Co-Q10's potential to help control heart arrhythmias and reduce symptoms of fatigue in skeletal muscle. However, its effects on endurance athletes have been mixed. One poorly designed Finnish study showed dramatic improvements in Nordic skiing performances, but other studies have not verified this in other endurance athletes. Further research is needed to substantiate use of Co-Q10 in sport.

Choline

Cholinergic nerves carry signals to the muscle fibers to induce muscle contractions. Acetylcholine is the signaling compound that the body synthesizes from choline. Choline has been shown to drop as much as 40 to 55 percent below normal resting levels during intense exercise; this may reduce acetylcholine release, causing a lowering effect on endurance and performance. Studies have indicated that choline blood levels may be better sustained using phosphatidylcholine rather than choline itself. One study conducted as a double-blind, crossover, placebo-controlled clinical trial showed increased choline levels in 10 runners receiving 2.8 grams of choline citrate versus the placebo one hour before, and again after, completing 10 miles (16 kilometers) of a 20-mile (about 32-kilometer) run. The treatment group improved the mean run time from 158.9 minutes to 153.7 minutes. The subjects were well-trained endurance athletes ages 25 to 28 with a mean body mass of 75.3 kilograms (166 pounds). It is important to note, however, that in other research studies in which the athletes did not deplete choline levels during exercise, the supplementation of choline did not delay the onset of fatigue.

Buffering Agents

It is well known that intense exercise produces considerable amounts of metabolic acids that inhibit muscle contractions. Buffering agents are compounds used to buffer the hydrogen ions and ease the acidic burden within the muscles, in the blood, or in both. Numerous studies have used the intake of sodium bicarbonate (baking soda), sodium citrate, phosphates (sodium or calcium phosphate, creatine phosphate), and others.

Investigation of the use of phosphates in athletic performance began as early as the 1920s. Here are three plausible benefits of ingesting phosphates:

1. **Buffering metabolic acids.** Studies have determined that some benefits to performance come from acidic metabolites such as lactate. Phosphates and the amino acid carnosine (not to be confused with L-carnitine) are key components in muscle buffering. Carnosine is a naturally occurring dipeptide in both skeletal and heart muscle. It contains two amino acids, alanine and histidine, and has been shown to have buffering and antioxidant properties. However, bicarbonate works on blood acidity rather than by effectively buffering intramuscular acidosis and fatigue.

2. **Increasing available oxygen.** Research shows that increased concentrations of an important compound in red blood cells, 2,3-diphosphoglycerate (2,3-DPG), can be obtained through buffering. This compound speeds the release of oxygen from hemoglobin transporters to muscle cells.

3. **Replenishing the creatine-phosphate system.** Additional phosphate may provide phosphorylation of creatine to form creatine phosphate, the body's chief source of fuel in the first several seconds of high-intensity exercise. German researchers were aware of these fatigue-reducing properties during World War I and reportedly gave one to three grams of sodium phosphate to soldiers to reduce battle fatigue.

Extensive research on the effects of 2,3-diphosphoglycerate and sodium phosphate on athletic performance is credited to Dr. Richard Kreider. His studies have found 9 percent increases in maximal oxygen uptake ($\dot{V}O_2$max) and 10 percent rises in anaerobic threshold levels in highly trained cyclists during maximal testing. During a 40-kilometer (24.8-mile) simulated race, buffered subjects showed an average of 18 percent higher $\dot{V}O_2$max values and 17 percent higher mean power outputs, resulting in an 8 percent improvement in performance time (Kreider 1992).

Dr. Kreider indicates that endurance performance improves with three to four grams per day of sodium phosphate (rather than calcium phosphate) for three or four days (Kreider 1999c). However, some have suggested that a chronically high intake of phosphates interferes with calcium absorption. Further confirmation of these findings should precede widespread use of phosphates by distance runners.

Sport Energy Drinks

Supplying adequate fluids is critical. Gatorade advertises that a 6 percent carbohydrate solution (6 grams of carbohydrate per 100 milliliter) is optimal for rehydrating the body during competition. Apparently, the speed at which the body absorbs carbohydrate for fuel and water depends on the concentration and composition of the solution consumed. Research studies have documented that the rate of absorption of certain fluid replacements may exceed the absorption rate of plain water when the solution approaches the same concentration as the body's fluids. Considerable sports-medicine research has been conducted to confirm this. Refer to the ACSM resources listed in the references that provide detailed recommendations for sport drinks. However, be aware of the high levels of sugar in some prepared electrolyte formulas, especially if using them in hot-weather competition; drinks high in sugar or salt cause water to be drawn from the bloodstream into the GI tract to be absorbed.

The following discussion provides basic information that runners may use when deciding which sport drink is best for them. Follow the directions on the product label when doing intense or long workouts. Of the energy drinks commonly used for competition, several have been researched (see table 8.3).

Cytomax Energy and Recovery Drink is a unique product containing a designer-engineered carbohydrate molecule, alpha L-polylactacte that was patented because of its ability to buffer lactic acid. Most of the available research has been conducted by Dr. G.A. Brooks and has indicated that Cytomax helps prevent fatigue with its alpha L-polylactacte and additional components: maltodextrins from corn hybrid, antioxidants, sucralose, and electrolytes. Independent verification of these findings is not currently available.

VAAM (Vespa Amino Acid Mixture) comes from Japan. Biochemist Takashi Abe observed that the giant killer hornet has incredible endurance, gained from a nutrient containing a unique combination of 17 amino acids and secreted by wasp larvae. The adult hornets hunt at flying velocities in excess of 15 miles per hour (24 kilometers per hour) all day long, covering distances of about 60 miles (96 kilometers)! Dr. Abe successfully clarified the composition of the

Table 8.3 Common Sport Hydrating and Energy Drinks

Product*	Ingredients (to be mixed with water)	Calories per 6 oz	Grams of protein per 6 oz	Grams of carbohydrate per 6 oz
Accelerade	Sucrose, fructose, maltodextrin, whey, sodium, potassium, magnesium, vitamin C, vitamin E, glutamine, branched-chain amino acids	60	3	10.5
All Sport	High fructose corn syrup, sodium, potassium	40	0	11
Cytomax	Alpha L-polylactacte, maltodextrins from corn hybrid, sucralose, L-glutamine, antioxidants, natural flavors, sodium, potassium	36	0	7.5
Endurox R4	Glucose, complex carbohydrates, whey protein concentrate, crystalline fructose, citric acid, L-arginine, natural flavors, ciwujia, d-alpha tocopheryl acetate, ascorbic acid, sodium chloride, L-glutamine, magnesium oxide, paprika (natural color), potassium phosphate, lecithin	60	2.5	10.5
Enervit G	Fructose, maltodextrin, glucose, sucrose, magnesium, vitamin C	45	0	10.5
Enervit R2	Dextrose, sucrose, maltodextrin, branched-chain amino acids (leucine, isoleucine, and valine), L-glutamine, sodium bicarbonate, polycosanols, vitamins (B_6, niacin, riboflavin, thiamin, C, E), potassium, magnesium	83	0.75	15

*Manufacturer's suggested serving sizes vary; columns three through five of this table list information per 6 oz serving for each product for comparison purposes.

Product*	Ingredients (to be mixed with water)	Calories per 6 oz	Grams of protein per 6 oz	Grams of carbohydrate per 6 oz
Extran Thirstquencher	Fructose, dextrin maltose, citric acid, lemon (or other) flavor, minerals (sodium chloride 1.37%, tripotassium citrate 1.20%)	45	0	11
Gatorade Hydrating Formula	Carbohydrates, sodium, potassium, chloride, calcium, magnesium	50	0	11.3
Gatorade Thirst Quencher	Carbohydrate, sodium, potassium, chloride	46	0	10.5
GU2O	Maltodextrin, fructose, sodium and potassium nitrate, citric acid, all-natural flavors and colors	37.5	0	9.8
Powerade	High-fructose corn syrup, glucose polymers, sodium, potassium	80	0	21
Ultima	Maltodextrin, sodium, potassium, vitamin C	10.5	0	2.7
VAAM	Cane sugar, amino acids (proline, lysine, glycine, tyrosine, threonine, leucine, valine, phenylalanine, arginine, isoleucine, alanine, glutamic acid, tryptophan, histidine, serine, methionine, aspartic acid), flavoring, acidifier, sweetener (stevia, thaumatin)	42	2.6	7.6

165

larvae-produced amino acids and formatted a sport drink based on his analysis. VAAM has a carbohydrate-to-protein ratio of approximately 3:1. It supplies 2.6 grams of protein (as amino acids), 7.6 grams of carbohydrate, and 42 calories of energy per six-ounce serving.

A significant volume of research has been generated on this product, particularly among Japanese researchers (see references). VAAM has a unique composition of amino acids, containing large amounts of threonine, proline, glycine, and tryptophan. Most of the research has focused on VAAM's effects on endurance and blood chemistry in swimming mice and in exercising humans. Promising research findings have indicated that in humans the product increases blood levels of gamma-hydroxybutyrate and acetoacetate both pre- and post-exercise and boosts glucagon and serum glycerol levels during recovery periods. Glucogon and glycerol are significant energy sources that provide additional metabolic substrates during critical stresses found in endurance performance. Animal research shows prolonged swimming times to exhaustion for mice, with significantly more stable blood glucose levels and lower lactate levels.

Endurox R4 is a drink that contains a 4:1 ratio of carbohydrate to protein and possibly the only drink commercially available that has an adaptogen herb, *ciwujia*. Ciwujia (acanthopanax), a close cousin of eleuthero ginseng, is a root grown in the northeast section of China, where it has been used safely for almost 1,700 years to treat fatigue and improve physical work tolerance. One randomized trial in cyclists found that it reduced fatigue (as determined by recovery heart rates) and boosted the use of fat during exercise. Several other studies on Endurox and on a related product, Accelerade, indicate that Accelerade helps reduce free radicals, assists with muscle-glycogen recovery, and prevents muscle-protein breakdown. Other researchers have yet to confirm these findings (Cheuvront et al. 1999). The Endurox research design has been criticized; refer to the article "Magic Potion" by Owen Anderson at his Web site (see Web site section of reference list).

Sport Gels

In recent years, sport gels have become popular as an energy source during competition. Basically, the greater the glucose (simply sugar) intake once the race or event has started, the more fatigue is delayed. During races that last for hours, you may want to consume one or two gel packets per hour followed by water to maintain sufficient energy levels. Depending on your training preparation and the racing conditions, you may find that your need for this energy varies from session to session. The greater the relative effort and event duration, the greater the need for supplemental energy and hydrating drinks.

Refer to table 8.4 for common examples of sport gels and their contents. Most have easily absorbed carbohydrate and electrolytes; some contain caffeine and botanical ingredients to enhance the boosting effect.

Table 8.4 Common Sport Gels

Product	Ingredients	Calories per packet	Grams of protein per packet	Grams of carbohydrate per packet
Accel Gel (chocolate, strawberry-kiwi, vanilla)	Water, maltodextrin, high fructose corn syrup, whey protein concentrate, trehalose (Ascendä), cocoa powder, sodium chloride, monopotassium phosphate, ascorbic acid, vitamin E acetate, caffeine, potassium sorbate, sodium benzoate, polysorbate 80	90	5	20
Carb-BOOM (strawberry, kiwi, banana, chocolate, cherry, vanilla orange)	Maltodextrin, water, fruit puree (see flavors) and fruit concentrate, citric acid, potassium citrate, sea salt, potassium sorbate, sodium benzoate	110	0	26-27
CLIF Shots (vanilla, raspberry, cocoa powder, chocolate liquor)	Brown rice syrup, natural flavors (see flavors), sea salt, potassium citrate, magnesium oxide	100	0	24
PowerGel (chocolate, green apple, lemon lime, raspberry cream, strawberry, banana, tangerine, tropical fruit, vanilla)	Maltodextrin, water, fructose, dextrose, natural flavoring, citric acid, PowerBar Amino Acid Blend (leucine, valine, isoleucine), potassium chloride, sea salt, sodium citrate, sodium benzoate, potassium sorbate, antioxidant vitamins C and E; PowerGel comes in caffeinated and noncaffeinated flavors; all varieties include vitamins, amino acids, and electrolytes, and the caffeinated flavors also have a PowerGel Booster Blend of caffeine, kola nut extract, and ginseng	110	0	28

(continued)

167

Table 8.4 *(continued)*

Product	Ingredients	Calories per packet	Grams of protein per packet	Grams of carbohydrate per packet
GU Energy Gel (vanilla bean, chocolate, banana blitz, just plain, tri-berry, orange burst)	Maltodextrin (glucose polymers), filtered water, fructose, leucine, valine, natural and artificial flavoring, sodium, potassium citrate, pectin, calcium carbonate, fumaric acid, sea salt, histidine, citric acid, potassium sorbate, sodium benzoate, GU herbal blend (astragalus, chamomile, kola nut extract [has caffeine], ginseng), GU antioxidant blend (vitamins C and E)	100	0	25
Extran Carbohydrate	Water, glucose syrup (36%), citric acid, citrus (or other) flavors	284	0	71

Recovery Aids

Nutrition plays a vital role in recovery from intense training or competition. Several new supplements have been found that may assist in the recovery process.

Ribose is a compound that the body produces from glucose. Supplementation with ribose has been granted patent protection that covers a broad range of nutritional and pharmaceutical uses. More than 20 patents have been awarded for uses in energy enhancement and prevention of muscle soreness, stiffness, and cramping. Although ribose has been shown to enhance ATP production under low-oxygen conditions, there has yet to be a clear demonstration that ribose enhances athletic performance. Beginning exercisers may find it helpful in reducing initial muscle soreness. Taking three to five grams of ribose every day should put enough in the bloodstream to ensure that the heart and skeletal-muscle cells have an adequate supply. Serious athletes and people concerned about their circulation may want to take more. In fact, these people may require 10 to 20 grams or more per day. Experienced runners may not see dramatic effects; more research is needed. Some have suggested that ribose taken in combination with the cordyceps mushroom may have synergistic effects on the availability of ATP (high-energy phosphates) to the muscle cell.

Inosine is a precursor to uric acid in the muscle with specific cellular functions and has been theorized to have an ergogenic (work-producing) effect on performance. However, at least three controlled studies have demonstrated no benefit to athletic performance and suggest that inosine may actually impair performance. The use of inosine is therefore not recommended.

Alpha-lipoic acid, a popular antioxidant, has reportedly been helpful in reducing muscle soreness and improving recovery following competition. Similarly, adaptogenic herbs have been reported to speed recovery and reduce soreness. Bromelain, papain, and proteolytic enzymes are digestive enzymes that have been shown to assist in reducing inflammation and swelling in athletes following intensive training or injury. Other digestive enzymes that might assist in general digestion are available as common food supplements. These include lactase to digest milk, lipase to digest fat, alpha amylase to digest carbohydrate, and cellulase to digest fiber.

The use of supplements by runners is a vast and ever-changing area that illustrates the complexity of nutrition. It is little wonder that many supplements available in the market are driven more by sales than science. The decision to use specific supplements should be made after carefully considering professional opinions and advice and after reviewing published findings. Unfortunately, the majority of currently available supplements show inconsistent results in studies, probably because of bio-individuality, the shifting nutritional status of subjects, and the biochemical characteristics, such as quality, of the supplement in question.

The central factor for improving performance is the long-term use of nutritional supplements that synergistically develop all the body's physiological systems rather than the short-term use of one particular supplement during athletic competition or laboratory testing. Long-term studies examining the role of nutrition need to be funded and initiated. We can only hope that reliable studies using well-controlled, crossover designs will continue and will help runners sort through the myriad nutritional supplements available. Table 8.5 provides a summary in support of informed, controlled supplement use for runners.

Table 8.5 Summary of Support for Supplement Usage

Available research and support	Product or nutrient common name	Actions
Substantial positive results	Carbohydrate, maltodextrin, polycose	Energy, endurance, antifatigue Recovery, therapeutic
	Electrolyte replacement drink	Energy, endurance, antifatigue Recovery, therapeutic
Some positive results	Antioxidant vitamins C, E, A, folate, B complex	Antioxidant, antimetabolite, buffer; general well-being
	Creatine monohydrate	Energy, endurance, antifatigue
	Creatine, carbohydrate, sodium phosphate	Energy, endurance, antifatigue
	Phosphates (2,3,-diphospho-glycerate)	Energy, endurance, antifatigue
Mixed results	BCAA and other amino acids, e.g., glutamine, arginine	Muscle development, strength, mass; energy, endurance, anti-fatigue Recovery, therapeutic
	HMB (hydroxymethylbutyrate)	Muscle development, strength, mass Injury prevention, joint function Recovery, therapeutic
	Caffeine	Energy, endurance, antifatigue
	Glucosamine	Injury prevention, joint function
	Adaptogen herbs, e.g., ciwujia, Siberian ginseng	Stress tolerance and adaptation Increased energy, endurance, antifatigue; general well-being
	Sodium bicarbonate	Antioxidant, antimetabolite, buffer
	Glycerol	Hydration; energy, endurance, antifatigue
	Choline	Energy, endurance, antifatigue
	Alpha L-polylactate	Anti-oxidant, antimetabolite, buffer Increased energy, endurance, anti-fatigue
	Ribose	Increased energy, increased ATP production Endurance, antifatigue
	Fat intake prior to carbohydrate loading	Energy, endurance, antifatigue
	Calcium citrate	Energy, endurance, antifatigue

Available research and support	Product or nutrient common name	Actions
Mixed results	Coenzyme Q10	Energy, endurance, antifatigue Anti-oxidant, antimetabolite, buffer
	NADH (nicotinamide adenine dinucleotide)	Energy, endurance, antifatigue
	Bee pollen	Energy, endurance, antifatigue Immune system, general well-being
	MSM (methylsulfonylmethane)	Injury prevention, joint function
	Electrolyte drinks with amino acids and adaptogens	Energy, endurance, antifatigue Stress tolerance and adaptation
	Cordyceps (mushroom)	Stress tolerance and adaptation Increased energy, endurance, antifatigue
	Multivitamins	Recovery, therapeutic; injury prevention, joint function; general well-being
	Minerals: calcium and magnesium	Muscle development, strength, mass, general well-being
	Trace minerals: iron, copper, manganese, zinc	Energy, endurance, antifatigue Injury prevention, joint function; general well-being
Few studies—negative results or no effect	Pyruvate	Energy, endurance, antifatigue
	MCT (medium-chain triglycerides)	Energy, endurance, antifatigue
	Inosine	Energy, endurance, antifatigue
	Phytosterols and sterolins (beta-sitosterol)	Immune function, general well-being
Unknown effect on athletic performance; other physical benefits possible	Guarana	Energy, endurance, antifatigue
	Milk thistle	Energy, endurance, antifatigue; recovery, therapeutic; general well-being
	Ashwaganda (Indian ginseng)	Stress tolerance and adaptation; energy, endurance, antifatigue; general well-being

(continued)

171

Table 8.5 *(continued)*

Available research and support	Product or nutrient common name	Actions
Unknown effect on athletic performance; other physical benefits possible	Astragalus	Immune function; stress tolerance and adaptation Increased energy, endurance, antifatigue; general well-being
	Hawthorn berry	Blood flow stimulant, vasodilator Immune function
	Fish oils and polyunsaturated fatty acid	Energy, endurance, antifatigue Stress tolerance and adaptation; general well-being
	Grape seed extract, pycnogenol	Anti-oxidant, antimetabolite, buffer Injury prevention, joint function Recovery, therapeutic
	Gingko biloba	Blood flow stimulant, vasodilator Mental performance

CHAPTER 9

Revving the Cardiovascular Engine

JOHN KELLOGG, MAT

The late Kiyoshi Nakamura, coach of 2:08 marathoner and former Fukuoka and Boston champion Toshihiko Seko, was fond of comparing a distance runner's development to a steady fall of raindrops slowly forging a hole in a huge rock over a period of many years. On some days the rain falls hard, on other days it falls gently, and on some days it does not fall at all. But in the final analysis, the process cannot be rushed, and we must wait patiently for the natural order of events to run its course before we can admire the finished product.

Too many runners are in search of "magic" workouts, when in fact the real secret to ultimate success is the patient, prolonged cardiovascular development alluded to in the rain analogy. Other runners and coaches pay mere lip service to concepts such as *base training* and *long-term improvement* without realizing how much running is actually required to fulfill a runner's ultimate career potential. Of course, you must love running or know that you can come to love it to sustain the kind of dedication embodied in Nakamura's analogy. By taking a proper long-term approach, progress will often be slower, but it will be more complete.

When deciding on a long-term path for your running, it is important to consider *universal* principles (those that work for everyone) before examining experiment-of-one success stories or principles that might apply only to certain types of athletes. Several principles apply across the spectrum of body types. These include the following:

- Gradually work toward base mileage levels that are as high as can be safely tolerated (obviously, this figure varies from athlete to athlete and depends on factors such as experience and age).

- Learn to stay comfortable on easy runs to ensure proper recovery.

- Spend an optimal amount of time at a high-end aerobic pace (at or near the lactate threshold); see chapter 3 for a suggested breakdown of different types of workouts.

- Include regular speed maintenance (in the form of short, alactic strides—that is, bursts of speed too brief to incur lactic acid buildup—drills, and hills; see chapter 2 for specifics).

- Build toward a seasonal peak with limited injections of oxygen-uptake training and harder, faster anaerobic-tolerance training.

This chapter focuses on how to implement all of these concepts into your training over not just a single season but over a period of years; I discuss how each relates to aerobic development, which for our purposes equates to cardiovascular strength.

Build Base Miles Gradually

For any distance runner, there is a distinct correlation between acquired lifetime training mileage—particularly during base-training periods—and subsequent race performances. This raises a question: Is talent for fast performances in the distances also accompanied by the ability to handle high training mileage? Possibly, but *most* runners can safely increase their mileage over time by running more slowly for much of it and by applying other principles to their training to increase their speed. Some of these principles involve common sense. Getting adequate rest, nutrients, and fluids; wearing appropriate shoes; and varying the running terrain are obviously important. Also crucial is making smooth, safe, and gradual transitions when running on new terrain, when wearing new shoes, or when training at speeds you have not touched on for some time.

It is always best to establish the highest base mileage that continues to provide a favorable cost-to-benefit ratio—that is, figuring out the highest mileage you can attain without injury or without detriment to your other training. You will find your own personal mileage sweet spot only by trial and error and by patiently building your fitness through the years. Then and only then will the training "secrets" widely sought by distance runners everywhere begin to reveal themselves to you.

In the 1970s, it was common for many American high school distance runners to average more than 100 miles per week during their preseason base-building period. This was not considered outrageous at all; it was merely the kind of thing serious runners did if they had big dreams. It was no coincidence that high school marks in the distance events were at an all-time high during this period, followed by a banner crop of American road runners and long track–event specialists in the ensuing years. This higher mileage fell out of favor among high schoolers in the 1980s and the first half of the 1990s, apparently as a result of media influences. Subsequently, both top-end performances and the depth of these performances seemed to significantly decline during this period. Since

© Empics

Top distance performers routinely rack up high training mileage; the trick is to gradually build a high-mileage foundation rather than pushing for too much too soon.

the late 1990s, there has been a return to higher mileage and more aerobically based training, and performances as of 2004 have returned to pre-1980 levels.

Upon closer inspection of the careers of the 1970s and 1980s elites, it becomes apparent that the runners who used high-mileage training *year-round* in high school tended to outperform all others during their high school years, but were often surpassed later in life by athletes who had been somewhat slower in their youth. What is common among the elite adults of that era is the fact that most were exposed to high mileage in restricted amounts during their teenage years (which likely enabled them to safely make the jump to marathon-type training later in life), yet they saved their bodies for more year-round high mileage in adulthood. The implication here is that a gradual progression toward higher mileage, with brief forays into high-mileage territory during the teen years, sets a runner up for a long and maximally efficacious competitive career.

Regardless of training volume, frequent use of intense anaerobic interval training and racing in youth is a surefire way to thwart a runner's future development. So if you're a younger runner or a youth coach concerned about burnout, be far more wary of extravagant training intensity than extravagant training mileage.

The lesson here for younger runners is: Be patient! It takes years to create a sufficient mileage foundation for truly effective training and for reaching your ultimate potential. For example, Kyle Heffner had personal bests of 4:27 for the mile and 9:42 for the two-mile in high school—well above average performances, but nowhere near the national level. Kyle was only able to handle an average training load of 50 to 55 miles per week in high school and was not structurally comfortable running 100 miles in a single week until his senior year of college, when he was barely able to run six miles at 5:00 per mile. Yet he dedicated himself to full-time training after college and patiently continued to build his mileage until he could run up to 145 miles per week, much of it at 8,000 feet of elevation and on difficult terrain. The increased training load enabled him to make huge improvements in all his personal bests from 5,000 meters up to the marathon. He went on to earn a berth on the 1980 Olympic marathon team with a 2:10:55 (4:59 per mile) and was ranked 17th in the world at the marathon distance. By gradually increasing his base mileage as he matured physically into his mid-20s, Heffner, who wrote chapter 8 of this book, extracted the most out of himself as a distance runner.

During each new preseason, experiment with slightly higher mileage than you have previously run; for example, you may try an additional 50 miles or so spread out over a one-month period if you've got a few years of experience under your belt. Start by bumping up the volume for a few days at a time. This doesn't have to be done in seven-day blocks; two to four days at a time of higher mileage—say, 10 to 20 percent above your daily norm over the past several months—is sufficient at first. Recover from that injection of volume with a lower block of mileage for two to four days or as long as it takes to feel some "snap," then increase again for several days. An example for a runner accustomed to 40 to 45 miles a week might include a pattern of days with mileage like this: 6, 5, 6, 10, 7, 10, 8, 5, 6, 5.

Run extremely relaxed when you are increasing your mileage to previously unattained levels. Do not increase the mileage and the intensity (speed) of your base-building runs simultaneously until you have completed several seasons while incorporating each separately. You can and should run some short (15- to 30-second) buildups or strides every second or third day to provide variety, but avoid intense anaerobic work and races during these introductory high-mileage stages.

With each passing year, you should be able to increase the mileage itself and the length of the high-mileage blocks, so that you are eventually capable of several weeks in a row of very high volume without the need to reduce your mileage and without incurring stress-related problems because of the volume. With each season, your average pace may also become faster than it once was, but don't force this. Just allow the faster running to come to you over time as your body becomes ready for it. During base training, most of your effort should come from the mileage and the monotony of it all, not from a series of hard workouts. Through an increased number of muscle capillaries, a higher density of oxygen-processing muscle mitochondria, more red blood cells, and other changes directly and indirectly related to the cardiovascular and circulatory systems, you will lay the groundwork for strength that will ultimately sustain you not for a season, but for the duration of your running career!

Begin introducing the higher mileage in short doses, particularly if you are still growing or in your first two or three years of running, allowing your body to absorb the training by dropping back in volume for a while between high-mileage segments. This plan follows the stress–recovery or stimulation–adaptation principle. Expand your boundaries with higher mileage and with longer installments of high mileage from year to year as you mature. In short, keep Kiyoshi Nakamura's raindrops analogy in mind and do not try to rush things too quickly. Start at the bottom rung of the fitness ladder and gradually work your way up.

Some sessions (and how they fit together to form an overall training program) actually facilitate future mileage increases by reducing injury risk and by enhancing the effectiveness of the high-mileage training itself. Particularly important are alactic strides and other speed maintenance workouts (see chapter 2), which provide variety in footstrike characteristics, rhythm, and muscle fiber recruitment. These sessions also help increase lower-leg integrity and allow you to segue seamlessly to faster-paced running as the competitive season approaches. Spending certain time periods at the high end of aerobic effort (near the lactate threshold) is also very cost-effective; I describe this in more detail later in this chapter.

Maximize Recovery on Easy Days

Runners often reach a point in their training when everything goes smoothly and a fairly quick pace seems surprisingly easy. During these times, improvements may be rapid; however inserting slower easy days can yield better results over a period of several years, although short-term gains may not come as quickly. In practical terms, if you are nearing your prime racing years—around 28 to 32 for men, perhaps a bit older for women—you may benefit from running a little quicker average pace on your daily runs. If you are in your teen years, however, you will likely be better served in the long term by incorporating more *slow* running, especially if you are in the process of increasing your mileage. In so doing, you may sacrifice a modicum of high school glory, but will likely achieve more in adulthood; this holds true whether your event of primary focus is the mile or the marathon.

Much of your running during the preseason or base-building periods should not only be perceptually easy; it should actually be slower pacewise than you may think is beneficial. Running "slowly"—even two minutes a mile slower than marathon pace—confers cardiovascular benefits while still allowing recovery; blasting along at close to marathon pace will not introduce significant additional cardiovascular benefits but will almost certainly interfere with recovery if sustained over days or weeks. Of course, short strides (for speed maintenance) and some faster tempo runs during this base-building phase of training are necessary on occasion, but going too fast too often—even if it feels good at the time—can backfire by the time the peak of the competitive season arrives, as you likely won't be well-rested often enough to perform the quality sessions necessary for maximal competitive success. It is certainly possible to be fit enough from an aerobic standpoint to override your structural integrity and create overuse injuries without feeling as though the pace is fast. That is, a fairly quick pace on daily runs may seem easy to you if everything has been "clicking" on recent outings, but the impact stress, cellular overload, and muscle contractile force required usually cannot be sustained for months on end; staying close to 60 to 65 percent of max heart rate is more advisable.

Peaking for your most important competitions later in the season does not require you to be in better racing shape during a preseason than you were at the same point in previous preseasons. If you do things intelligently, you will often run better at the end of a competitive season after being slightly slower at the beginning of that season. Keeping the pace extremely relaxed and slow on many recovery days acts as a kind of insurance policy toward this goal. Most people run too fast on their easy days and never get adequate recovery; thus, they accumulate and experience chronic fatigue, often without realizing that they could be feeling much fresher. Most of your easy runs should give you the sensation of storing up energy for your next faster effort.

In 2003, Weldon Johnson ran 28:06 for 10,000 meters and placed fourth in the U.S. track championships in 2001 and 2003. He often does easy runs at 7:00 to 8:00 per mile, a pace that even many 35:00 10K runners might consider too slow to be of benefit. Yet this pace is functionally comfortable for him. Because of his overall high mileage (between 100 and 150 miles per week) and because of his accumulated lifetime volume (and buildup to this volume), even this slower pace is sufficient for maintaining capillarization of his muscles and some fitness as long as other crucial training bases are covered regularly. This last point is important. Weldon does not *always* run slowly; otherwise he would risk being a plodder and would never maximize his potential. He performs his share of challenging workouts leading up to competitions (even performing intense anaerobic ones during his base phase), but he always makes sure he is reinvigorated for his faster sessions when they are scheduled, even taking an extra (unplanned) easy day from time to time. Meanwhile, many midpack runners run at medium speeds on easy days and are rarely relaxed and rested when it is time to run hard. As the Japanese standouts of both sexes have long demonstrated, extremely slow miles—even if done at a pace most would consider jogging—really do have a beneficial effect as long as they're supported by the requisite sharpening work, particularly, but not only, for marathoners. It's all grist for your mill.

Spend Time at Your Lactate Threshold

To understand the cardiovascular benefits of training, you need to understand what occurs in your body—in particular your heart and bloodstream—when you run at specific intensities for specific periods of time. Properly allocating the amount of work you do among various well-defined intensity levels is vitally important in terms of your long-term development as a competitive athlete.

When examining specific training speeds, familiarity with a few terms promotes better understanding and facilitates discussion of the involved physiology; among these terms are lactic acid, blood lactate, and lactate threshold.

Lactic acid is the end product of anaerobic glucose metabolism (glycolysis). During intense efforts ranging from 200-meter track sprints to hour-long road races, glucose is converted to pyruvic acid, which is in turn reduced to lactic acid. Lactic acid dissociates quickly into lactate (its negative ion) and free protons, and it is usually referred to as lactate. It was long thought that the protons were responsible for interfering with muscular contractions, causing the "tying up" experienced during all-out efforts lasting longer than about 40 seconds (e.g., 400 meters and 800 meters or a long sprint at the end of a 5,000-meter race). More recent research (Robergs 2001) shows that this may not be the case. However, excessive lactic acid production during exercise goes hand in hand with the experience of tying up, and thus it is prudent to limit the amount of time at the effort level that results in this production; otherwise, chronic soreness, staleness, and possible injury may result.

Crucial to limiting the amount of time you spend with excessive lactic acid production is knowing your lactate threshold (LT). Your lactate threshold is the point during increasing exercise intensity at which a rapid accumulation of lactate entering the bloodstream (blood lactate) follows an "inflection point," or a change in the normal level of blood lactate. When lactate is produced faster than it can be cleared and begins to accumulate in the blood, a state of oxygen debt sets in and exercise intensity must drop; if it doesn't, biochemical obligation will cause activity to grind to a halt. Thus learning to stay just on the "safe side" of lactate production is absolutely invaluable (see the discussion of lactate threshold velocity).

Lactate threshold velocity (LT pace) is the speed (expressed in meters per second or kilometers per hour) or, more commonly, the pace (expressed in minutes and seconds per mile or kilometer) required to bring a runner to his or her LT or just below the point of rapid lactate accumulation. Most well-trained runners can maintain their LT pace (what could loosely be called high-end aerobic pace) for about 20 minutes before surpassing this point. A near-LT pace may be maintained for an hour or more, but once the threshold is reached, the accumulation of lactate is inevitable, so the effort will likely alternate between high levels of aerobic metabolism, and anaerobic metabolism, and the pace will eventually have to slow. At such times, the runner will reach the **respiratory compensation point,** resulting in extreme hyperventilation. Experiencing this point in training may help the athlete learn to monitor the pace just below the LT in a tempo run during training. From the runner's point of view, the effort level just below the LT could accurately be called "maximum steady state," because all systems usually remain perceptually in equilibrium until the LT is reached. The ability to recognize the pace corresponding to LT—and by extension, the physical signs of reaching LT—is critical; the benefits of training as frequently as possible at this pace are substantial, while training at faster than LT pace can only be done in relatively short bursts because of lactate accumulation and its deleterious effects on working muscle.

So how can you determine your own lactate threshold? You can use data from a heart rate monitor to estimate where your LT occurs, but it is usually best to rely on sensory feedback (running by feel) to find that high end of aerobic effort. Many runners try to rush the process and begin doing hard tempo runs without first becoming attuned to the finer sensory signals that indicate that they are reaching their threshold. With enough background training at speeds somewhat slower than your maximum steady state (which you achieved with proper base building), you can turn your own body into an exquisitely tuned "lactate analyzer." This is something you must do to get the most out of your threshold workouts, especially when you begin to phase in sessions that might cause you to slightly exceed your threshold.

One of the first noticeable changes occurring at the lactate threshold is in the breathing pattern. Depending on the ability of the fibers of the working muscles to take in and use oxygen and to store fuel (also depending on the intensity of the work itself), you begin to breathe either harder or faster or both once you reach your LT. This is due to the fact that extra carbon dioxide is produced from the buffering of lactate by bicarbonates in your blood, from increased burning of carbohydrates to produce energy, and from lactate affecting chemoreceptors in the brain. Once you begin breathing harder and faster (hyperventilating), you've reached your respiratory compensation point and have *already surpassed* your LT. You also begin getting the first hint of tightness, perhaps in the legs, but possibly in the arms or abdomen, when you've operated above (faster than) your LT for several minutes.

At some point, you will want to find the fastest pace that keeps you feeling relaxed and in a good groove, the pace that trains you yet doesn't strain you. This strong, purposeful running is often referred to as a "high-end aerobic pace." This effort level is not a hard pace if sustained for only 20 minutes or so, but it certainly isn't jogging, either. The most effective training speed is at (or slightly slower than) that which you can maintain for about an hour in an all-out, evenly paced race. Beginners will not be able to run at a strong pace for a full hour or more, yet they have a high-end pace, too. They just cannot maintain it very long and may have to run in short segments with walking or jogging breaks when training at this effort level. Lengthening the amount of time you can maintain your high-end pace is part of what cardiovascular development is all about.

Some experienced runners can spend time training at their LT, or high-end, pace nearly every day, but most people are better served by including a greater number of very easy days in between their high-end outings, with perhaps one and one-half to two easy days for every high-end day. Again, cardiovascular development may take somewhat longer with these very easy days included, but it is usually more thorough after several years. Also the baseline fitness you establish with slower runs will contribute to a more ideal running weight; this will allow you the most productive high-end tempo runs.

A good high-end run should feel like one of those outings that begins as a planned easy day but then spontaneously progresses into a memorably awesome, fast run because you begin to get a floating, weightless feeling. As you become more fit, the pace should feel as though it is establishing itself, and you are just along for the ride. One of the keys to achieving this enjoyable and effective state is to start extremely slowly and to remain at this slow pace longer than you think is necessary. Your transition from slow shuffling to faster running should be so gradual that there is no definable point of effort increase. Conscious relaxation assists in achieving a near-effortless maximum steady state. As you gain fitness, you may find that you can reach the high end of aerobic effort sooner during your runs without a conscious attempt to do so. You may also find that you can summon the magic at will and summon it more frequently.

On most high-end runs, you should have the discipline to pull the ripcord, i.e., bring the fast portion of the run to an end, *before* you experience undue struggling or tying up. The amount of time you accumulate *before* struggling actually contributes *more* to your aerobic development than does the time spent fighting on after beginning to suffer. You can occasionally go ahead and release the hounds with a very fast finish to a continuous tempo run if you really feel awesome and want to fly, but try to avoid doing this too often or the effect will be similar to overracing. Of course, if you are extremely tired and cannot find the groove you want, you should stay at an easy pace throughout the entire run.

You can and should perform lactate threshold training for different lengths of time and at various speeds. On continuous threshold efforts, you may skirt right on the brink of struggling and run for a moderately short time (20 minutes or so) or you might hold back slightly from that pace and stay even more controlled for up to an hour. Performing runs of various lengths in this fashion provides a slightly different stimulus for improvement from workout to workout and relieves the possible monotony of grinding out the same pace on every high-end run. Most coaches and physiologists agree that 20 minutes seems to be the "ideal" duration of a true lactate-threshold run, although marathoners often go twice this long. Track athletes typically de-emphasize threshold runs in favor of faster interval work during the competitive season, whereas road racers—especially marathoners—keep them as a staple throughout. For specific suggestions on incorporating threshold runs into your training program, see chapter 3.

Do not hammer these sessions in an attempt to hit a predetermined pace; just allow perceived effort (sensory feedback) to dictate the speed. By all means, avoid racing your high-end runs, either against your training partners or against your times from previous outings. Your aim is to lock into the pace that will train you, yet force a slower runner to strain, i.e., relax a runner, kill a jogger. This pace may vary from day to day, so focus instead on your effort level.

One final note, it is a good policy to wear racing flats for most high-end workouts. Doing so ensures a more natural footstrike and fosters better foot, ankle, and lower-leg strength and flexibility, which will ideally reduce injury risk. Wearing racing flats also affords you the opportunity to achieve the fastest pace for any given effort level.

Finally, regardless of your distance of choice, include year-round, regular speed maintenance in the form of short alactic strides and drills; see chapter 2—in particular the section on neuromuscular training—for details on how to accomplish this.

Build to a Peak of Higher-Intensity Training

When you first experience a nonlinear increase in lactate as a result of increased running intensity, bicarbonates in the blood buffer the lactate entering the bloodstream, which precipitates an increase in CO_2 production. This stage of exercise is known as the *isocapnic buffering period*. At some point, as the intensity increases (or as moderate intensity is prolonged), lactate production exceeds the buffering capacity of the system, resulting in an additional drive to breathe, which marks your respiratory compensation point. In practice, this means you begin hyperventilating and start to have a tight, straining feeling, a sign that you've crossed your lactate threshold.

Isocapnic Buffering Zone

The isocapnic buffering zone is a highly effective training zone that is also fairly safe for many hard workouts at slightly faster than your maximum steady state (at or slightly above your threshold). This involves a very thin window of effort intensity, i.e., even the slightest misjudgment in pace or in duration of effort can send you sailing into distress. The state you want to achieve is a pleasantly challenging or barely uncomfortable feeling that is just short of the onset of hyperventilation. You should be pushing, but should not quite be in trouble. Particularly competitive runners tend to make these workouts harder than they need to be for maximum effectiveness. As with continuous high-end, or LT-pace, running, you might need to experiment to get the effort intensity just right. Consequently, you need to spend some months improving and learning to recognize your maximum steady state before focusing on training in this nebulous area between comfortable and uncomfortable.

You can train most effectively in the isocapnic buffering region by using repeats that feature short rest periods relative to the run periods. An example of such a workout is 10 to 15 × 3 minutes at about 8 to 12 seconds faster than the pace you could run for one hour in an all-out, evenly paced race, with 30 to 60 seconds recovery between each 3-minute bout; less experienced runners should gravitate at first toward the longer recovery interval. Just take enough rest that you are ready to go again and achieve that same nearly uncomfortable feeling by the end of each bout, but pace yourself so that you need only 30 seconds or so between reps. If you feel you are going over the intensity after 8 reps, you can end the session when you finish the 10th rep. If you feel great through 10, you could do 12 or even 15 reps. Remember—do not be a slave to numbers written on a workout schedule. Other sample sessions that achieve this training include 5×7 minutes at slightly faster than one-hour race pace (LT pace) with about 2 minutes of walking or jogging recovery or 3×15 minutes with 3 minutes recovery of mostly jogging. Regardless of the parameters you choose, remember to monitor your physical signs to determine what "zone" you're in and whether you're pushing too hard for the workout.

Breaking up a workout into segments in this fashion allows you to spend more time in the isocapnic buffering zone than would be prudent in a continuous run (although continuous high-end runs are important in their own right and should never be neglected). For example, if you ran longer than, say, 25 minutes at your LT pace, you might drift from being under control to a state of hyperventilation and suffering. However, you could amass more than 30 minutes at a marginally *faster* pace with less distress (and with less continuous pounding) by running those medium-length segments with short rests as outlined previously. Trial and error shows that spending a total of 30 to 45 minutes at your LT pace or slightly faster with these short rests between the work bouts is most effective. Of course, you must first have enough background running to be capable of running at a fairly strong pace for about an hour!

$\dot{V}O_2$max Zone

To produce energy aerobically, your working muscles must *consume* oxygen. **Oxygen uptake** (also known as $\dot{V}O_2$) is a measure of how much oxygen your body is consuming at any given time. It is usually expressed in milliliters (or sometimes in liters) of oxygen consumed per minute of exercise. The $\dot{V}$ in $\dot{V}O_2$ stands for ventilation. The dot over the V represents "per minute" oxygen uptake.

There is an upper limit to how much oxygen your body can consume. This figure varies according to hereditary factors, with training (including childhood activity), and sometimes with living conditions such as high altitude. This maximal oxygen uptake is customarily referred to as $\dot{V}O_2$**max** and can be expressed in either absolute terms (usually milliliters of oxygen consumed per minute) or in relative terms (milliliters of oxygen consumed per minute per kilogram of body mass) to compare values between individuals. Running performance at $\dot{V}O_2$max is strongly assisted by anaerobic energy production, which means that lactate levels can be very high after several minutes of running at maximal oxygen uptake.

Exercise physiologists normally take measurements of an individual's $\dot{V}O_2$max using a maximum effort running test on a treadmill. When following most testing protocols, in which the subject begins at slow speeds and then increases the intensity at regular intervals, there is a speed associated with working at $\dot{V}O_2$max, that is commonly referred to as **velocity at $\dot{V}O_2$max** (or $\dot{V}O_2$max pace). Of course, this value varies from runner to runner, but it is normally the pace that a runner could sustain for roughly nine minutes in an all-out, evenly paced effort.

When training at your $\dot{V}O_2max$, you want to minimize the negative effects of lactic acid accumulation so that your movements remain efficient, muscle groups are recruited in harmonious concert, and aerobic energy production dominates your efforts as long as possible. Therefore, prudent use of training in this zone involves shorter repeats of 2 to 4 minutes each at this pace, with nearly equal rest-to-run ratios and with about 15 to 20 minutes total time spent at the pace. Examples of $\dot{V}O_2max$ workouts would be 8 to 10 × 2 minutes on, 2 minutes off (jogging some or all of the rest period) or 5 × 4 minutes on, 3:30 off. This format works the respiratory muscles, improves the ability of the left ventricle to deliver more blood per stroke, induces maximal oxygen uptake, and provides a small (but not excessive) degree of anaerobic tolerance training. As with easy runs and high-end continuous runs, you can perform these "$\dot{V}O_2max$ repeats" on a cross country course or on a track. These workouts are quite challenging after accumulating 15 to 20 minutes at this pace, but with adequate recovery periods your lactic acid levels should stay somewhat under control, so that you will not tie up and resort to flailing, struggling movements, or even slow down while increasing your effort. For maximum effectiveness, you should pace yourself so that you can run the last few reps in a $\dot{V}O_2max$ session *faster* than you ran the early reps.

It is normally best to keep the run distances or durations constant within the workout, i.e., use all 800s or use all four-minute runs rather than using ladder (also called pyramid) sets or step-down sets. This trains you to monitor effort better and to mount rising fatigue with additional effort in a more linear fashion. It is also desirable to vary the distances from session to session. This provides variety in duration of effort and prevents you from obsessively comparing times from previous workouts, which leads to forcing too fast a pace too early in the session.

If you are feeling pleasantly "itchy" and want to run a little faster than your usual $\dot{V}O_2max$ pace, an effective session consists of running repeats of 30 to 60 seconds each at the speed you could maintain for about six minutes in a race, with equal rest periods in which you jog exactly *twice* as slow as the speed you are using on the work bouts. For example, a high school runner with recent bests of 4:35 for 1,600 meters and 10:00 for 3,200 meters might choose to run repeats of 200 meters in 36 seconds each (about midway between 1,600 race pace and 3,200 race pace), with a jog of 100 meters in 36 seconds between each 200. He continues until it becomes difficult to maintain the pace of the faster segments without tying up. High schoolers are invited to do such workouts; they just shouldn't form the cornerstone of a younger runner's training program, as too often happens.

As with most timed sessions, oxygen uptake workouts should be those in which you let a strong, challenging rhythm come to you, not sessions in which you write down times and hit them at all costs. Most people make enormous improvements in their race times or places once they add a few weeks of these (and faster) workouts, then they incorrectly conclude that hard interval running is the most important type of training. Do not adopt the attitude that killer workouts automatically create fast races; this is not entirely correct. Superior aerobic fitness plus a few judiciously spaced fast workouts (including a killer one here and there) create fast races. Once you have built an adequate base, you can do fast workouts as often as once per week, and "killer" ones perhaps once every three weeks.

Optimize Your Running Time

The reason you should work at certain percentages of parameters such as LT pace and $\dot{V}O_2$max pace is to optimize your time spent running. Over a few months, the person who spends a fair amount of time training within the most favorable guidelines—at speeds that are proven to provide the best return for the investment—gains an advantage over an equally talented fellow runner who strays outside of these boundaries and trains haphazardly too often. This advantage may be minimal during the course of one or two seasons, but if you follow the correct guidelines, the differences become more pronounced after several years of persistent and methodical training.

Having offered that advice, it is crucial that perceived effort almost always trump rigid numbers. Your LT pace and your $\dot{V}O_2$max pace will not be exactly the same every time you attempt to run at some percentage of either of those parameters. Weather conditions, recent diet and hydration, recently run sessions, and so forth all add up to produce workout-to-workout fluctuations in your rate of lactate production or rate of oxygen consumption. It is also all too common for runners to use all-time personal bests or atypical performances when determining their training paces from charts, rather than relying on recent races or on performances they normally produce.

When given the option, runners with big goals are usually headstrong about hitting specific times rather than applying principles to their workouts, but it is more important to get the desired effect than it is to satisfy the stopwatch. Times should be guidelines only. Making a daily practice of hitting fixed times at all costs is often a prescription for reckless overtraining and subsequent burnout.

In the same vein, regimented, canned "systems" that lay out, months in advance, an unmodifiable list of specific daily workouts are about as effective in running as a similarly inflexible scheme is in monetary investment. You may profit a few times by visiting a casino and applying an algorithmic system, but the odds are not in your favor over a longer time frame. You are much better served by diversifying your portfolio while following proven long-term investment principles. Using this approach, you may have seasonal ups and downs, but you will come out ahead in the long haul if you keep your cool. Once you have enough in the bank, you can then use some of your resources to take those really big risks on occasion.

© Empics

For consistent results, let proven principles guide your training.

With that in mind, be wary of strictly paced cookie-cutter training systems offered in books or magazines. Instead, be somewhat flexible and think of critical training speeds (and percentages of them) as a kind of road map, a way of pointing you to the neighborhood the pace should be in on certain workouts. The more often you can hit the exact level of effort that yields the desired result for each session, as opposed to merely adhering to precise pace-per-mile constraints, the more cumulative benefits you will reap over the course of several seasons.

No aspect of fitness stands alone. All physiological systems must be optimized. This is where rigorous, controlled laboratory studies often muddle the training picture by examining only a few factors at once, therefore being of limited scope, particularly if the test subjects are rats, whose "running careers" last only a few months. What is best is to experiment with these restricted findings to see if they blend in favorably with the greater context of long-term training. It is myopic, for example, to believe that raising maximal oxygen uptake is the Holy Grail of training and that 40 miles per week is sufficient total mileage for a serious distance runner. Drawing that conclusion is analogous to quaffing a soft drink, getting a quick energy burst, and reasoning that simple sugars and caffeine are the nutrients that matter most in meeting day-to-day energy requirements. Yes, this will provide a quick fix, but it is not optimal over an extended period. In order for you to reach fruition as a runner, you must incorporate the full spectrum of training, with each energy system worked at its proper time and in satisfactory balance with the training of other systems. To quote Kiyoshi Nakamura, "When you break down a car, it is nothing more than pieces of iron, rubber, plastic, and glass. But when they are all put together in a correct way, it becomes a car. What would happen if even one of many screws is deformed?"

186

Each workout should have a purpose. A well-placed easy, shake-out run is just as important a training tool as a seven-mile run at a strong pace, and (depending on the time of year) it's likely more important than 10 stomach-knotting 400s as far as long-term development is concerned. Do not merely train harder than your competitors; train smarter! Follow the proven principles that have elevated great runners to the pinnacle of the sport. Above all, you must be a runner, not just a person who runs, to achieve your full potential. That is, if you love training and racing enough to persevere through the difficult times, you will likewise relish those magic moments of effortless soaring.

CHAPTER 10

Peaking for a Key Race

GWYN COOGAN, PHD, AND MARK COOGAN

In any given year, there are usually one or two races at which you really want to run your best—in running parlance, to "peak" at the right time. We provide you with both general and specific strategies that Olympians and everyday runners alike have successfully implemented in their training programs to be ready to rip at just the right moment. These address both the physical aspects of preparation such as key workouts, tapering, and nutrition and the mental aspects such as positive visualization, course familiarity, and knowing the competition. This comprehensive package will greatly increase your chances of success at your next big race.

Before we delve into things that will help you peak perfectly, you need to start by determining well in advance the race at which you'd like to be most ready to perform well—be it the state high-school championship meet or the Olympic Trials—and marking the event date on your calendar. By working backward from the date of your peak race to the present, you can establish not only the *whens*, but also the *whats*, and *hows* of your training, and from there, you can put specific training strategies into play. For example, if you have a year until your big event, you can effectively use periodization in your training by establishing base work or foundational miles, shift into intervals or faster-paced training, and then work on peaking at the right time for your event. If, on the other hand, you have only four months, you need to spend correspondingly less time building your base before moving into the sharpening and peaking phases.

It's important to remember that improvements in distance running typically don't come quickly. Depending on your age, experience, and ability level, the process of getting faster may mean carving only a few seconds from your personal best time in your event of choice every year. Do not let this be a cause for dismay; in fact, these small improvements are what you want to look for; in simplest terms this means your hard work is paying off.

189

Plan Your Training

Now that you've set an event to peak for, you can more effectively plan your training to optimize your performance at that race. If your peak race is nine months or more away, then doing three or four months of base work now is the key to successful racing later. If your goal race is four months away, you'll still want to spend half of that time base-building. This type of training, as the name implies, serves as a foundation for the rest of your training program. You can't benefit from the hard interval workouts required for quality racing late in the season without first doing base work; your body won't be able to handle the more intense work, and injury and illness usually pursue runners who don't allow adequate base training. Base work gradually strengthens muscles, joints, and tendons and effects the necessary cardiovascular adaptations needed for faster training during the racing season.

Many runners who want to go straight into hard interval training overlook the importance of base work. For a world-class marathoner, base building might mean distance runs of 8 to 12 miles plus a long run of 90 minutes to three hours on the weekend. Base work also includes drills, plyometrics, weightlifting, or other cross-training that allows you to strengthen supporting muscles. By the end of the base-work phase, you should feel as strong as an ox. You might occasionally run a great race at this stage of your training, but don't expect to run your fastest during this phase.

When doing base work, it's helpful to be more concerned with the time spent on your feet running than the total miles you're covering. Keep in mind that you're laying the foundation for the rest of your season. In response to some of his runners' ideas regarding summer road races, former University of Maryland coach and current Lasalle College coach Charles Torpey was known to say, "No way are you racing. You're putting money in the bank so you can make a major withdrawal next spring at nationals." He was right—base work makes runners better able to move forward with their training programs. You may, however, need to race occasionally during this time to stay motivated, for the camaraderie, or to show support for the cause of a given race. But if you must race during this phase, remember your primary goal—the races at the end of the season that you are peaking for—and realize that you may have to race while tired. You may even have to eat the dust of your archrival. If, however, you can bear in mind that the race you need to be best prepared for is still several months away, swallowing your pride should pose no problem.

After your base is solid, you'll move into more specific preparatory phases—typically strengthening, when you begin longer interval work, tempo (or lactate-threshold) runs, and possibly hills; sharpening, when you begin racing and add shorter intervals to build speed and a strong finishing kick; and peaking, when you spend several weeks preparing for that all-important goal race. Specifics on planning these phases in the context of your own program and race goals are found in chapter 3; chapter 9 deals with some of the underlying physiology.

Consider Race Conditions

It's wise to consider what conditions you're likely to face at your goal race: hot and humid versus cold and windy, hilly versus flat, evening versus morning, road versus track versus some other type of surface. If, for example, you're training for a certain marathon in Boston, you should be aware of the marked downhill stretches leading up to the "Heartbreak Hill" series of climbs beginning in the town of Newton. For this reason, in preparing for the Boston Marathon, it's extremely important to incorporate not only lots of uphill running but also plenty of downhill into your training program; experienced runners targeting Boston all make sure that their long runs include some major climbs and descents.

One 22-mile training loop in Boulder, Colorado—a storied training mecca for world-class marathon aspirants from around the world—is known locally as "over the top" or "Old Stage." Sixteen miles into the run, the loop climbs a small mountain for the next five miles. The uphill climb starts gradually but increases in pitch and difficulty to the point that you feel as if your nose is nearly scraping the road before you. After reaching the top, it's a quick and steep descent back into Boulder. I (Mark) feel that this was my "make-or-break" workout in training for the Boston Marathon and the 1996 Olympic Trials. If I could feel like I was still running and not simply dragging at the top of the mountain, and I wasn't too beat up the next day, then I knew my fitness was such that I was in a position to have a good marathon race. This is the kind of mental and physical workout you want to do to prepare for your peak race. The cardiovascular and structural strength gained from running over these hills helps you withstand the continual pounding in a race such as the Boston Marathon, or, for that matter, any hilly marathon.

In preparing for the Boston Marathon, or any long race with significant downhill stretches—especially toward the end—include hard running on a slight downhill, such as 1,000-meter repeats at approximately 10K race pace. This prepares your quads for the pounding they'll take during the marathon; as long as you don't overdo it, the added muscle strength and resiliency gained from these types of intervals helps prevent some of the damage that comes from running a hilly course. Another useful workout for preparing for a hilly marathon course is an 18-mile run that includes three long repeats. Do a 20-minute warm-up, then 15 minutes at marathon race pace or slightly faster, followed by 5 minutes of easy recovery running. Do this three times, then complete the run at an easy pace. This workout can be done anywhere, of course, but doing it over undulating terrain is great mental and physical preparation for a rolling racecourse. In a long run, 15 minutes is a long time to concentrate for a single interval, and doing three of them requires, and builds, concentration, a necessity for any marathoner. When you can complete this session, you can be confident that you can notch a good marathon.

Be sure to take into account aspects of your goal race that might be unusual. For example, in specifically preparing for Boston, try to do some of your long runs at noon, which is when the race starts; because this is an unusual start time for any long-distance race, it's important to see how a midday race affects your digestive system and vice versa so that you can plan your meals accordingly. What will your body tolerate for breakfast before your peak race? It's important to know in advance.

The same thing is true of an evening race. It takes practice to figure out what type of food works well for a race late in the day. If possible, run a few interval workouts at the same time your peak race is scheduled. Can you sneak in a nap on race day if the event is happening at night? Moreover, can you take a nap and not be drowsy later? You need to answer questions like these in training well before the event.

If you're preparing for an event like the LaSalle Bank Chicago Marathon, certain aspects of your approach will be different. Chicago's pancake-flat course is more reminiscent of a 10K on the track than it is of the ups and downs of the Boston Marathon. In this scenario, it would be reasonable to do many of the same track or short-interval workouts you would if your goal race were a 10K, but you should also throw in long runs of 20 to 23 miles at a good clip. When you run a flat marathon after a sound period of training, you don't get beat up physically so much as you become exhausted simply from running out of energy,

Each competition presents unique challenges. Prepare and train for the specific conditions you will face on race day.

whereas on a hilly course mechanical factors can slow you long before you're actually out of gas. A staple "aerobic power" workout for a Chicago-type course would be 10 to 12 × (1,000 meters at about 10K race pace with two minutes rest). Pace and rhythm are very important components of a successfully run marathon on the flat.

Of course, not everyone is a marathoner, but the same principles apply—be ready for anything your race is apt to throw your way. If you're getting ready for a cross country race, ask yourself what the course is like: Might it be muddy? Do the hills appear early on, late in the race, or both? Does the course narrow right away, necessitating a fast start for establishing position, or is it wide open? What's the probable range of weather conditions? Are you certain your shoes are appropriate for the terrain and distance? How large will the field be? Leave no stone unturned!

Another great way to prepare for a road or cross country event is to run some sections of the course well before race day if possible. If you live close to the race site, you may even get a chance to run a shorter race on the same course at some point in the year. If possible, visit a friend who lives near your race site and run a section of the course with him or her. It's helpful during a race to have mental associations with certain points along the course, especially the last 10 miles of a marathon. You can also manufacture these benchmarks if you have to; see "Stay on Task the Day Before" later in this chapter.

Know Your Competitive Environment

Thinking about the competitive environment you will face on race day, is also important. Will you be able to choose a spot near the starting line or be packed in tight with 10,000 others? Will you have a chance to hit the bathroom at the last minute, or will you be required to stand behind the line 30 minutes before the gun?

If you are a male 2:30 marathoner, there will be women ahead of you at Boston or Chicago. If you are a female 3:00 marathoner, there will be men your same height but twice as heavy running the same pace as you with impossibly long, ungainly strides; these people will likely try to outkick you at the end of the race. If you are running a cross country race, 90 percent of the field will go out too fast. You have a choice; you can also go out too fast but try to minimize the length of your sprint, or you can learn how to be extremely disciplined and self-aware and work your way up through the field as the race progresses. Either way, you need to train for your anticipated competitive environment so that you know how to respond and what tactic works best for you. You can even practice crowded track or cross country starts with teammates or clubmates so you won't be thrown (or thrown to the ground!) by rough starts on goal race day.

If you're running a megarace such as the New York City Marathon, you may have to stand in the cold and rain for two hours before you race. If this is the case, learn some stretches or maybe yoga that can help you simulate a running

193

Doing Right by Accident: Mark's 1996 Olympic Trials Marathon

I was living in Boulder, Colorado, toward the end of 1995. I had just come off of a wonderful track season in which I'd run 13:23 for 5,000 meters and finished second to Bob Kennedy in the U.S. Championships. In the fall, I made the World Cross Country team at Boston's Franklin Park despite having a terrible wipeout five miles into the 10K race, slipping on a cobblestone and hurting my hip. I had four cortisone shots in that hip over the next four months leading up to the Olympic Marathon Trials in Charlotte, North Carolina.

Boulder is a training base for many excellent runners from all over the world. Runners seem to come and go constantly. When I started preparing for the Trials race by doing lots of distance work in the fall, there were plenty of people to train with. At least 10 guys showed up for long runs at the Boulder Reservoir, sessions we'd start at either Mark Plaatjes's house (he was the World Champion in the marathon) or at my home. It was a great fall.

As it turned out, it was a snowy winter in Boulder for marathon training. I remember a lot of guys suddenly saying right after Christmas that they were going to go away and train for the Trials in Mexico or somewhere else with dependable weather. I thought, "Wow, these guys are so lucky—they're going away to train." I was jealous of them for being able make running their number one priority. I felt as if I were stuck in Boulder by myself.

Although I couldn't see it then, in the end, staying put worked out great because I was in the most comfortable environment for me at that time. We had a two-year-old daughter, and Gwyn was wrapping up her PhD and training for the women's Olympic Marathon Trials, so training away from home would have been impossible. When I think about the situation now, I see that I made the correct decision, not because I wanted to, but because I had to. The reasons? For one, I knew every one of my training runs. I knew my loops. I knew what a time meant on a certain run. I didn't have to adjust to a new training environment. If I went out to the reservoir and did my 10.3-mile loop in 58 minutes, I knew I was flying; if it took 70 minutes, then I knew was a bit tired and should think about backing off. I was sleeping in my own bed. I had no problems sleeping, no jet lag, and no sickness from traveling. I knew what food I could eat and that the water was safe to drink. I could continue to see Al Kupczak, my excellent massage therapist. If we had a major snowstorm, I could go to the fitness club and run on a treadmill. In short, I had everything I needed right there in Boulder, even if I didn't realize it at first when faced with the superficial glamour of training abroad.

My training went well. I still had a few good friends to run with a few days a week, and even the cold weather turned out to be a blessing because the Trials race was run in freezing-cold conditions in Charlotte. I remember eating lunch at the Trials and listening to loads of people complain about the cold and telling myself, "It's just like Boulder. You'll be fine, Mark."

In the Trials race my strategy was very simple. I thought Bob Kempainen was the best runner in the field and also the most consistent. I don't think he ever had a bad marathon. I decided to watch him and try to cover any move he made, but gradually. If Bob made a big move, I told myself I had one mile to reel him back in. I did this once in the middle of the race and again when Bob broke the race open to make it a three-person affair at 19 or 20 miles. Bob led me to a second-place finish at the Trials, a spot on the U.S. Olympic Team.

By staying put and training in Boulder, I prepared correctly, not because I wanted to, but because it was in the hand I was dealt. In the end, the best environment for Mark Coogan turned out to be exactly the one I started in. The lesson? Don't change what works, and don't follow up successes with radical changes. Chances are, if you keep doing what you've done, you'll continue getting what you need to perform well.

warm-up and practice this routine before one of your long runs to see how it makes you feel during the run. Alternatively, practice using the first two miles of a long run as a race warm-up.

Another aspect of the competitive environment to consider is your buddies. Will your best buddy be at the race? Will you have people who know you along the course like you did in the race at home? Prepare for this—a little support can mean a lot in terms of your performance. If you're traveling alone, visualize all of the sources of support—human and otherwise—that helped get you to the line intact and ready to roll. Running for causes is a ready source of midrace strength and inspiration; in today's racing world, companionship and camaraderie are there for the taking.

Fine-Tune During the Last Month

In the last four weeks before your goal race, focus on details that will deliver you to race day as prepared as you can be. Giving yourself several weeks to rehearse important details minimizes your chances of omitting something crucial.

Although the following checklist centers on the marathon, it's applicable to a variety of distances. Many items may appear to be common-sense points, but a surprising number of experienced runners neglect the "little essentials" when looking at the big picture as race day looms.

195

- Select your racing shoes. Make sure you have run in them at least three times before race day to be sure they're suitable and broken in, particularly if you are running a marathon.

- Practice drinking fluids. Have you tried in training taking in the fluids you'll consume during the race? It's important that you try your preferred drinks (or gels) during harder interval efforts and faster distance runs to simulate how they will affect you in a race—it always feels a bit funny to run at top speed with a belly full of fluid that's bouncing around. If necessary, switch brands or mix your drink at a stronger or weaker concentration; for some, this can make all the difference in the world. Experimentation is the only way to find out what works.

- Choose your clothing. Wear the singlet and shorts you'll use during the race in a "practice race" during the buildup to your goal event. Pay attention to how the uniform feels. If it chafes or clings to your body when it's wet from either sweat or rain, change uniforms. If the race will likely be held in cold conditions, choose a suitable hat and gloves. Is it easy to hold a cup of water with these gloves on? At what temperature will you consider wearing a T-shirt under your singlet? It's important to answer these questions, and putting them off until race week rolls around will add to your stress level.

- Visualize the race as it approaches. Don't think about it only on runs or when talking to a coach; start to think about it at night when you go to bed. Visualize yourself in good position throughout the race and sticking to your splits and your plan. See yourself running up to your potential and striving for a great run regardless of your finish. Picture yourself breaking the tape. In the last week before the event, try to run the race in your head at least once a day. It is impossible to mentally "run" an entire marathon, but you can run a 5K or 10K in your head and see yourself through a great performance from wire to wire. If you are running a marathon, imagine the feeling you'll have at the start. How do you feel when you see other racers and runners you recognize as well as those who are strangers? How will a large crowd affect you? Try to concern yourself only with things you can control (and will therefore have taken care of) before the race; beyond these, try to go with the flow. For example, don't get too worked up if your ride to the start is late or if there's a line at the bathroom. Try to keep your routine, but don't stress out if you have to improvise a bit. If you can visualize things happening smoothly in advance, it is more likely that they will go smoothly on race day.

- Get your rest. During the week of the race, you should cut back all unnecessary activities. Try to get extra rest as your body recharges from the hard training you've done. If you ordinarily work full-time and are able to take a couple of days or half-days off during the marathon week, resist the temptation to burn off extra energy by doing work around the house. It's common to hear of people training for a marathon and finally getting to the week of the race feeling so good that they start a new project at home. Couch time with a book or some movies is a good race-week "project," whereas painting the house or doing landscaping is not.

- Don't make significant changes to your eating or sleeping routines. The athletic body thrives on predictability and patterns.

- Focus on the positive aspects of your training. This is a good time to take stock of all the training you've done and to focus on the effective features of your training plan. You can't change the past, but you can accept it. Don't get caught up comparing your long runs and interval sessions with those of your friends. This will drive you crazy, and worse, it may drive you to do silly things, like squeeze in one last long run that you don't need, or run all of your final week's mileage at marathon pace. Look at your training and tell yourself that you have done a good job. No matter what, you're going to have to work hard on race day, so focus your energies on that day, not on wondering whether you've trained well enough.

Stay on Task the Day Before

If you've had to travel to your race, you're probably at the race city a day early, and you may be tempted by your surroundings—tempted to enjoy the local food or the local tourist sites, tempted to stand in line at the runners' expo to get Amy Rudolph's autograph. Resist these temptations unless you're somehow sure that partaking in them will improve your race. A quick trip through the walk-through heart at the Franklin Institute before the Philadelphia Half-Marathon, for example, might actually inspire you, but you might pull something exploring the submarines docked in the harbor. Instead, send your buddies out to these sites so that you can be lazy.

You may also be tempted to run with people you don't usually train with, such as an old buddy from college the day before the race. Admit it—you are competitive or you wouldn't be doing this in the first place, and you may feel the need to prove yourself even in the last few days before the race. There is nothing you can do here but hurt yourself. Let your buddies think that you are slow and weak. Then amaze them on race day.

As far as whether or not to take the four-hour bus tour of your marathon course, it's a matter of personal preference. It may help you to see the whole course, but it might help you more to take that time and walk the last three miles of the course. Or pick out distinct spots along the course that you'll look forward to the next day, like the cute coffee shop or the park where you had a chance to play with your children while checking out the surroundings. Another idea is to drive an often troubling section of the course—miles 13 to 18 or miles 17 to 21 of a marathon course, for example—and then focus on your plan for these miles.

197

Gwyn: Little Things Mean a Lot

I wish I could say that my all-time favorite race was the 10,000 meters at the 1992 Barcelona Olympics. But despite the obvious honor and prestige of that race, the truth is that just as with most runners, certain "small" races resonate more strongly in my mind. These races have motivated me to train harder than before, have rewarded hard training, and have justified the sacrifices that staying in racing shape requires—races that, in short, have kept me racing.

The races that fit this category share a few attributes. Understand that I have always tended toward pessimism regarding my own capabilities. Like many runners, I worry. It's not the weather that worries me. Nor is it how my shorts are going to look. It's me, all me. I worry about whether I'll feel good, whether I'm fit enough, whether I'm strong enough, whether I am fooling myself by even entering the race, whether I'll run intelligently, and whether this whole escapade is, in fact, a waste of human endeavor and natural resources. I truly love to run and train; running has introduced me to many interesting people, given me the chance to get to know them in the crazy, intimate way that results from training together. But the worries can really get to me at times and cast a shadow over all the fun.

So my favorite races are the ones that my worries drove me to train for effectively, but not stupidly. The ones in which I was able to maintain a positive mental and emotional outlook despite my worries and any negative feedback I might have received. The ones in which I truly surprised myself, mostly by letting go of that ever-lurking mental storm cloud.

I spent the spring semester of my sophomore year of college at Harvey Mudd College in Claremont, California. It was then that I first ran track. John Goldhammer was my coach, and the meet that sticks in my mind was a dual meet against our biggest rival, Occidental College. Like most distance runners, I often ran two or three races in each meet—1,500s, 3,000s, and 5,000s—but because this was our next-to-last meet before the conference championships and the NCAA Division III Nationals, I had asked Goldhammer if I could run just the 800 meters for a change of pace.

I had never run the 800 before, and I was worried about running with the "real" runners. As a result of this concern, I rested up the week before the race; other times I might have reacted to the same situation by overtraining, but not this time—I knew I couldn't train for an 800 in a week and that my best option was to go in fresh.

I had never started on a stagger before. In fact, I wore cross country racing flats for this race. I was in lane six or seven.

Let me take you through it. It is evening in Los Angeles. I pretend that I am fast and that I belong in this race, and I lean over. A gun is fired, and I take off. There are horses to my right and my left as we approach the man with the flag, where the stagger ends. I am going to have to either slow down and find a place behind all of the other runners on the inside or speed up just a tad to move smoothly and efficiently over to the rail before the next turn begins. I do it—I speed up, and before I know it, I am at the front of the race, running for my life.

I round the turn and head down the straightaway, knowing that I'm out of my mind, that I don't belong in the front of this race; but I also know that slowing down would have cost me too much. I can hear my teammates and Goldhammer cheering wildly. They can't believe that this is the same conservative girl who has won the races she has won by steadily doling out her energy lap by lap, checking her reserves and modifying her pace accordingly. I hear my 400-meter split: 65, my fastest ever.

I suddenly realize: This, racing, is fun. The team isn't counting on my points, and there is no pressure, just me and my spirit. Four runners go around me just after the next turn, with 300 meters to go, and a few others pass me on the final bend, but I hold on as best I can. I know I am slowing down, but still I hold on, thinking that my endurance might come into play in the homestretch. This was staying positive.

I did not set any records; I ran 2:18, and got sixth or seventh. But because I prepared properly, conquered my doubts, and ran for the finish line rather than from phantom fears, I still have fun thinking about this race, which propelled me to greater heights during my competitive career just as strongly as my training did.

It's a good idea to check out the location of the starting line the day before the race. It's good to know how long it will take you to get to the start whether you're walking or driving. Make sure you also find out exactly where the finish line is. Take a good look at it; this is your target.

The night before the race, make sure you have everything you need for the race ready and packed before going to sleep. If possible, have your number already pinned on your singlet. Have your racing shoes ready, your sweats laid out, and everything else you need for the race all set to go. This should give you some peace of mind when you settle in for your last night of sleep.

Your last large meal should be lunch the day before, not dinner; stay away from pasta buffets at 8:00 p.m. when your race is at 7:00 a.m.! By the time you hit the sack, your urine should be clear, but don't go so heavy on the liquids that you're forced to clamber out of bed and into the john every hour.

Don't be surprised if, just as with kids on Christmas Eve, excitement keeps you from sleeping well the night before the race. It's normal to toss and turn a bit and make a few bathroom trips; rest is more important the week leading up to the event as a whole than it is on the last night. Stories abound of people getting up in the middle of the night to eat something before a race so that they feel as if they have enough energy in their system.

© David Gonzales/Icon SMI

Spend the final hours before the race in calm and deliberate preparation. Maintain your focus, and you'll be rested and ready for the main event.

Go Get 'Em on Race Day

On the morning of the race, try to maintain your normal routine. It's a good idea get up at least two and a half hours before the start. Take a relaxing shower and then eat a light breakfast two hours before the gun goes off. If you drink coffee, do it early (and don't overdo it). A bagel or toast makes an easily digested meal; by this time you should have tried several things and know what works for you. You may have received a new type of energy bar in your expo packet—don't even think of eating anything for the first time on race day!

If you can, get to the race site 60 to 90 minutes before the start so you can get your bearings. Hopefully you will have seen the course, or at a minimum, the start and finish area, the day before. It is important to avoid making your prerace regimen a social hour; this is a time to gather your thoughts and energy for the race. Tell family and friends that you'll see them at the finish line. If you're a caretaker by inclination, then it will be hard to resist making sure everyone around you is happy, so avoid putting yourself in this position. For mothers especially, it's fun to have your children around you, but you will all be happier in the end if you can find someone else you trust to care for them in the last hours before the race. Let them know it's important for you to be able to focus beforehand so they don't unwittingly interrupt your last-minute preparations (most people familiar with competitive runners quickly come to understand this).

By this time, you've figured out what it takes for you to feel warmed up and ready to go. Stick to the same warm-up routine as always. A suggestion: One hour before the start, stand up and do some very easy stretching. Then go for a 10- to 15-minute jog. When you're done jogging, head to the bathroom, but don't count on this being your last trip. Then find a quiet area where you can relax, continue stretching, and change into your racing gear. Try to select a quiet place, but be in a position to hear prerace announcements. Do a few easy strides, put your racing flats on, and do a few more strides of 100 meters or so, then head for the starting line. This is a time for positive self-talk: Tell yourself to be tough or that you'll try to stay with so-and-so.

Finally, remind yourself that it is a privilege to train and race. Go get 'em!

CHAPTER 11

Making Your Recovery Count

PETE PFITZINGER, MS

Hard workouts are necessary for your body to achieve a higher fitness level, but an adequate amount of time is needed to recover from these hard workouts to allow your body to adapt. Gradually, as you put in a series of hard workouts, the fatigue incurred during a workout decreases and the rebuilding response from the training stimulus makes you a slightly better runner; however, the key word here is *gradually*.

Imagine the benefits, in terms of improved running performance, you can realize if you recover more quickly. If you are a serious runner who puts a great deal of effort into planning and executing your training, then also take the time to plan your recovery. In fact, it can be argued that your improvement as a highly motivated runner is chiefly limited by your ability to recover. This chapter focuses on the science of recovery as well as on training strategies to improve recovery, prevent injury, and make you an overall stronger runner.

How the body adapts to training is simple. First, you must train hard enough to provide a stimulus for some aspect of your body's physiology to improve. In the short term, hard training actually causes negative effects—fatigue, energy depletion, and tissue breakdown. All of these reduce your ability to train hard or race. A period of time is required to return your body to the level it was before the workout. With continued recovery, supercompensation—the improvement resulting from the training stimulus—occurs. Breaking down the training adaptation process into these steps makes it clear that getting the training stimulus right and optimizing your recovery are equally important.

Your muscles and cardiovascular system adapt over days and weeks because of the cumulative effect of repeated training. The precise balance among the intensity, duration, and frequency of your training influences the rate at which your body adapts. The changes in hormone levels, fat burning ability, capillary density, and so on that result from endurance training occur through repeated training bouts and your body's response to these workouts.

The physical and mental fatigue, energy depletion, and tissue breakdown caused by training limit your ability to handle an increased training load. Therefore, in developing an optimal training program, you must only train hard when your body is ready to train hard; otherwise, your rate of improvement will be suboptimal and your running performance may actually deteriorate. If you can increase your recovery rate, you will accelerate your body's rate of positive adaptation to training. When you start to view overtraining as *underrecovery*, you are well on your way to understanding how to improve your training program, and therefore, your running performance.

At the simplest level, the hard–easy principle of training allows recovery by always following hard training efforts with one or more easier training sessions. Recovery training is simply lower-intensity exercise done between hard workouts or after a race to enhance your recovery. This easy training enhances recovery primarily by increasing blood flow to and from your muscles, which removes waste products (accumulated during harder training) while providing an influx of essential nutrients to these muscles. These processes help muscles rebuild and recover more quickly—reducing the amount of time before you can resume hard training.

Genetics and lifestyle factors are responsible for the great variation among runners in how long it takes them to recover from and adapt to a workout. Your genetics determine your predisposition to adapt to training; it is a cruel fact that some runners are "programmed" to adapt more quickly than others. Lifestyle factors such as diet, quantity and quality of sleep, general health, age (we tend to recover more slowly as we get older), gender (women tend to recover more slowly than men because of lower testosterone levels), and various life stressors such as work and relationships all influence how quickly you recover from and adapt to training. The stress created by lifestyle factors is difficult to evaluate and depends in large part on your reaction to that stress. Your individual psychological makeup determines whether a given amount of stress is too much or can be tolerated relatively easily. Although you may not have a great deal of control over certain stresses in your life, how you manage the lifestyle factors you *can* control may determine whether your running performance improves or whether it stagnates.

These factors combine to create a large variation among runners in how many hard training sessions they can positively adapt to in a given period of time. By having a plan to optimize your recovery, you can help ensure that you improve as a runner as quickly as your genetics will allow.

Understanding Overtraining and Overreaching

Fatigue for a couple of days after a hard training session isn't necessarily a sign of overtraining. In fact, it is a necessary step in the recovery and development process. When a runner applies training stress in the appropriate amounts and with adequate recovery, he optimizes his rate of improvement. If training stress is above the optimal level, or recovery is less than optimal, improvement may still occur, but more slowly. Only above a runner's individual "training threshold" and over time does true overtraining occur. We call the zone between optimal training for improvement and the point at which performance decreases *overreaching*. This zone—often a precursor to overtraining—is where many dedicated runners spend much of their time.

Overreaching occurs when a runner violates the hard–easy principle and strings together too many days of hard training without allowing the body to rest between these sessions. The muscle fatigue you experience when you overreach is most likely due to glycogen (carbohydrate) depletion, and when this happens, you simply need time for metabolic recovery; a few days of easy training combined with a high-carbohydrate diet should quickly remedy the situation. The combined effects of dehydration, lack of sleep, and the addition of other life stresses on top of normal training—all of which can hinder recovery from hard training—can also cause overreaching. In all of these cases, runners can and should rebound within a few days of removing the offending stressors. Cross-training can provide much-needed mental variety to help recover from overreaching.

However, if you don't remove the stressors, repeated or prolonged overreaching eventually leads to overtraining syndrome, which takes substantially longer to correct. If a few days of reduced training and increased rest do not help correct the fatigue and poor running performance that result from overreaching, then it's likely that illness or overtraining syndrome is involved. Overtraining is at least partly regulated by the hypothalamus, which is essentially the brain's master control center for dealing with stress and regulating body temperature, sugar and fat metabolism, and the release of a variety of hormones. When the capabilities of the hypothalamus are overwhelmed by a combination of hard training and general life stressors, the result is overtraining syndrome. The symptoms are fatigue, decreased motivation, irritability, and poor running performance.

The physiological and psychological components of overtraining are inseparable. Physiological recovery from overtraining, which can take weeks or months depending on the severity of the situation, is obviously essential, but equally important is rekindling the desire and mental energy for training and competition. Most athletes with overtraining syndrome have symptoms of depression and disturbed sleep (the role of sleep in recovery is addressed later in this chapter). Other symptoms such as fatigue have both physical and psychological aspects; overtrained athletes almost invariably report that even moderate training sessions are harder than they should be. Recovery from overtraining generally requires training and lifestyle changes that increase the variety of training and provide general relaxation as well as physical recovery.

Incorporating the Five Periods of Recovery

Adequate recovery is necessary within a training session, between hard workouts, and over the weeks, months, and years of your running career. You need to manage your training and recovery over five different lengths of time, and each of these periods requires different strategies to optimize your running performance. The following are training considerations and recovery strategies for each of the five recovery periods.

Within a Training Session

The recovery options available to you during a training session are limited, but important for optimal training. During a workout, your recovery strategies should ensure that you complete the training session at the desired pace.

For a long run, your recovery plan should include taking in fluids and carbohydrate to prevent dehydration and carbohydrate depletion. During an interval session, the length of recovery between hard efforts should be short enough to keep your metabolic rate from decreasing too much (excessive recovery reduces the quality of your workout), but long enough to allow you to complete the workout at the intended pace. If your pace judgment is reasonably accurate, then interval sessions in which your pace progressively slows are generally the result of insufficient recovery. Cooling down at the end of a hard training session is an important first step in preparing for your next workout and is discussed later in this chapter.

Between Hard Workouts

Your ability to recover between hard workouts is critical in improving your running performance because it determines your ability to train hard again. The recovery strategies between hard workouts include recovery training such as easy days of running or cross-training, replacement of nutrients, and a variety of supplementary recovery methods. Recovery training sessions improve blood flow to and from the muscles, which helps to improve recovery and prepare you for your next hard workout. Recovery runs and cross-training recovery options are discussed in detail in later sections in this chapter.

Dietary strategies for recovery between hard workouts include drinking fluids for rehydration, ingesting carbohydrate to replace glycogen stores, and consuming protein for optimal regeneration of muscles and other tissues; these are covered in the next section. Finally, most of the supplementary recovery strategies discussed later in this chapter—such as massage and hot–cold contrast therapy—are used primarily to improve recovery between hard workouts.

Scheduling a minirecovery block of two successive recovery days each week helps you avoid overreaching and allows continued progression in your running performance. Fatigue is often due to glycogen depletion, and two days of recovery provide enough time to refill your glycogen stores. Scheduling two recovery days in a row allows you to regain your physical and mental energy levels and provides time for muscle tissue repair.

Successive recovery days are particularly appropriate for recovery from delayed-onset muscle soreness (DOMS), which occurs particularly after a race or hard workout that includes downhill running. (Chapter 1 delves into the mechanics of downhill running and its potential hazards; chapters 2 and 10 offer suggested workouts incorporating downhills.) DOMS is caused by microscopic damage to muscle fibers and the surrounding connective tissue as a result of eccentric muscle contractions. An eccentric muscle contraction is a lengthening or "braking" contraction. When you run downhill, your quadriceps muscles contract eccentrically to keep your knees from buckling when your feet strike the ground, and the steeper and longer the downhill, the worse the damage.

DOMS is generally most severe 24 to 72 hours after hard downhill running, because inflammation—and thus pain—does not set in immediately after muscle-damaging exercise. "Running through" DOMS delays the repair process; your muscles' resiliency—and thus their resistance to injury—are at all-time lows during DOMS, so avoid running until the soreness

© Empics

Adequate recovery between hard workouts allows for the replenishment of vital nutrients and the repair of damaged tissue.

diminishes. Low-impact cross-training during this time, however, will increase circulation through the damaged muscle fibers, facilitating the removal of waste products and accelerating the repair process. A light massage while your muscles are sore may also help reduce the symptoms of DOMS.

Recovery Weeks

With each successive week of training, you provide additional stimulus for improvement but also become progressively more fatigued, so that after a few weeks your body needs a recovery week to continue to adapt positively. The number of weeks of hard training before a recovery week that is right for you depends on how hard you train as well as on individual lifestyle and genetic factors determining your overall ability to recover. The optimal pattern for most runners seems to be two to four high-effort weeks followed by one recovery week; the most commonly successful ratio is three harder weeks to one easier week.

Recovery weeks are vital for progress as a runner—they allow your body to adapt to the key workouts during your harder training weeks. Almost invariably, when runners break down in training, it is at least partially attributable to violating the recommended training pattern of two to four hard weeks followed by a recovery week. After several hard weeks without more complete recovery, a weak link breaks down and one or more weeks of training are lost to injury or illness. Useful guidelines for a recovery week are to do 60 to 70 percent of your previous week's mileage, replace one or more runs with cross-training, and eliminate hard sessions such as intervals.

As with the other periods of recovery, recovery weeks address mental aspects of training as well. After several hard weeks of training, it is refreshing to be able to go out for relaxed, enjoyable runs and cross-training sessions without having to produce a purposeful effort. By the end of your recovery week, you should feel energetic and look forward to the next string of hard weeks. If you have not recovered after one week, reevaluate your overall training program to assess whether you are doing too much high-intensity training or are not allowing enough recovery between hard sessions.

Recovery Blocks

Build at least two recovery blocks of several weeks' duration into your training over the course of a year to allow complete recovery from training and competition. It is ideal to insert recovery blocks after you have trained seriously for, and competed successfully in, a goal race. The recovery is a well-earned physical and mental reward. When training or racing do not go so well, however, is when you really need a recovery block. Without recovery blocks, you can almost guarantee that you will eventually lose enthusiasm for hard training, and your racing performances will suffer.

Distance runners who are highly successful year after year invariably include low-key recovery blocks in their training programs. A recovery block can include as few as 3 weeks or as many as 10 weeks of scheduled downtime before you prepare to reach new goals. Recovery blocks are not necessarily periods in which you do not run; rather, they are stretches in which your running or activity level is stress free. During a recovery block, avoid intervals, tempo runs, long runs, and monotonous training. You may want to take a complete break from running during part of your recovery block, and instead, stay active by trying other activities that you usually do not have time for. Recovery blocks rejuvenate your body and help you regain a hunger for hard training and competition. Many runners find that after a week or so of not running they go stir crazy and start back running seriously too soon. Trying other types of physical activity during this period will help ensure that you enjoy these planned breaks from training.

Recovery Years

For optimal running success, also schedule harder and easier years of training and racing. If not planned for, the body generally dictates its own recovery year by breaking down, leading to weeks or months of frustration. Or, you might just find that you have a year in which no matter how hard you try, your hard training sessions are mediocre and your racing performances are lackluster.

While the need for extending the hard–easy principle over multiple years is most obvious for world-class runners preparing for a peak effort at the Olympics, it is also useful for runners who want to maintain enthusiasm for training and competition over the many years of their running careers. By planning a less-intense training and racing schedule every two to four years, you can help ensure that your running progresses throughout your competitive career.

Optimizing Recovery Runs

As you now see, easy running can improve your recovery from races or hard training and help prepare your body to train hard again more quickly. Too much mileage or too much effort between hard sessions, however, can leave you dragging for your next planned hard session, which will hinder your progress toward your racing goals. One of the most common, if not *the* most common, training error made by distance runners is not allowing their bodies to recover between hard efforts such as long runs, tempo runs, and long-interval sessions. This section looks at the appropriate intensity and duration of recovery runs, whether it makes sense to train twice per day, and the all-important first step in recovery after any workout—the cool-down.

Intensity. It takes discipline to run easily when you feel good on a planned recovery day. But, if you train too hard on a recovery day, you will be a bit tired for your next hard day, so that workout will likely not go as well as intended. You may then decide to run a bit harder than planned on the next recovery day to "make up for" the suboptimal hard training session. This creates a vicious cycle in which the easy days are too intense and the quality of the hard days is diminished. The result is a lack of improvement and mediocre race performances.

Of course, at one end of the intensity spectrum is the option of cross-training or taking days off from exercise altogether. Cross-training can be an excellent way to enhance recovery, and the benefits of cross-training are discussed later in this chapter. Days off provide "passive" recovery in which the body repairs and develops without the beneficial blood flow effects of easy running or cross-training. Taking days off from exercise is the appropriate option if you are building up your mileage after an injury or illness or have not yet built up your overall training program to the point at which you can train every day without progressively increasing fatigue.

The greatest value of using a heart rate monitor is preventing yourself from accidentally training too hard on your recovery runs. Keeping your heart rate below 75 percent of your maximal heart rate (or 70 percent of your heart rate reserve, explained later in this chapter) lets your body recover so you can perform higher-quality workouts on your scheduled hard training days. Keeping your heart rate a few beats per minute below this level allows you to recover without having to run at an uncomfortably slow pace. (One workout to accurately determine your maximum heart rate is to warm up thoroughly and then run three high-intensity repeats of two to three minutes up a moderate hill, jogging back to the bottom immediately after each. If you run the first hill at 90 percent effort and the last two all-out, your heart rate should reach its maximal level during the second or third repeat.)

For example, say Katrina's resting heart rate is 50 beats per minute and her maximal heart rate is 187 beats per minute. Using the maximal heart rate method, Katrina would keep her heart rate below 140 beats per minute (187 × 0.75). Heart rate reserve is the difference between maximal heart rate and resting heart rate, so it represents the amount that heart rate can increase in response to exercise. In this example, Katrina's heart rate reserve is 137 (187 − 50). Using the heart rate reserve method, Katrina would keep her heart rate below 146 (resting heart rate of 50 + [137 × 0.70]) during her recovery runs. By setting her heart rate monitor to beep at this limit, Katrina has an automatic reminder to keep her recovery runs at the correct intensity.

Duration. How long to run on your easy training days depends on whether the objective of those runs is primarily to enhance your recovery or to increase your total mileage. If the objective is recovery, then keep the run at no more than 50 minutes for high-mileage (70-plus miles per week) runners, and scale it down accordingly for lower-mileage runners. During the buildup phase of a marathon training program, the tension between recovery and total mileage is not as great a factor because the major efforts consist of long runs rather than high-intensity workouts. During the high-mileage phase of a marathon buildup, you can extend recovery runs up to an hour assuming that you do not get carried away and run too fast. Avoid the trap of adding mileage to your recovery days for the sole purpose of boosting your weekly mileage; this simply makes your recovery less complete for your subsequent hard-training days.

Daily frequency. Many runners introduce two runs per day before it is necessary. If you are preparing for races of 10,000 meters or longer, avoid double workouts until you have maximized the mileage that you can positively recover from in single workouts. Staying with longer single runs builds endurance and gives you more time for recovery between training sessions.

As your total weekly mileage increases, however, you reach a point at which incorporating double runs into your training program can speed

Cooling Down

Cooling down after a hard run helps return your body to preexercise conditions, such as reduced heart rate, breathing rate, and core body temperature. This is the critical first step in managing your recovery. A thorough cool-down improves your recovery by removing lactate from your muscles and blood more quickly, reducing adrenaline levels, and reducing muscle stiffness, which decreases your likelihood of future injury. Cooling down works in the following ways:

1. It improves lactate removal. After hard intervals or races of 10K or less, a cool-down removes the lactate that has accumulated in your muscles and blood. Lactate levels decrease much more quickly when you do a cool-down run because you maintain blood flow at a higher level, which increases movement of lactate out of your muscles and increases the rate at which your muscles use the lactate to produce energy aerobically.

2. It reduces adrenaline levels. Adrenaline and noradrenaline are hormones that increase the rate and force at which your heart contracts, increase blood pressure, increase your rate and depth of breathing, and increase the rate at which your muscles break down glycogen, among many other things. Adrenaline and noradrenaline levels in your blood increase rapidly when you run hard. After you stop running, adrenaline levels typically decrease to resting levels in less than an hour, but noradrenaline levels can take several hours to return to resting levels. An active cool-down helps get these hormones out of your system, which helps your body recover more quickly.

3. It reduces muscle stiffness. Cooling down also improves recovery by reducing muscle stiffness. A relaxing cool-down makes the muscles more resilient, which can reduce the risk of injury following a race or hard workout.

Start your cool-down with 10 to 20 minutes of easy running (if you're too tired to run, then walk for an equivalent amount of time, or try easy cross-training). The optimal clearance of lactate, adrenaline, and so forth occurs if you start your cool-down run at about 60 to 75 percent of your maximum heart rate, and slow down to a slow jog or walk for the last 5 minutes. After running, your muscles are warm and have very good blood flow, which increases their ability to stretch without injury, thus, this is the perfect time to gently stretch your muscles; there is evidence that postexercise recovery stretching can reduce the likelihood of injury.

your recovery from hard training sessions. If you do an easy recovery run in the afternoon after long intervals, speedwork, or a tempo run in the morning, you will likely feel more recovered the following day. Similarly, an easy recovery run in the morning can help prepare you for a hard effort in the evening.

Keep the minimum time for an added second run at 25 minutes. If you run for fewer than 25 minutes, it is hardly worth the extra time and effort both physiologically and in terms of the time it takes to shower and change clothes. As discussed below, it may be wiser to increase your aerobic recovery training by adding cross-training to your program rather than by increasing your risk of injury with more miles of running. When your mileage increases to the point at which your recovery runs last more than 50 minutes (or more than an hour during high-mileage marathon training), then it is time to switch those days to easy double-workout days. Doing two runs of 35 minutes rather than one 70-minute run is easier on your body and enhances your recovery.

Including Aerobic Cross-Training

Aerobic cross-training is another useful way to improve your recovery, avoid injury, and enhance aerobic fitness. (Other types of supplementary training, such as core stability training, flexibility training, and weight training are discussed in chapters 4, 5, and 6.) Perhaps the greatest challenge for highly motivated runners is to achieve optimal fitness while remaining injury free. The number of running steps you take determines the amount of impact forces that your body must deal with. Research on running injuries has shown that although running experience is associated with a decreased injury rate, weekly mileage is the strongest predictor of a future running injury. (Chapter 9 provides insights on safely and effectively working toward greater workloads and finding your own ideal mileage level.)

Aerobic cross-training is an intelligent way to reduce the likelihood of injury by reducing the accumulated impact forces that the muscles, tendons, ligaments, and bones are subjected to, without compromising your aerobic fitness or recovery. With cross-training, you decrease your weekly running mileage, replacing it with conditioning that helps you maintain your fitness and enhance your recovery. For runners with a history of injury—or better yet, runners with the foresight to avoid injuries in the first place—cross-training can be a vital strategy for optimal running performance. Each runner needs to perform his or her own individual risk–benefit analysis to evaluate the aerobic fitness gains and the increased injury risk associated with increased mileage, and then estimate when it would be wise to include cross-training into the overall training program. In evaluating when to include aerobic cross-training in your training program, review your old training diaries to see if there is a specific mileage level above which your likelihood of injury increases sharply.

Cross-training's main benefit is to improve blood flow through the muscles. Because recovery days are generally scheduled after hard training days—when fatigue levels are highest and muscles' resiliency is at its lowest—your risk of injury decreases if you do low-impact exercise on your recovery days. Many runners follow their Sunday long runs with cross-training on Mondays as an alternative to running seven days per week.

The one downside to replacing recovery runs with cross-training is that your training diary will show lower weekly mileage. Unfortunately, there is no foolproof way to equate time spent cross-training to running mileage (take a deep breath and get over it). You can, however, "convert" the cardiovascular benefits of various forms of cross-training into those gained from running by using heart rate. The relationship between a given heart rate and the cardiovascular benefits it confers is similar across a spectrum of activities—running, cycling, in-line skating, cross-country skiing, elliptical training, rowing, stair climbing, and walking. For example, if you want to keep your heart rate between 130 and 140 beats per minute during recovery training, the physiological effects of these various types of cross-training will be reasonably similar to those of running. During both swimming and running in water, however, your heart rate will be lower compared to a similar effort while running because of the pressure of the water around your body and the horizontal body position swimming entails. If you are cross-training primarily to enhance recovery, it is not worth getting too concerned with the precise intensity of your cross-training; it is better to enjoy the session rather than to be concerned with maintaining a specific intensity. Also, remember that weekly mileage is not a goal in itself—race results are what really count.

If you are replacing some of your running mileage with cross-training because of a history of injury, select an activity that closely simulates running; this ensures that you train the most relevant muscle groups. Deep-water running, elliptical training, and cross-country skiing are good options. Because your muscles adapt specifically to the type of training you do, no activity is a "perfect" substitute for running. Even deep-water running, despite its close similarity to running in terms of movement patterns, doesn't come close to replicating the muscular demands of running on land because of buoyancy factors and the absence of impact stresses. (More on water running can be found in chapters 7 and 12.)

If you are already putting in high mileage and are adding cross-training purely to enhance recovery, select an activity that works a wide variety of muscle groups and does not increase the fatigue of your running-specific muscles. Purely in terms of recovery, swimming is a better option than stair climbing or in-line skating.

There are many different ways to cross-train. Table 11.1 lists some of the advantages and disadvantages of popular methods of cross-training for runners.

Table 11.1 Recommended Cross-Training Options

Type of training	Advantages	Disadvantages
Cross-country skiing	Very low impact Total-body exercise	Requires equipment and correct technique Can add to fatigue of quadriceps
Cycling	Nonimpact Enhances recovery if using low resistance and high cadence	Requires a bike or gym Can add to fatigue of quadriceps
Deep-water running	Nonimpact Simulates running movement Total-body exercise	Requires a pool or body of water
Elliptical training	Very low impact Simulates running Total-body exercise	Requires equipment and correct technique Can add to fatigue of quadriceps
In-line skating	Low impact	Requires equipment and correct technique Can add to fatigue of quadriceps
Rowing and kayaking	Nonimpact Total-body exercise	Requires equipment and correct technique Can add to fatigue of quadriceps
Stair climbing	Low impact	Requires equipment Difficult to keep effort in recovery range Can add to fatigue of quadriceps
Swimming	Nonimpact Total-body exercise	Requires a pool or body of water and correct technique Runners may initially fatigue quickly
Walking	Low impact Convenient Good transition to running	Low intensity

Using Diet to Enhance Recovery

Running uses up your body's carbohydrate stores, causes cellular damage in your muscles, and makes you sweat out water and various minerals. To recover optimally, you need to ensure adequate intake of macronutrients (protein, carbohydrate, and water) as well as important micronutrients, such as antioxidants and iron, to maximize the rebuilding and repairing process. If you train hard and do not plan your recovery strategy, then you put your running performance at risk.

Protein

Protein supplies at most 10 percent of your energy needs both for day-to-day living and for training, and considerably less when your glycogen stores are full; it is critical, however, for ongoing recovery from training. Protein is needed for rebuilding your muscles and forms the building blocks for tendons, enzymes, hormones, and hemoglobin, among other things.

The average sedentary person needs approximately 0.8 to 1.0 grams of protein per kilogram of body weight per day. Over the past 10 years, studies have shown that endurance athletes have a greater protein requirement than previously thought because of ongoing repair of the training-induced breakdown of muscles and connective tissue ("muscle turnover"). Today, it is generally accepted that a distance runner doing moderate mileage needs 1.2 to 1.4 grams of protein per kilogram of body weight per day, while more serious runners need approximately 1.4 to 1.6 grams of protein per kilogram of body weight per day (see table 11.2). Recent evidence indicates that ingesting a moderate quantity of protein (10 to 30 grams) within the first hour after a training session can help speed the rebuilding and recovery process and—if taken with carbohydrate—also assist in the replacement of your glycogen stores.

The typical American diet contains more protein than an endurance athlete needs, but if you restrict meat, dairy products, or both in an effort to restrict calories, fat, or cholesterol, you may not be getting the optimal amount of protein. The most at-risk group is casual vegetarians, who might not be diligent about properly balancing the nutritional components of their meals. But with reasonable planning, vegetarian runners can also easily meet their protein requirements.

Table 11.2 Daily Protein Requirements

Approx weekly mileage	Protein/kg body weight/day	Protein/day for a 150-lb (68-kg) runner
<50	1.2-1.4 g	82-95 g
50+	1.4-1.6 g	95-109 g

Good sources of protein include the following: one egg = 6 grams; one pint of skim milk = 19 grams; one 1/4-lb. serving of lean meat (e.g., chicken or beef) = 25 grams.

Carbohydrate

Carbohydrate is your muscles' major source of energy. When you do a hard workout, a long run, or a race, you deplete your body's glycogen stores. The farther you run and the more intense the workout, the more glycogen you use. Glycogen is your body's stockpile of carbohydrate for energy; part of the recovery process required before you can run hard again is replenishing these stores.

Your muscles replace their glycogen stores at the fastest rate during the first 30 minutes to an hour after you stop running. Glycogen resynthesis continues at a higher-than-average rate for up to 12 hours after a glycogen-depleting run. The degree of glycogen depletion depends on how fast and how long the run is and how much glycogen was stored before the run. You recover more quickly if you eat and drink carbohydrate soon after your hard efforts. This is important! Try to consume at least 50 grams of carbohydrate within an hour after training or racing. Foods with a high glycemic index increase blood sugar levels more quickly and will therefore enhance glycogen resynthesis. (For a list of foods with a high glycemic index, refer to *Endurance Sports Nutrition* by Suzanne Girard Eberle. For further explanation of glycemic index, refer to chapter 8.) If your stomach does not feel up to a meal within an hour or so after running, you can take in 50 grams of carbohydrate (200 calories) relatively easily by eating a bagel, two bananas, or an energy bar or by downing a 20-ounce sport drink to start the replenishment process. Later, when your stomach can handle it, eat more carbohydrate to completely replenish your glycogen stores.

Hard running and carbohydrate depletion have both been shown to depress runners' immune systems. By taking in a carbohydrate drink soon after a hard run, you maintain your blood sugar level, which may help reduce this temporary immune-system suppression. To improve your recovery from long runs and hard interval workouts, it also helps to glycogen load for one or two days before the workout. This reduces the degree of glycogen depletion resulting from your workout, which in turn reduces your recovery requirements.

The more you run, the more carbohydrate you use for energy and, therefore, the higher your daily carbohydrate requirements. Table 11.3 shows the approximate carbohydrate needs for runners undertaking various amounts of training.

Table 11.3 Daily Carbohydrate Requirements

Weekly mileage	Carbohydrate/kg body weight/day	Carbohydrate/day for a 150-lb (68-kg) runner
<40	6-7 g	408-476 g
40-60	7-8 g	476-544 g
60-80	8-9 g	544-612 g
80+	9-10 g	612-680 g

Good sources of carbohydrate include the following: one cup of fruit juice = 25 grams; one large bagel = 50 grams; one banana or one slice of bread = 20 grams.

Fluid Intake

Sweat contains water and electrolytes. As you sweat, your blood volume decreases and your heart pumps less blood per contraction; your heart rate must therefore increase to pump the same amount of blood per unit of time. The result is that less oxygen-rich blood reaches your working muscles, so you produce less energy aerobically and cannot maintain as fast a pace. Becoming dehydrated also increases the amount of time you require for recovery, so preventing dehydration is a recovery-enhancing strategy as well as a performance-enhancing one. In addition, replacing fluids quickly after exercise helps to speed your recovery because your blood and other bodily fluids help remove waste products and bring nutrients to tissues for repair purposes.

To help minimize dehydration, concentrate on drinking enough fluids to ensure that you are fully hydrated before races and workouts. Even experienced runners often neglect their fluid needs. Unfortunately, you cannot just sit down and drink a half-gallon of fluid and head out the door for a run. It takes time for your body tissues to absorb water, so drink 8 to 16 ounces of fluid at a time throughout the day rather than a lot at once.

A good practice is to weigh yourself before and after running, calculate how much weight you have lost during a run, and drink fluids with the objective of bringing your weight back up to what it was before the run. Because your body excretes some of the water that you drink, you need to drink up to one and a half times as much fluid as you lost to become fully rehydrated. Your food should adequately replace your electrolytes, but if you are doing high-mileage training in the heat, a sports drink with electrolytes can be a good source of both carbohydrate and electrolytes. If you typically limit your salt intake, be a bit more liberal with the salt shaker during hot weather.

Antioxidants

There is evidence that after high-intensity running of an hour or more, the immune system is suppressed for several hours, creating an "open window" during which runners are at an increased risk of infection. For healthy, well-trained runners, evidence suggests that the immune system is only suppressed following exercise of more than one hour at an intensity greater than 80 percent of $\dot{V}O_2max$ (about marathon pace) or from a hard interval session.

Taking an antioxidant supplement containing vitamin C, beta-carotene, vitamin E, and zinc the day before, the day of, and the day after a hard workout may help reduce the risk of infection, thereby enhancing your recovery. If your diet is only so-so in terms of vitamins and minerals, taking a multivitamin supplement can also ensure that you get enough of the various vitamins required for optimal recovery from training. Although the results of studies on antioxidant supplementation have been mixed, with some indicating a benefit of supplementation in preventing postexercise infections and others indicating no effect, taking moderate doses of antioxidants such as those found in commercially available supplements may help and are unlikely to cause harm.

Iron

Maintaining adequate iron levels is critical in maximizing running performance and recovery. Iron is necessary for producing the protein hemoglobin in your red blood cells (RBCs). Hemoglobin is the RBC component that carries oxygen from the lungs to the muscles. If your hemoglobin level is low, less oxygen reaches your muscles, and this reduces your aerobic capacity and running performance. In addition, iron is a component of many other substances in the body, such as the enzymes in muscle cells responsible for aerobic energy production.

Runners tend to have higher iron requirements than other people because of footstrike hemolysis (the breakdown of red blood cells when the foot hits the ground during running), iron loss through sweat, and iron loss through the gastrointestinal (GI) system. Many runners also avoid red meat and therefore take in relatively little dietary iron. The highest risk of iron deficiency is found in premenopausal women runners, whose iron intake often does not meet their needs. Ensuring adequate iron intake is an important part of every serious runner's strategy for optimal training and recovery. Serious women runners should have their iron levels checked at least twice per year and consult with a health professional regarding dietary changes and supplementation if their iron levels are low. (See chapter 8 for a thorough discussion of nutritional supplements.)

Getting Enough Sleep

Adequate sleep helps you recover from, and positively adapt to, training. Exercise generally improves both the quantity and quality of sleep, but overtraining can interfere with sleep patterns. How exercise leads to improved sleep is not well understood, although it is believed that one mechanism may be a decrease in the ratio of sympathetic to parasympathetic nervous system activity. Stimulation of the sympathetic nervous system increases heart rate, blood pressure, metabolic rate, and mental activity, all of which are counterproductive to falling asleep; parasympathetic activity has the opposite effects. During running, sympathetic activity increases, but endurance training leads to a decrease in sympathetic activity relative to parasympathetic activity during rest (one example of this is runners' low resting heart rates as compared to untrained people). This alteration in the balance between sympathetic and parasympathetic activity may allow you to fall asleep more quickly and to sleep more deeply. Running or exercising too close to bedtime, however, can leave the sympathetic nervous system stimulated for several hours, making it more difficult to fall asleep.

A change in your sleeping habits is an early warning sign of overtraining. The physical and psychological stresses of training beyond your individual threshold may overstimulate the sympathetic nervous system, leading to irritability, and reducing the quality and quantity of sleep. A reduction in sleep is a double-edged sword for a runner, because much of the body's recovery and rebuilding occurs during sleep. If you train hard, you need to be particularly careful about getting adequate sleep, or you may experience a decline in performance, immune system depression, and increased susceptibility to injury. If you sleep well most of the time, however, you do not have to worry if you have trouble sleeping the night before a race; there is no evidence that one night of poor sleep is detrimental to performance.

When you have uncharacteristic difficulty sleeping, you could be training hard too frequently. You may be able to improve your sleep fairly easily by backing off your training and not running too late in the day. The harder you exercise, the greater the stimulus to your nervous system, so cutting back your training intensity will likely benefit your ability to sleep more than cutting back your mileage will.

To improve your sleep pattern, develop and maintain a routine that works for you. The mind and body thrive on a regular routine. Eating dinner and going to bed at approximately the same time each night will help to set your body clock, so that your body and mind automatically shut down at the same time each night. Avoid bright lights at night, and avoid lying down until you are ready to go to sleep. This way, when you do lie down, it will serve as a signal to ease your mind toward sleep.

Using Other Strategies to Recover and Prevent Injury

In addition to the strategies related to training, diet, and sleep for optimizing your recovery and preventing injury, this section covers a variety of additional methods and factors that influence your ability to stay healthy and adapt positively to training.

Hot–Cold Contrast Therapy

Athletes in a wide variety of sports use hot–cold contrast therapy to speed recovery. Contrast therapy is an extension of the use of heat and cold for physical therapy for injuries, but the benefits of contrasting these in one therapy to improve recovery are not well documented. Claims for contrast therapy include the following:

- Improved blood flow, which increases elimination of lactate and other products of hard exercise
- Reduced inflammation
- Reduced delayed-onset muscle soreness (DOMS)
- Enhanced relaxation, which reduces the metabolic rate and improves the psychological state to enhance recovery

The best time to use contrast therapy is usually within 20 minutes after exercise. The athlete then alternately submerges himself or herself in hot and cold water, generally using bathtubs, portable tubs, or wheelie bins. Team-sport athletes typically submerge up to the neck, but for runners submersion to the waist should be effective. The hot water is ideally about 35 degrees Celsius (95 degrees F), and the cold water is in the range of 10 to 12 degrees C (50 to 54 degrees F). Athletes typically stay in the hot water two to three times longer than in the cold water. For example, a typical protocol is two to three minutes hot followed by one minute cold, repeating the cycle three or four times. Athletes often finish in hot in the winter and cold in the summer.

Three somewhat more practical alternatives for contrast therapy are (1) to fill the bath with cold water, and alternately soak in the bath for one minute followed by a hot shower for two to three minutes; (2) on a hot day, to alternate a cold bath (or a dip in the ocean or a lake) with simply getting out into the warm air; and (3) to alternate hot and cold water in the shower. Although showering does not seem to be as effective as water submersion, it is far easier and more practical for most people.

Massage Therapy

Muscle injuries occur when muscle fibers are stressed after a hard workout or race before sufficient recovery has occurred. Whether or not overworked muscle fibers develop spasms and strains, therefore, depends in large part on the recovery process. Competitive distance runners widely use massage therapy to improve their recovery time and prevent injury. Unfortunately, it is difficult to design a scientific study to evaluate the benefits of massage. As a result, there is little scientific evidence but much anecdotal evidence for the benefits of massage therapy for athletes and for distance runners in particular. However, the following benefits have been established:

- Improvement in blood flow to the massaged area
- Relaxation of the muscles
- Improvement in mobility and flexibility of the muscle and surrounding connective tissue
- Relaxation of the athlete
- Breakdown of scar tissue
- Identification of tight areas before they become injuries, which could lead to physical therapy or modifying training to prevent injury

Interestingly, research with horses has shown that massage therapy can increase both range of motion and stride length. These results with horses eliminate the placebo effect that causes one of the problems with massage studies conducted on human subjects, and indicate that correct massage technique can benefit running performance.

Many competitive runners use weekly massage to improve recovery, to reduce the likelihood of injury, and to generally relax. It is beneficial to supplement these sessions with more frequent self-massage on tight muscles that can be easily reached, such as the quadriceps, calf muscles, and muscles in the feet.

There are many different types of massage therapy, and as with any discipline, a wide range in expertise among massage therapists. As a relatively unregulated industry, find a massage therapist who is a member of the American Massage Therapy Association and has been recommended by other runners so you can be confident that the sessions will be effective.

Running Surfaces

The total force absorbed by your body during running is equal to the amount of force per step × the number of steps you take. Adjusting either of these factors reduces your risk of injury. The surface that you run on can make a substantial difference in the amount of pounding your body absorbs, and this difference may determine whether or not you cross your threshold for injury.

Concrete is the least forgiving surface for running. Often you can prevent shinsplints and stress fractures by running instead on a softer surface. Blacktop or asphalt, while slightly softer than concrete, is far from an ideal surface. Our bodies did not evolve while running on a uniform hard surface. The joints, muscles, tendons, ligaments, and bones are not designed to withstand hundreds of miles of running on roads. The higher the percentage of your training that you do off-road and off-sidewalk, the lower your likelihood of developing an overuse injury. Search for natural surfaces such as dirt paths, grass fields, golf courses, and trails. Tracks are not a good option except for interval sessions because repetitively running the curves can lead to injury, and because some tracks are not particularly soft.

Running off-road also reduces injury risk by reducing the repetitiveness of your footsteps. The uneven surfaces require you to make many small adjustments to your stride, and this increased variety spreads the accumulated impact forces over a greater area, which should, at least in theory, help to reduce repetitive stress injuries. Take care during off-road running to avoid sprained ankles from holes and roots.

Shoes

Keeping your shoes in good condition can make a big difference in the amount of shock that your body absorbs. The cushioning properties of all running shoes on the market break down significantly after less than 800 miles of running. For those running 100 miles per week, this represents only eight weeks of training, while a pair of running shoes may last a 40-mile-per-week runner up to five months. Depending on your size, running mechanics, and what model of shoe you wear, you may need to replace your running shoes after as few as 400 miles.

It is also a good idea to use different pairs of running shoes on different days. Different shoes somewhat alter the forces your body must deal with. By switching shoes, the shock that your feet, legs, and back receive becomes somewhat less repetitive. This reduced repetitiveness may slow the development of an injury. It takes time for the resiliency of your shoes to completely return after running, so rotating pairs of shoes ensures that the cushioning properties have fully recovered before you run in them again.

Monitoring Your Recoverability

There are many ways to monitor your recovery, but the simplest measures are often the most useful and the easiest to adhere to. In combination, these measures provide insight into your adaptation to training, your risk of injury or illness, and how ready you are for the next hard training session. Typically, when the results of these measures decrease, running performance and recovery deteriorate between 4 and 10 days later. In addition to keeping track of the details of your actual training, consider recording the following details in your training diary and reviewing them periodically to find the patterns that predict overtraining, illness, and injury. You can then use this information to improve your recovery by modifying your training schedule.

Weight. Check your weight at the same time each day or several times per week. Decreases in weight over a few days usually indicate dehydration. Decreases in weight over a few weeks can indicate that you are not eating enough calories, have an illness, or are overtraining.

Morning heart rate. Your heart rate when you first wake up in the morning provides an indication of your recovery state. It is important to check your heart rate soon after you awaken and while still lying down, because it increases as soon as you start thinking about your plans for the day, and by about 10 beats per minute when you get up. In addition, waking to an alarm can increase your heart rate and make this information less reliable. To find your resting heart rate, therefore, take your pulse immediately upon waking for several consecutive days. Your true resting heart rate is the lowest rate you measure. Once you've established your true resting rate, if your morning heart rate is more than four or five beats per minute higher than usual, this may indicate illness or inadequate recovery. An elevated morning heart rate can be a particularly useful sign in preventing illness because an increased heart rate is often the first sign that you are not altogether well. This early warning signal allows you to modify your training so that you avoid trying to do a hard session, which may prolong your recovery.

Environmental conditions. Record the temperature and humidity on hot days and the temperature and wind chill factor on cold days. Your body undergoes substantially more stress when, for example, you run at 80 degrees Fahrenheit and 80 percent humidity than when you run at 60 degrees and low humidity; this is due to increased core body temperature and dehydration. If you train hard or compete on a hot, humid day, the heat you generate can overwhelm your body's ability to eliminate it, causing your core temperature to climb, which can greatly increase recovery time. This is especially true as you acclimate to warmer temperatures; that is, your first run of the year in 90-degree weather takes a much greater toll on your body than a similar run later when you are acclimated. Similarly, dehydration also increases recovery time. With cold weather and wind chill, the important factor is avoiding extreme conditions, both of which are dangerous to your health and can require increased recovery time. Sometimes it is better for your overall running progress for you to take a day off or train indoors rather than risk wearing yourself out in extreme environmental conditions.

Hours of sleep. The number of hours of sleep that you get in any one night is not particularly important. Over the course of several nights, however, your quantity of sleep can affect your recovery and ability to adapt positively to training.

Quality of sleep. The quality of your sleep is arguably more important than the number of hours you sleep. Evaluate the quality of your sleep each night on a scale from 1 to 10, and try to be as consistent as possible in your assessment. A reduction in the quality of sleep is often associated with overtraining. Reduced sleep quality can also be caused by nonrunning stresses, but the resulting impact on your running performance is the same.

Diet quality. Evaluate the overall quality of your diet each day on a scale from 1 to 10; again, try to be as consistent as possible in your assessment. Often, you can trace a lack of energy to a poor diet over the previous few days. Evaluating the quality of your diet also provides a gentle reminder of the importance of good nutrition for runners.

Hydration level. Dehydration has an immediate effect on running performance and slows recovery. Evaluate your hydration level each day on a scale from 1 to 10, and try to be as consistent as possible. Your daily weight provides a good indication of your hydration level. Evaluating your hydration level will make you less likely to forget to stay hydrated.

Muscle soreness. It is not unusual for runners to have slightly sore muscles most of the time. An increase in muscle soreness from this baseline can be caused by a race, a hard workout, or by running downhill. Evaluate your general muscle soreness each day on a scale from 1 to 10, trying to be as consistent as possible. If increased general muscle soreness lasts more than four or five days, then it is likely that you are ill or overtrained. Soreness in a specific muscle indicates a potential injury, whereas more general muscle soreness indicates your adaptation to training and need for recovery.

Energy level. An assessment of your energy level is one of the best indications of recovery from training. Consistently evaluate your energy level each day on a scale from 1 to 10. If you find your energy level is reduced for more than three days, it is important to determine the cause—dehydration, lack of adequate carbohydrate intake, training hard too many days in a row, illness, low iron levels, lack of sleep, and so on. By reviewing your training diary and considering your various lifestyle factors, you should be able to find the likely cause of a low energy level.

Heart rate at a standard pace. If your heart rate at a set pace is more than five beats per minute higher than usual, then you may not be recovered from your previous training session or sessions. For example, if your heart rate at eight minutes per mile is typically 145 beats per minute under given conditions, and one day you find it is 153 beats per minute at that pace under similar conditions, then you likely need additional recovery before doing your next hard training session. Listening to your body in this way can help curtail overreaching before long-term staleness sets in. Heart rate during running at a given pace varies naturally by a few beats per minute from day to day and is also influenced by factors such as dehydration and hot or humid conditions, so take these factors into consideration in evaluating the implications of a higher-than-usual heart rate.

CHAPTER 12

Retaining Fitness While Recovering From Injury

SCOTT DOUGLAS

For dedicated runners, there are few darker periods than those of prolonged injury. Out of nowhere, it seems, your legs go from being one of your primary sources of pleasure to being traitors, failing parts of a once smoothly operating machine that now provide only pain and heartache. Despite what experts and well-meaning friends might tell you, you just know that, with every passing minute of an injury that keeps you from running, your hard-won fitness is decreasing while your body-fat percentage is increasing. Racing plans must be altered; cherished group runs are missed. Meanwhile, what is usually one of your main means of stress relief is now a major source of stress, and no end seems in sight.

Of course, nearly all injuries are eventually overcome. In the meantime, what can you do to maintain some semblance of fitness and not go crazy? In most cases you will be able to find an aerobic activity that won't aggravate your injury but will provide some of the same physical and psychological benefits of running. This chapter is for those times when you need to find such an activity because you won't be able to run for at least two weeks. Therefore, my advice about cross-training for runners is different from advice on how to incorporate cross-training into your normal running program (see chapter 11 for information on that type of cross-training). In this case, the assumption is that you'll do nothing but cross-training for (you hope) a short time.

Another up-front caveat: We've all heard stories of someone who was injured soon before a key race, cross-trained extensively, resumed running a few weeks before race day, and did great in the race. Bob Kempainen's cross-country ski machine routine shortly before placing third at the 1992 Olympic Marathon Trials is an example. Sorry, but the advice in this chapter isn't tailored to such situations. Those of us not of Kempainen's caliber have the luxury of picking new goal races when serious injury intrudes in the month or two before our originally planned event. In the long run, you're almost always better off regaining your health, resuming normal training, and revising your plans. Use the information in this chapter to maintain your physical and mental fitness during the "regaining health" part of that process.

Before looking at each cross-training activity in detail, let's continue with a few general considerations applicable to all of them.

Judging Your Effort

It's often tough for longtime runners to gauge their efforts in other endeavors because of the mismatch between their highly developed cardiovascular fitness and lack of experience with alternative aerobic activities. If you doubt this, head out for a bike ride and try to stay with the next chubby cyclist who passes you. It's quite likely that your quads will tire rapidly, even though your breathing seems under control. Fortunately, while injured, you're not looking to keep up with the Joneses; you just want to get in a good workout most days. How do you judge that during new activities?

The best way, especially in your early days as a cross-trainer, is by using a heart rate monitor. Shooting for 70 to 80 percent of your maximal heart rate on noninterval days—more on that in a moment—will ensure that you're working hard enough to make the cross-training worth your time. (Granted, using a heart rate monitor while deep-water running can be tough; later we'll look at how to judge your effort in the pool.)

Once you become more familiar with your cross-training activity, the signals from your heart and leg muscles will be more in synch, and you can more reliably use perceived effort as a guide for whether you're working hard enough. At the same time, many injured runners like to use a heart rate monitor throughout their cross-training exiles because it gives them something to focus on beyond the tick-tick-tick of the clock. Speaking of which . . .

Getting Your Mind Around It

If nothing else, after an extended cross-training bout, you'll understand how a lot of people feel about running. One of the hardest aspects of cross-training is the mental one, namely, *How in the world can you occupy your mind while waiting for the daily dose of drudgery to end?* Learning how to get through 90 minutes on a stationary bike is indeed a tough adjustment for runners used to touring trails at sunset and otherwise moving freely through nature.

The overarching advice is this: Do what you need to do to get yourself to cross-train for as long as you have planned to. Listen to music, play games with the time to break it up, set up little rewards for yourself that you can claim only if you make it through the planned session, whatever it takes. Learn which tricks motivate you, and exploit them. Find ways not to cut your cross-training short, and you'll be much happier with yourself when you go to bed at night.

Have a plan for each day. Before you start, tell yourself the minimum amount of time you're going to work out that day. Tell others, too, to provide extra motivation. (Nobody likes having the, "No, I cut the bike ride short because . . ." conversation.)

Also have a plan for each week. Keeping the structure of your normal running week—a longest workout, a medium-long workout, a lactate-threshold workout, an interval workout, and so forth—adds the variety needed to keep the days from blending together into one great glop of cross-training monotony. Frequent hard and long workouts, of course, also help to maintain your fitness better than several weeks of nothing

Serious runners who cross-train their way to renewed health should approach their substitute training as they approach their running: They should set goals, formulate a plan, and commit to the task at hand.

but running-out-the-clock, medium-effort days. At the same time, try not to think too much further ahead than a week at a time, because it can be tough to stay motivated if you focus on the fact that you'll be cross-training for, say, two months.

On the plus side, just like when you were a new runner and the PRs came easily, you can make great improvements quickly as a nascent cross-trainer. Maintain motivation by marking your cross-training superlatives—longest pool workout, fastest sustained speed for an hour bike ride, and the like—and frequently trying to better them.

Converting Cross-Training

A word about converting cross-training to running miles: Don't bother. Sure, you can find formulas that supposedly equate one form of exercise with another,

227

such as every 10 minutes of cycling counts as one mile running. These conversions, however, stem more from injured runners' psychological needs than from hard data.

I came to accept this way of thinking after a two-hour bike ride with Pete Pfitzinger, the author of chapter 11 of this book, who was also injured at the time. As we pulled into his driveway, I asked, "So two hours pretty hard—what is that? A 10-mile run? 8? 12?" Pete said, "It is what it is—a two-hour bike ride."

In other words, rather than wondering how many running apples your cross-training oranges are worth, focus on the quality of your oranges. There will be plenty of time to be obsessive about documenting running mileage when you're healthy.

That's not to say you should disregard any sort of cross-training measurement. In general, plan to spend more *time* cross-training than you normally do running if you want to maintain any semblance of the fitness you had before becoming injured. Unfortunately, the usual advice—if you usually run X number of minutes per day, cross-train for that amount of time when injured—is misguided, because it ignores how much of a workout you can get out of a short run. Anyone who has compared how she feels after a 30-minute run with how she feels after a half-hour bike ride could tell you that. In the next section, we look at rough estimations for each of the activities.

Choosing Your Poison

Okay, so you're injured and can't run. How do you not turn into Jabba the Hutt by sunset? The key is to find at least one aerobic activity that fulfills the following criteria:

- Won't aggravate your injury
- You can do at a high heart rate—at least 65 percent of your maximum—for a long time
- You can tolerate psychologically
- You can reasonably count on doing most days for the next however many weeks

That last point is crucial. Spend any time on running message boards on the Web, and you'll see desperate injured runners asking, "What cross-training is the best while I'm hurt?" Certainly, exercise physiologists could relate in great detail whether deep-water running or cycling more improves your heart's stroke volume, or whether cross-country skiing or using an elliptical trainer better replicates the neuromuscular demands of running. But does it really help to hear that you absolutely must spend your downtime doing deep-water running if the nearest pool is a 45-minute drive away? Can you really count on the elliptical trainer as your savior if the only gym in your town requires a costly annual membership before you can even try the machines? No, as an injured runner, what you need is not the Platonic ideal of a cross-training routine, but the one that will work within the constraints of your available resources, schedule, and finances. As with your running, the easier it is to regularly cross-train, the greater the chance that you'll stick with it.

Another point: An injury-induced break from running is a good time to do those extra activities that seem to take a perpetual backseat when you're healthy. Starting a core-strengthening program, doing a yoga or Pilates video, or embarking on a weightlifting routine will not only give you another outlet for the energy you usually devote to running, but will also help you build a sounder body (see chapters 4, 5, 6, and 7 for more on these important topics). The gains you make from this supplementary work will make you less susceptible to injury when you resume normal training. If your injury stems from chronic weakness or tightness of some area of your body, choose a supplementary activity that will address this underlying problem.

In this chapter I detail three cross-training options: deep-water running, cycling, and using an elliptical trainer. I focus on these because, on the basis of conversations with scores of serious runners and my too-vast experience with being injured, they're the three that are most likely to meet the above criteria.

So, which of the big three is best for you? Assuming none of them aggravates your injury, the simple answer is whichever you realistically think you'll do most often. And, of course, you needn't pick just one—if you can regularly do more than one type of cross-training, go for it. The variety will help to keep you motivated. Let's look at how to approach each as an injured runner.

Off the Deep End

Maybe because it includes the word "running," the first alternative exercise that many runners turn to is deep-water running (or pool running—I'm using the terms interchangeably). Pool running is a viable cross-training choice for almost any running injury. If you have a stress fracture, especially in your foot, it should be your first choice. But pool running has benefits besides sounding like a kissing cousin of the real thing. Several short-term (four to six weeks) studies have shown that a runner's fitness level, as measured by parameters such as lactate threshold and running economy, holds steady when real running is replaced by pool running. And although the motion doesn't mimic that of land running, it's close enough to maintain some muscle memory.

Nonetheless, many injured runners find that pool running isn't their best long-term solution. For starters, you have to work extraordinarily hard to sustain a high heart rate. Studies have found maximal heart rates while deep-water running to be 16 beats per minute lower than during land running. That's because the water's pressure on your body returns more blood to your heart, meaning that more blood is pumped per contraction. The bottom line is that it's nearly impossible to find a pool-running equivalent of your medium-paced 45-minute run. Instead, you'll have to do interval workouts almost every day to sustain an intensity level that will maintain your fitness.

Deep-water running is also far from fascinating, to say the least. You will need all of your runner's discipline and then some to get through daily workouts of an hour or more. If you can do some of your deep-water running in an outdoor pool or natural body of water, the time won't seem to drag as much. (See chapter 7 for a visualization strategy aimed at easing the ennui of pool running.)

Water Works

If you choose pool running as your main cross-training activity, plan to spend at least as much time on it as you usually do running. In this case, more probably is better, and won't increase your injury risk, given the supportive, nonweight-bearing environment of the pool. Spend your first few pool-running sessions getting the motion down. Then the fun starts.

As mentioned, you'll need to do intervals almost every day in the pool to get in a decent workout. Although this might make pool running sound that much more dire, it's actually a positive, because intervals make the time pass more quickly. Of your pool-running workouts each week, plan to make all but one interval workouts; reserve one day a week for a steady-effort pool run.

What types of intervals should you do in the pool? Sets of several short intervals with even shorter rests are best. These will make it easier to sustain a high heart rate than doing fewer, longer repeats; once your hard bouts are longer than five minutes, it's difficult to maintain the proper intensity. Simulating tempo runs, such as a continuous "comfortably hard" 25 minutes, is an especially tough task.

How many intervals you do depends on how long you intend to stay in the pool that day. Here are some combinations of intervals and following rest periods:

50 seconds hard, 10 seconds easy

1:30 hard, 30 seconds easy

1:45 hard, 15 seconds easy

2:30 hard, 30 seconds easy

5:00 hard, 60 seconds easy

If you're doing shorter intervals, break them into sets, such as 10 repeats of 1:30 hard, 30 seconds easy, followed by 2:00 easy, followed by another set of 10 repeats of 1:30 hard, 30 seconds easy. Another nice way to break up the time is by starting a workout with shorter repeats, such as $10 \times$ (50 seconds hard, 10 seconds easy), take an easy 2:00, then $8 \times$ (2:30 hard, 30 seconds easy), take another 2:00 easy, and finish with $10 \times$ (50 seconds hard, 10 seconds easy).

Yes, the recovery times you see are for real. Your heart rate starts to return to normal much more quickly in the pool than when you're really running, so you need to do workouts that would be nearly impossible on the track.

Once you get used to running in the pool, you'll find that you can sustain close to the same intensity for longer repeats, such as those lasting five minutes, as on shorter ones of, say, 90 seconds. Therefore, as you become more accustomed to deep-water running, spend more of your days doing longer intervals.

Pool running is also unique in that you need barely any warm-up or cool-down time. Five minutes of easy deep-water running on each end of your interval sessions is plenty to prepare for and recover from the hard work that constitutes the bulk of your time in the pool.

Expect your breathing to be more shallow and rapid while pool running, especially when you're doing intervals. If you're able to get a heart rate monitor to work in the water, don't be surprised if your perceived effort at a given heart rate is higher in water compared to when running on land. (Again, this is because the water pressure makes it nearly impossible for you to reach your true maximum heart rate.)

Although it's the least intense day of the week, the one nonintervals day is the toughest day mentally for most runners. Shoot for between one and two hours at a steady, not-too-easy effort. At times, you'll really need to concentrate to keep your heart rate up.

Sansabelt?

Although you can run in the pool without a belt or vest, you're better off attaching one of the flotation aids. Without one of the devices, you work harder just to keep your head above water—especially if you have a single-digit body-fat percentage—and this can distract you from getting in your best possible interval sessions.

As for your form in the pool, try to mimic your land-running form as much as possible, while bearing in mind that an exact replica won't be possible. In the pool, your turnover is going to be slower, and your legs are unlikely to come up behind you to the degree they do on land. Find the form that feels kind of like running but that also allows you to work hard. Most runners find that moving their legs in a piston-like motion, while not identical to their running stride, feels close enough and allows a decent workout.

You'll find that the more you lean forward, the more you move around in the water. Some movement is inevitable, but try to keep your trunk erect enough to minimize your wandering. You might want to make an exception on your steady-run day in the pool—lean forward a little more than usual so that you can do slow laps or figure eights. This helps the time pass more quickly.

Because of the shorter stride and the piston-like motion you use while deep-water running, the front muscles of your body will get tighter in the pool than during land running. Spend at least five minutes after your workout stretching your quads and hip flexors. Yoga poses that incorporate back bends, such as the camel, are also a good choice for regular pool runners. Refer to the exercises in chapter 4—in particular the walking lunges and the combination quadriceps, hip flexor, iliotibial band, latissimus dorsi stretch—for specifics on loosening up before and after workouts.

231

Stroll With the Changes

When healthy, most runners think that walking is to working out as microwaving frozen entrees is to cooking—it's not completely antithetical, but it doesn't really count as the real thing. As with so many other aspects of athletic pride, though, that attitude can quickly change when you're hurt. Many injured runners come to appreciate the simple pleasure of a vigorous stroll around the neighborhood. (Or farther—Japanese marathon great Toshihiko Seko used to walk for hours a day when injured, as did 1980s road race stalwart Herb Lindsay. During one injury bout, once a week I walked a 12-mile route home from work.)

Walking, of course, doesn't count as a "real" workout in the context of the other cross-training types I discuss. As a fit runner, you'd be hard-pressed to get your heart rate much above 90 on any walk other than one straight up a mountain. But taking regular walks, in addition to doing more-intense alternative workouts, can help you through your down time in several ways.

First and perhaps most important, walking brings many of the same aesthetic pleasures as running. You're outside; you're moving under your own power; you're covering some of your regular running routes; and unlike during indoor cross-training, you're not staring at a clock waiting for your allotted time to end.

Walking also burns roughly the same number of calories per mile as running. So if you're concerned about gaining weight while you're injured, consider that a one-hour walk will burn about the same number of calories as a three- or four-mile run. Do this several times a week, and you'll be much less likely to put on unwanted pounds. In addition, regular walking will help you to maintain muscle memory for when you begin running again, whereas several weeks of nothing but pool running or cycling will make your return to running that much more difficult.

Probably the biggest drawback of walking is that it takes so much more time than running to get in a worthwhile jaunt. If your schedule is tight during the workweek, set aside a couple of hours on weekend days for a nice hike, and squeeze in short walks during your lunch break on weekdays.

Going in Cycles

Even a casual viewer of the Tour de France can tell that cycling builds incredible fitness. But it does so only if you devote tons of time to it; runners used to calling a half-hour tour of the neighborhood a decent workout can be in for a shock if they turn to cycling when injured. So although cycling is compatible with nearly all running injuries—stress fractures of the foot and shin, and some knee problems, are prime exceptions—it's still not for everybody. Plan to cycle as your main cross-training choice only if you can devote at least twice as much time to it as you usually do running, and have easy access to a good bike.

"Good bike" can mean either a stationary bike, a road bike, or, best, a road bike that you can convert to a stationary bike with a training stand or rollers. For runners who haven't spent years developing their bike-handling skills (which using rollers requires), an effective setup is to attach the rear wheel axle of the bike to a training stand. Cycling shoes are another worthwhile investment; they provide a stiff sole—helpful in transferring power efficiently from foot to pedal—along with a snug, comfortable fit not available from running or cross-training shoes. All of this equipment can be purchased for less than $250 (US).

More so than running, cycling is affected by weather and time of day. That's why it's best, if possible, to be able to count on outdoor and indoor riding. If you already own a decent road bike, you can cheaply convert it to an indoor stationary bike with a training stand. Alternatively, you could ride a stationary bike at a gym most days and go mountain biking on other days.

As I keep stressing, you'll increase your chance of successful cross-training by encountering as few barriers as possible to easy exercise. The road bike with training stand is what worked best for me during one three-month stint because I could get in an hour ride in the garage before and after work during the workweek, and take long rides outside on the weekends. This was during the winter, so having an indoor option vastly increased my ability to get in an effective workout despite bad weather and darkness, and thinking about a pleasant long ride outside on the weekend helped to keep me going during the workweek. You might find that committing to a gym will help your motivation, as will finding group rides to take part in. Do whatever it takes to maintain regularity.

Spinning Class

You won't be surprised to hear that riding outside is far more aesthetic than spinning in place in a garage for two hours. Nonetheless, for injured runners, outdoor cycling has a few drawbacks that you should consider when deciding where to ride.

Most important, you have a lot more control over your workout when riding indoors. Outside, factors such as hills, stopping for traffic, wind, and other cyclists—that's why they draft in cycling competitions—can make significant differences in your heart rate. Depending on where you live, it can also be tough to find cycling routes for sustained, unimpeded workouts. Consider that in a three-hour ride, you'll cover between 45 and 75 miles, a far cry from most runners' ability to get by with access to just a few miles of suitable roads. Even if your area has an extensive bike-path network, you probably know from running that cycling on them at a good clip isn't the way to go. All of these factors are another reason to be able to ride indoors and out. If you can, do the hard workouts described later on a stationary bike, and head outdoors for your longest rides and some of the day-to-day workouts.

Another thing you've probably noticed about the Tour de France is that the participants go hard (and long) almost every day for three weeks. Because of the lack of pounding and subsequent muscle damage, you recover much more quickly from cycling than running. As with pool running, this means that injured runners on the bike can and should do hard workouts more often than in their normal running schedule. Again, as with pool running, the more-frequent workouts not only better maintain your fitness, but also break up the cross-training time mentally.

Using a heart rate monitor is helpful during your cycling cross-training. Even once you become accustomed to the cycling motion, it can be tricky to accurately rate your effort level. The workouts that follow assume you'll be using a heart rate monitor. If you won't, base your efforts on how your breathing compares to a hard running effort of half the time (e.g., on the five-minute repeats, you should feel like you're breathing as hard as you would on a running interval of 2:30).

Core workouts for injured runners who are cycling include the following. Be sure that before any of the first three workouts you warm up with 15 to 20 minutes of progressively faster spinning. Follow that with a few fast spins of 15 to 20 seconds or add a couple of 1-minute pickups toward the end to start to elevate your heart rate. Cool down after each workout with 5 to 10 minutes of easy spinning.

- Repeats of 4 to 5 minutes, with 1 minute of easy spinning between. Do these at 90 to 95 percent of your maximal heart rate. Start at 5 repeats, and work up to 10. Do this or the workout described next once a week. On these intervals, you should feel like you're running half-mile repeats.

- Repeats of 8 to 12 minutes, with 2 minutes of easy spinning between. Do these at 85 to 90 percent of your maximal heart rate. Do this or the previous workout once a week. Start at three repeats, and work up to five. On these intervals, you should feel like you're running mile repeats.

- "Tempo run" efforts of up to 60 minutes. Start with shorter segments, such as 2 × 20 minutes or 3 × 15 minutes, with 3 to 5 minutes of easy spinning between. As your cycling fitness improves, move toward one long sustained ride. Do these at 80 to 90 percent of your maximal heart rate. Do this once a week. On these rides, you should feel like you're running an absurdly long tempo run.

- Fast spins of 15 to 20 seconds, starting every minute. Do 10 of these toward the end of an otherwise normal ride twice a week. Don't worry about heart rate on these. On these fast spins, you should feel like you're running striders.

As for the rest of the week, set aside one day for a long ride of two hours or more. (More is definitely better.) On the other days, ride as much as your schedule allows at a moderate effort level. Again, plan to spend at least twice as much time cycling as you normally do running.

Other Cycling Considerations

The following are a few things to be mindful of while playacting as a cyclist:

- For the first few days to a week, your legs, especially your quads, will tire more easily than you might think they should. This might be partly caused by trying to ride in too high a gear. During your first few days of cycling, be sure to ride in an easy enough gear to maintain the proper cadence (see next bullet).

- When riding indoors, maintain a cadence of at least 180 pedal strokes per minute (i.e., your right foot comes down 90 times a minute). This helps to maintain the turnover you need for good running, and ensures that you're not trying to push too hard a gear. Hills, wind, and so forth will greatly affect your cadence outdoors, so don't worry about counting turnover when you're riding outside.

- Stand up out of the saddle frequently. This not only more closely simulates running, but also provides relief to your low back, which can easily get tight and sore in runners who aren't used to spending hours on a bike seat.

- Do lots of quad and low back stretching after your rides.

- Get some real cycling gear. Skinny runners' butts very much appreciate padded cycling shorts.

Straight Talk About Elliptical Trainers

The elliptical trainer is the best addition to the injured runner's arsenal in recent years. It's readily available at most gyms, provides something close to the running motion, gives an effective workout, and can be safely used during most running injuries.

The biggest caution concerning ellipticals is that, like stair machines, they involve some degree of weight bearing. Therefore, if you have a stress fracture, you'll have to cross train elsewhere.

A lesser caveat: Although there's not much of a learning curve for runners new to the elliptical, your perceived exertion on it can still be a little off. Ellipticals are renowned for inducing huge amounts of sweat—after all, you're working hard in a warm gym without wind—so you might be fooled into thinking you're getting more of a workout than you are. Steve Holman, America's best miler in the 1990s, used an elliptical trainer during two injury stints and found after putting on a heart rate monitor that he wasn't working as intensely as he had thought. Holman thereafter wore a monitor during his elliptical workouts.

Although the discrepancy between how much time it takes for an effective workout on an elliptical trainer and during a run isn't as severe as that between cycling and running, plan to spend more time on the elliptical than you do on running when healthy. Shoot for one and a half times your normal running time to maintain a good level of fitness. Because it can be difficult mentally and logistically to stay on ellipticals for more than 90 minutes—many gyms have time limits—look to cycling or pool running as your long-run substitute.

Holman and others have found that, as with pool running and cycling, they did interval workouts more often on the elliptical than they did in their normal running schedule. If the elliptical is your main cross-training choice, shoot for four hard workouts a week. Emphasize shorter repeats to ensure that your heart rate stays elevated.

Keep your rests a little shorter than if you were running repeats of the same duration. Try to reach at least 85 percent of your maximal heart rate, with the last few closer to 95 percent. Some examples follow:

$20 \times$ (1:30 hard, 30 seconds easy)

$10 \times$ (2:00 hard, 1:00 easy)

$8 \times$ (3:30 hard, 1:30 easy)

$5 \times$ (5:30 hard, 2:30 easy)

Precede these workouts with at least a 10-minute warm-up, and follow them with at least a 5-minute cool-down.

Because your motion on an elliptical is fairly close to that of running, your adjustment period should be minimal. You should be able to start hard workouts after one or two getting-the-motion-down sessions, and you shouldn't be unusually sore after your initial workouts.

You'll get a better workout if you use the elliptical trainer hands free; leaning over and supporting your weight with your arms provides less benefit to you as an injured runner. You'll also maintain better form and get a workout more appropriate for a runner by keeping the incline settings on low.

Returning to Running

As tempting as it might be to ditch the pool belt or cycling shoes as soon as you can jog for 10 minutes, don't. Keep cross-training as an integral part of your program until you're back to your normal running schedule. After all, when healthy, you wouldn't count on staying fit if you cut your mileage in half for several weeks. The same is true when starting from scratch—just because you've gone from zero to 20 miles a week, there's no reason to think that, without some cross-training, this is as good as your normal 40-mile weeks.

While making the transition back to normal running, it's especially important to stick with your longest and hardest cross-training workouts. If you're being smart in your return to running, you'll start with nothing but easy, short runs, and it will probably be at least a few weeks before you feel ready to run for more than 90 minutes or to try speedwork. Therefore, you'll need to keep hammering out those long bike rides or intense elliptical-trainer sessions for the special endurance and high-end fitness boosts that only those sorts of workouts provide.

Knowing that you get to do a real run the day after a long, hard interval session in the pool should help you to stay disciplined about the tougher cross-training workouts. Stop doing them only when you can safely resume the running equivalent.

A final thought about returning to running: If you have access to a treadmill, do at least your first few runs back on it. That way, if your injury speaks up, you can stop immediately, rather than be 15 minutes from home and tempted to convince yourself that you'll be fine to finish the run.

Funny, You Don't Look Like a Runner

For many runners, one of the hardest aspects of an extended time away from running is the growing sense that they're, well, growing. Some of those concerns are unfounded; some are worth tending to.

On the one hand, don't freak out that your musculature will radically change because of four or eight weeks of no running and lots of cross-training. That's simply not enough time to build the massive quads that are great for cycling but are a hindrance to distance running, or to become the next Schwarzenegger in the gym. Any minimal muscle gains that might come about will gradually be lost as you return to regular running.

On the other hand, if you're not careful, it can be easy to add pounds of fat during your downtime, especially if you're a high-mileage runner used to eating a lot. Your appetite might not noticeably change, even though you're likely not burning as many calories as when you were running. Although there's no need to get obsessive about weight gain while you're hurt, be honest with yourself—if your clothes start to fit differently, you might want to up your cross-training, cut back on your food more, or both. Returning to running after several weeks off is hard enough under any circumstances; don't make it even more difficult by gaining unneeded fat.

Selected Readings and Resources

Abe, T., Y. Takiguchi, M. Tamura, J. Shimura, and K. Yamazaki. 1995. Effects of Vespa Amino Acid Mixture (VAAM) isolated from hornet larval saliva and modified VMM nutrients on endurance exercise in swimming mice: Improvement in performance and changes of blood lactate and glucose. *Japanese Journal of Physical Fitness and Sports Medicine* 44(2):225-238.

American College of Sports Medicine (ACSM). 2001. *ACSM's Resource Manual for Guidelines for Exercise Testing and Prescription*. Philadelphia: Lippincott, Williams, and Wilkins.

American Dietetic Association, Dietitians of Canada, and the American College of Sports Medicine. 2000. Nutrition and athletic performance: Position of the American Dietetic Association, Dietitians of Canada, and the American College of Sports Medicine. *Journal of American Dietetic Association* 100:1543-1556.

Antonio, J., and J. Stout. 2002. *Supplements for Endurance Athletes*. Champaign, IL: Human Kinetics.

Bandy, W.D., and J.M. Irion. 1994. The effect of time of static stretch on the flexibility of the hamstring muscles. *Physical Therapy* 64(4):491-497.

Barneveld, A., and P.R. van Weeren. 1999. Conclusions regarding the influence of exercise on the development of the equine musculoskeletal system with special reference to osteochondrosis. *Equine Veterinary Journal* 31(Suppl.):112-119.

Barr, S.I. 1999. Effects of dehydration on exercise performance. *Canadian Journal of Applied Physiology* 24:164-172.

Barr, S.I., and D.L. Costill. 1989. Water: Can the endurance athlete get too much of a good thing? *Journal of American Dietetic Association* 89:1629-1632,1635.

Barrette, E.P. 1998. Creatine supplementation for enhancement of athletic performance. *Alternative Medicine Alert* 1(7):73-76.

Birkmayer, J.G.D. 1996. *Energy for Life: NADH, The Energizing Coenzyme*. New York: Menuco Corp.

Birkmayer, J.G.D., and P. Vank. 1996. Reduced coenzyme 1 (NADH) improves psychomotoric and physical performance in athletes. *White Paper Report*. New York: Menuco Corp.

Bonetti, A., F. Solito, G. Carmosino, A.M. Bargossi, and P.L. Fiorella. 2000. Effect of ubidecarenone oral treatment on aerobic power in middle-aged trained subjects. *Journal of Sports Medicine and Physical Fitness* 40:51-7.

Bowerman, W., and W. Freeman. 1991. *High-Performance Training for Track and Field*. 2nd ed. Champaign, IL: Human Kinetics.

Brooks, G.A. 1997. Importance of the "crossover concept" in exercise metabolism. *Clinical and Experimental Pharmacology and Physiology* 24:889-895.

Brooks G.A., T.D. Fahey, and T.P. White. 1996. *Exercise Physiology: Human Bioenergetics and Its Applications*. Mountain View, CA: Mayfield Publishing.

Burke, E. 1999. *Optimal Muscle Recovery*. Wayne, NJ: Avery Publishing.

Burke, L.M., D.J. Angus, G.R. Cox, N.K. Cummings, M.A. Febbraio, K. Gawthorn, J.A. Hawley, M. Minehan, D.T. Martin, and M. Hargreaves. 2000. Effect of fat adaptation and carbohydrate restoration on metabolism and performance during prolonged cycling. *Journal of Applied Physiology* 89(6):2413-2421

Cade, R., M. Conte, C. Zauner, D. Mars, J. Peterson, D. Lunne, M. Hommen, and D. Packer. 1984. Effects of phosphate loading on 2,3 diphosphoglycerate and maximal oxygen uptake. *Medicine and Science in Sports and Exercise* 16:263.

Carey, A.L., H.M. Staudacher, N.K. Cummings, N.K. Stepto, V. Nikolopoulos, L. Burke, and J.A. Hawley. 2001. Effects of fat adaptation and carbohydrate restoration on prolonged endurance exercise. *Journal of Applied Physiology* 91(1):115-122.

Cavanagh, P. (Ed.). 1990. *The Biomechanics of Distance Running*. Champaign, IL: Human Kinetics.

Cheuvront, S.N., R.J. Moffatt, K.D. Biggerstaff, S. Bearden, and P. McDonough. 1999. Effect of ENDUROX on metabolic responses to submaximal exercise. *International Journal of Sport Nutrition and Exercise Metabolism* 9:434-442.

Clark, J.F. 1998. Creatine: A review of its nutritional applications in sport. *Nutrition* 14:322-324.

Conlay, L.A., R.J. Wurtman, J.K. Blusztajn, I.L.G. Coviella, T.J. Maher, and G.E. Evoniuk. 1986. Decreased plasma choline concentrations in marathon runners. *The New England Journal of Medicine* 315(14):892.

Coggan, A.R., and E.E. Coyle. 1991. Carbohydrate ingestion during prolonged exercise: Effects on metabolism and performance. *Exercise and Sport Sciences Reviews* 19:1-40.

Costill, D.L., G.P. Dalsky, and W.J. Fink. 1978. Effects of caffeine ingestion on metabolism and exercise performance. *Medicine and Science in Sports and Exercise*. 10: 155-158.

Cox, G.R., B. Desbrow, P.G. Montgomery, M.E. Anderson, C.R. Bruce, T.A. Macrides, D.T. Martin, A. Moquin, A. Roberts, J.A. Hawley, L.M. Burke. 2002. Effect of different protocols of caffeine intake on metabolism and endurance performance. *Journal of Applied Physiology* 93:990-999.

Coyle, E. 1994. Fluid and carbohydrate replacement during exercise: How much and why? *Sports Science Exchange* 50 7(3). Available: Gatorade Sports Science Institute at www.GSSIweb.com.

Davis, J.M., R.S. Welsh, K.L. De Volve, and N.A. Alderson. 1999. Effects of branched-chain amino acids and carbohydrate on fatigue during intermittent, high-intensity running. *International Journal of Sports Medicine* 20:309-314.

Eberle, S.G. 2000. *Endurance Sports Nutrition*. Champaign, IL: Human Kinetics.

Fahey, T.D. 1994. Endurance training. In *Women and Exercise: Physiology and Sports Medicine*, edited by M.M. Shangold, MD, and G. Mirkin, MD. Philadelphia: FA Davis.

Farnsworth, N.R., A.D. Kinghorn, D.D. Soejarto, and D.P. Waller. 1985. Siberian ginseng (Eleutherococcus senticosis): Current status as an adaptogen. *Economic and Medicinal Plant Research* 1:155-215.

Fiatarone, M.A., E.C. Marks, N.D. Ryan, C.N. Meredith, L.A. Lipsitz, and W.J. Evans. 1990. Intensity strength training in nonagenarians: Effects on skeletal muscle. *Journal of American Medical Association* 263:3029-3034.

Fleck, S.J., and W.J. Kraemer. 2004. *Designing Resistance Training Programs*. 3rd ed. Champaign, IL: Human Kinetics.

Fogt, D.L, and J.L. Ivy. 2000. Effects of post-exercise carbohydrate-protein supplement on skeletal muscle glycogen storage. *Medicine and Science in Sports and Exercise* 32(5):S60.

Fowles, J.R., D.G. Sale, and J.D. MacDougall. 2000. Reduced strength after passive stretch of the human plantar flexors. *Journal of Applied Physiology* 89:1179-1188.

Fredericson, M. 1999. A comprehensive review of running injuries. *Critical Reviews in Physical Medicine and Rehabilitation* 11:1-34.

Gibala, M. 2002. Dietary protein, amino acid supplements, and recovery from exercise. *Sports Science Exchange* 87 15(4). Available: Gatorade Sports Science Institute at www.GSSIweb.com.

Graham, T., and L. Spriet. 1996. Caffeine and exercise performance. *Sports Science Exchange* 60 9(1). Available: Gatorade Sports Science Institute at www.GSSIweb.com.

Häkkinen, K. 1994. Neuromuscular adaptation during strength training, aging, detraining and immobilization. *Critical Reviews in Physical and Rehabilitation Medicine* 6(3): 161-198.

Hankard, R.G., M.W. Haymond, and D. Darmaun. 1996. Effect of glutamine on leucine metabolism in humans. *American Journal of Physiology* 271:E748-E754.

Hickson, R.C., B.A. Dvorak, E.M. Gorostiaga, T.T. Kurowski, and C. Foster. 1988. Potential for strength and endurance training to amplify endurance performance. *Journal of Applied Physiology* 65:2285-2290.

Hickson, R.C., L.E. Wegrzyn, D.F. Osborne, and I.E. Karl. 1996. Alanyl-glutamine prevents muscle atrophy and glutamine synthetase induction by glucocorticoids. *American Journal of Physiology* 271:R1165-R1172.

Hurley, B.F., and S. Roth. 2000. Strength training in the elderly: Effects and risk factors for age-related diseases. *Sports Medicine* 30:249-268.

Inder, W.J., M.P. Swanney, R.A. Donald, T.C. Prickett, and J. Hellemans. 1998. The effect of glycerol and desmopressin on exercise performance and hydration in triathletes. *Medicine and Science in Sports and Exercise* 30(8):1263-1269.

Karlic, H., and A. Lohninger. 2004. Supplementation of l-carnitine in athletes: Does it make sense? *Nutrition* 20(7-8):709-715.

Kraemer, W.J., S.J. Fleck, and W.J. Evans. 1996. Strength and power training: Physiological mechanisms of adaptation. *Exercise and Sport Science Reviews* 24:363-397.

Kraemer, W.J., S.E. Gordon, J.M. Lynch, M.E. Pop, and K.L. Clark. 1995. Effects of multibuffer supplementation on acid-base balance and 2,3-diphosphoglycerate following repetitive anaerobic exercise. *International Journal of Sport Nutrition* 5(4): 300-314.

Kreider, R.B., G.W. Miller, D. Schenck, C.W. Cortes, V. Miriel, C.T. Somma, P. Rowland, C. Turner, and D. Hill. 1992. Effects of phosphate loading on metabolic and myocardial responses to maximal and endurance exercise. *International Journal of Sport Nutrition* 2:20-47.

Kreider, R.B. 1999a. Dietary supplements and the promotion of muscle growth with resistance exercise. *Sports Medicine* 27:97-110.

Kreider R.B. 1999b. Effects of protein and amino acids supplementation on athletic performance. *Sportscience* 3(1). Available: www.sportsci.org.

Kreider R.B. 1999c. Phosphate supplementation in exercise and sport. In *Macroelements, Water and Electrolytes in Sport Nutrition*, edited by J.A. Driskell and I. Wolinsky. Boca Raton, FL: CRC Press.

Kukulka, C.G., A.G. Russell, and M.A. Moore. 1986. Electrical and mechanical changes in the human soleus muscle during sustained maximum isometric contractions. *Brain Research* 362:47-54.

Lebedev, A.A. 1971. On the pharmacology of schizandra chinensis. *Materials for the Study of Ginseng and Schizandra Chinensis* 3:170.

Lininger, S. (Ed.) 1998. *The Natural Pharmacy*. Rocklin, CA: Prima Health Publishing.

Lydiard, A. 1978. *Running to the Top*. Princeton, NJ: Prentice-Hall.

Madsen, K., D.A. MacLean, B. Kiens, and D. Christiansen. 1996. Effects of glucose, glucose plus branched-chain amino acids, or placebo on bike performance over 100 km. *Journal of Applied Physiology* 81:2644-2650.

Mann, R.A., G.T. Moran, and S.E. Dougherty. 1986. Comparative electromyography of the lower extremity in jogging, running and sprinting. *American Journal of Sports Medicine* 14:501-510.

Martin, D., and P. Coe. 1997. *Better Training for Distance Runners*. Champaign, IL: Human Kinetics.

McAlindon, T.E., M.P. LaValley, J.P. Gulin, and D.T. Felson. 2000. Glucosamine and chondroitin for treatment of osteoarthritis: A systemic quality assessment and meta-analysis. *The Journal of the American Medical Association* 283(11):1469-1475.

McConnell, J. 1991. Advanced McConnell patellofemoral treatment plan. Course text (unpublished) from a course taken at Lindcombe NSW, Australia.

McNair P.J., and S.N. Stanley. 1996. Effect of passive stretching and jogging on the series elastic muscle stiffness and range of motion of the ankle joint. *British Journal of Sports Medicine* 30(4):313-318.

McNaughton, L.R., B. Dalton, and J. Tarr. 1998. The effects of creatine supplementation on high-intensity exercise performance in elite performers. *European Journal of Applied Physiology* 78:236-240.

Meredith, C.N., M.J. Zackin, W.R. Frontera, and W.J. Evans. 1989. Dietary protein requirements and body protein metabolism in endurance-trained men. *Journal of Applied Physiology* 66:2850-2856.

Montner, P., D.M. Stark, M.L. Riedesel, G. Murata, R. Robergs, M. Timms, and T.W. Chick. 1996. Pre-exercise glycerol hydration improves cycling endurance time. *International Journal of Sports Medicine* 17:27-33.

Murray, M., and J. Pizzorno. 1999. *A Textbook of Natural Medicine*. 2nd ed. London, UK: Churchill-Livingstone.

Murray, R., G.L. Paul, J.G. Seifert, and D.E. Eddy. 1991. Responses to varying rates of carbohydrate ingestion during exercise. *Medicine and Science in Sports and Exercise* 23:713-718.

National Strength and Conditioning Association (NSCA). 2000. *Essentials of Strength Training and Conditioning*. 2nd ed. edited by T.R. Baechle and R. Earle. Champaign, IL: Human Kinetics.

Nicodemus, K.J., R.D. Hagan, J.S. Zhu, and C. Baker. 1999. Supplementation with cordyceps Cs-4 fermentation product promotes fat metabolism during prolonged exercise. Abstracts from the 46th annual meeting of the American College of Sports Medicine. *Medicine and Science in Sports Exercise* May. (abstract 928). Available: www.acsm-msse-org.

Niles, E., T. Lachowetz, J. Garfi, W. Sullivan, J. Smith, B. Leyh, and S. Headley. 2001. Carbohydrate-protein drink improves time to exhaustion after recovery from endurance exercise. *JEPonline*, 4(1):45-52.

Nissen, S., R. Sharp, M. Ray, J.A. Rathmacher, D. Rice, J.C. Fuller, Jr., J.S. Connelly, and N. Abumrad. 1996. Effect of leucine metabolite beta-hydroxy-beta-methylbutyrate on muscle metabolism during resistance-exercise training. *Journal of Applied Physiology* 81:2095-2104.

Noakes, T. 2004. *Lore of Running*. 4th ed. Champaign, IL: Human Kinetics.

PDR Health. 2003. Boosting energy and fitness: Which foods really work? *PDR Family Guide to Nutrition and Health*. Available: http://www.pdrhealth.com/content/nutrition_health/chapters/fgnt21.shtml.

Pope, R. 1999. Skip the warm-up. *New Scientist*. 164:2214-2223.

Porter, M.M., A.A. Vandervoort, and J. Lexell. 1995. Aging of the human muscle: Structure function and adaptability. *Scandinavian Journal of Medicine and Science in Sports* 5:129-142.

Powers, S.K., and E.T. Howley. 2001. *Exercise Physiology: Theory and Application to Fitness and Performance*. Indianapolis: McGrawHill.

Ready, S.L., J. Seifert, and E. Burke. 1999. The effect of two sports drink formulations on muscle stress and performance. *Medicine and Science in Sports and Exercise*. 31(5):S119.

Roberts, R.A. 2001. Exercise-induced metabolic acidosis: Where do the protons come from? *Sportscience* 5(2). Available: www.sportsci.org.

Rosenbaum, D., and E.M. Hennig. 1995. The influence of stretching and warm-up exercises on Achilles tendon reflex activity. *Journal of Sport Sciences* 13:481-490.

Sadamoto, T., F. Bonde-Peterson, and Y. Suzuki. 1983. Skeletal muscle tension, flow pressure, and EMG during sustained isometric contractions in humans. *European Journal of Applied Physiology* 51:395-408.

Sandage, B.W., R.N. Sabounjian, R.White, and R.J.Wurtman. 1992. Choline citrate may enhance athletic performance. *Physiologist* 35: 236a.

Saunders M., M. Kane, and M. Todd. 2004. Effects of a carbohydrate-protein beverage on cycling endurance and muscle damage. *Medicine and Science in Sports and Exercise* 36(7):1233-1238.

Shrier, I., and K. Gossal. 2000. Myths and truths of stretching. *Physician and Sports Medicine* 28(8):57-63.

Snider, I.P., T.L. Bazzarre, S.D. Murdoch, and A. Goldfarb. 1992. Effects of coenzyme athletic performance system as an ergogenic aid on endurance performance to exhaustion. *International Journal of Sports Nutrition and Exercise Metabolism* 2:272-286.

Stanko, R.T., R.J. Robertson, R.W. Galbreath, J.J. Reilly, Jr., K.D. Greenawalt, and F.L. Goss. 1990. Enhanced leg exercise endurance with a high-carbohydrate diet and dihydroxyacetone and pyruvate. *Journal of Applied Physiology* 69(5):1651-1656.

Stanko, R.T., R.J. Robertson, R.J. Spina, J.J. Reilly, Jr., K.D. Greenawalt, and F.L. Goss. 1990. Enhancement of arm exercise endurance capacity with dihydroxyacetone and pyruvate. *Journal of Applied Physiology* 68(1):119-124.

Stanko, R.T., D.L. Tietze, and J.E. Arch. 1992. Body composition, energy utilization, and nitrogen metabolism with a 4.25 MJ/d low-energy diet supplemented with pyruvate. *American Journal of Clinical Nutrition* 56(4):630-635.

Stone, M. 1988. Implications for connective tissue and bone alterations resulting from resistance training. *Medicine and Science in Sports and Exercise* 20:S162-168.

Taaffe, D.R., C. Duret, S. Wheeler, and R. Marcus. 1999. Once-weekly resistance exercise improves muscle strength and neuromuscular performance in older adults. *Journal of American Geriatrics Society* 47:1208-1214.

Travell, J. 1992. *Myofascial Pain and Dysfunction, Volume 2*. Philadelphia: Lippincott, Williams, and Wilkins.

Van Koevering, M.T., H.G. Dolezal, D.R. Gill, F.N. Owens, C.A. Strasia, D.S. Buchanan, R. Lake, and S. Nissen. 1994. Effects of beta-hydroxy-beta-methylbutyrate on performance and carcass quality of feedlot steers. *Journal of Animal Science* 72:1927-1935.

Van Zyl, C.G., E.V. Lambert, J.A. Hawley, T.D. Noakes, and S.C. Dennis. 1996. Effects of medium-chain triglyceride ingestion on carbohydrate metabolism and cycling performance. *Journal of Applied Physiology* 80:2217-2225.

Varnier, M., G.P. Leese, J. Thompson, and M.J. Rennie. 1995. Stimulatory effect of glutamine on glycogen accumulation in human skeletal muscle. *American Journal of Physiology* 269:E309-E315.

von Allwörden, H.N., S. Horn, J. Kahl, and W. Feldheim. 1993. The influence of lecithin on plasma choline concentrations in triathletes and adolescent runners during exercise. *European Journal of Applied Physiology* 67:87-91.

Wagner, D.R. 1999. Hyperhydrating with glycerol: Implications for athletic performance. *Journal of American Dietetic Association* 99:207-212.

Weston, S.B., S. Zhou, R.P. Weatherby, and S.J. Robson. 1997. Does exogenous coenzyme Q10 affect aerobic capacity in endurance athletes? *International Journal of Sport Nutrition* 7:197-206.

Williams, M.B., P.B. Raven, and J.L. Ivy. 1999. Effects of recovery drinks after prolonged glycogen-depletion exercise. *Medicine and Science in Sports and Exercise* 31(5):S124.

Williams, M.H., and J.D. Branch. 1998. Creatine supplementation and exercise performance: An update. *Journal of the American College of Nutrition* 17:216-234.

Williams, M.H., R.B. Kreider, and J.D. Branch. 1999. *Creatine: The Power Supplement.* Champaign, IL: Human Kinetics.

Wilmore, J., and D. Costill. 2004. *Physiology of Sport and Exercise.* 3rd ed. Champaign, IL: Human Kinetics.

World Health Organization (WHO). 1994. Assessment of fracture risk and its application to screening for osteoporosis. *Technical Services Report 843.* Geneva, Switzerland: World Health Organization.

Other helpful Web sites describing research particularly on nutritional supplements include:

www.e-vitamin.com (E-Vitamin)

www.GSSIweb.com (Gatorade Sports Science Institute)

www.glucosamine-arthritis.org/glucosamine-research

www.healthnotes.com (Healthnotes, Inc.)

www.pponline.co.uk (Owen Anderson at Peak Performance)

www.pdrhealth.com (PDR Health)

www.vrp.com (Vitamin Research Products)

www.nal.usda.gov/fnic/Fpyr/pyramid.html (USDA Food and Nutrition Information Center)

Index

Note: The italicized f and t following page numbers refer to figures and tables, respectively.

Index

About the Editor

Kevin Beck has been a runner since 1984 and is currently a senior writer for *Running Times* magazine. He has also written about sports and health-related topics for *Marathon & Beyond, Men's Fitness, The Roanoke Valley Sports Journal*, and numerous other publications.

After running cross country for the University of Vermont, Beck ran 2:39:37 in his first marathon in 1994. Since then, the New Hampshire native has steadily carved his personal best down to 2:24:17, placing seventh among Americans and 28th overall at the 2001 Boston Marathon.

In 2003, Beck placed seventh at the USA Track & Field New England Half-Marathon Championship and ran 1:49 to win the Eastern States' 20-miler. He kicked off 2004 with personal bests in the half-marathon (1:08:22), ten miles (51:33), and 5,000 meters both on the track (14:58.2) and on the road (15:16). In November 2004 he placed second at the USA Track & Field National 50K Road Championship, running 3:06:22.

Beck has served as a distance-running coach at various levels and is coached by two-time U.S. Olympic marathoner Pete Pfitzinger. He also helped coordinate a research study on exercise and diabetes at the University of California at San Francisco, where he was a diabetes researcher and exercise technician for the Mount Zion Medical Center.

About the Contributors

Chris Chorak is the owner and founder of Presidio Sport & Medicine of San Francisco, California. A physical therapist for nearly two decades, Chorak is an Ironman triathlete, endurance coach, and injury consultant for the Leukemia and Lymphoma Society's Team in Training program. He is also a lecturer on various topics including sports medicine, injury prevention, race-day nutrition, and competition psychology. Chorak holds two bachelor's degrees, one in physical therapy from Northwestern University and another in athletic training from Purdue University.

Gwyn Coogan was a member of the 1992 U.S. Olympic 10,000-meter squad. After taking up running upon entering Smith College, the former swimmer, field hockey player, and lacrosse player became an All-American. Her first marathon was a 2:32:58 victory at Twin Cities in 1995. She also competed in the 1991, 1993, 1994, and 1995 World Cross Country Championships and was a member of the 1997 U.S. World Championship 10,000-meter team. Coogan holds a PhD in mathematics from the University of Colorado at Boulder and is a teacher and coach at Phillips Exeter High School in New Hampshire.

Mark Coogan is a 1996 U.S. Olympian in the marathon who also qualified for the U.S. Olympic Track and Field Trials in four events: the 1,500 meters, 3,000-meter steeplechase, 5,000 meters and 10,000 meters. A graduate of the University of Maryland, the Massachusetts native debuted in the marathon in Boston with a 2:13:22 and placed second the next year at the Pan American Games marathon. He also ran 13:23 for 5,000 meters, placing second at the 1995 U.S. Championships. Coogan and his wife live in Exeter, New Hampshire, with their three children.

Scott Douglas is a former editor of *Running Times* and coauthor of four books on running, including *Advanced Marathoning* and *Road Racing for Serious Runners*. He is a regular contributor to Runner's World, and his articles have been published in outlets as diverse as the *Washington Post*, Slate.com, and *Continental*, the in-flight magazine for Continental Airlines. Douglas has logged more than 80,000 miles since he started running in 1979. His personal records include 30:48 for 10K and 51:01 for 10 miles. Douglas lives in South Portland, Maine.

Mark Elliott is the director of high performance for Triathlon New Zealand's elite triathlon program, where he coordinates and educates elite athletes and coaches performing at the Olympic and World Championship level. He actively coaches triathletes and runners at all levels, including World Champion and Olympic triathlon silver medalist Bevan Docherty. A keen multisport athlete and dedicated runner, Elliott is also a qualified sports physiotherapist with a specific interest in strength and conditioning for endurance athletes. Elliott's interests include coffee, chocolate, and spending time with his wife, Jude, and son, Hamish.

Kyle Heffner is an exercise physiologist with more than 20 years of experience in exercise science, research, sports medicine, and lifestyle health management. He was a member of the 1980 U.S. Olympic marathon team with a personal best time of 2:10:55, and he represented the United States in the Fukuoka Marathon in Japan, finishing 11th in 2:12:35. Heffner has a master's degree in exercise science from the University of North Texas and a bachelor's degree in kinesiology from Texas A&M University. He frequently makes presentations to companies and organizations on health-related topics such as health and sports medicine, musculoskeletal concerns, and alternative therapies.

Colleen Glyde Julian is a 1997 graduate of the University of Colorado, where she was a three-time Division I All-American in cross country and track. After receiving her master's degree in kinesiology and applied physiology in 2001, she worked alongside coach and scientist Dr. Jack Daniels at the Sports Medicine Institute International in Palo Alto, California. Her research has involved utilizing simulated high-altitude exposure as a performance-enhancement tool and clinical exercise testing analyses. Julian is pursuing a PhD in medical anthropology at the University of Colorado, focusing on physiological adaptations and health issues among high-altitude populations. Julian lives in Boulder, Colorado, with her husband Pete, who is a runner for Team adidas.

John Kellogg is a full-time professional running coach. He has trained in the United States and in Europe with runners of all ages, abilities, and nationalities. For 15 years he has coached numerous elite athletes who have competed internationally. He is the coach of Weldon Johnson, who has twice finished fourth in the 10,000 meters at the U.S. National Championships and holds a personal best of 28:06 for the distance. A runner for 28 years, Kellogg was nationally ranked in the marathon as a junior (under age 20), has logged more than 70,000 miles, and holds times of 14:22 for 5,000 meters and 30:46 for a 10,000-meter cross country course.

Michael Leveritt is a lecturer in human movement studies at the University of Queensland, Australia, where he also earned his PhD in exercise physiology. An NSCA-certified strength and conditioning specialist, Leveritt has served as a consultant for many athletes and sporting organizations. His research has focused on concurrent strength and endurance training. Leveritt resides in Brisbane, Australia.

Greg McMillan is a USA Track and Field–certified coach and holds a master's degree in exercise physiology. He combines his experience as a competitive runner with his knowledge of exercise science to coach other runners. As a runner, McMillan has excelled at a variety of distances—first as a high school state champion in the mile and most recently placing 25th at the California International Marathon. His elite athletes have competed in the 1996, 2000, and 2004 Olympic Trials; the 2001 and 2003 World Track and Field Championships; and the 2003 Pan American Games. McMillan has successfully coached beginning runners and veteran runners through his online coaching program at www.mcmillanrunning.com.

Pete Pfitzinger, the top American finisher in the 1984 and 1988 Olympic Marathons, is currently a distance running coach and exercise physiologist. He established himself as one of the best marathoners in U.S. history by outkicking Alberto Salazar to win the 1984 U.S. Olympic Marathon Trials. That same year he received the Robert E. DeCelle award for America's best distance runner and was named Runner of the Year by the Road Runners Club of America. As a coach, Pfitzinger has more than 20 years of experience with athletes ranging from beginning runners to 2:10 marathoners. As an exercise physiologist, Pfitzinger specializes in working with runners, triathletes, and other endurance athletes. The coauthor of *Advanced Marathoning* and *Road Racing for Serious Runners* is also a senior writer for *Running Times*, which features his monthly column, "The Pfitzinger Lab Report." He is a graduate of Cornell University and earned his master's degree in exercise science from the University of Massachusetts. Pfitzinger lives in Auckland, New Zealand.

Joe Rubio is a two-time U.S. Olympic Marathon Trials qualifier with a personal best of 2:18:06. He holds a master's degree in physical education from Cal Poly at San Luis Obispo, and he has served as the head coach of the Asics Aggies running club since 1999. Rubio has also worked with several Olympians and members of World Championship teams, including Linda Somers Smith and Jill (Gaitenby) Boaz. An NCAA Division II All-American in the 5,000 meters, Rubio is the founding partner of Venue Sports.

Jack Youngren received his PhD from the University of California at Los Angeles with a major emphasis in cardiovascular function and adaptation and a minor emphasis in biomechanics. His research on exercise and carbohydrate metabolism led to a faculty position at the University of California at San Francisco, where he is investigating the effects of aerobic exercise on insulin action and glucose metabolism. Youngren is a lifelong competitive runner and has raced distances ranging from the 400 meters to the half-marathon. He has also trained and competed as an enthusiastic cyclist and a reluctant triathlete. Youngren provides coaching for members of the storied West Valley Track Club.